Teaching
Without
Tears

Teaching
Without
Tears

CHARLES PREECE

TEACHING WITHOUT TEARS

THE CLASSROOM TEACHERS' SURVIVAL BOOK

ISBN 0-9619349-3-X
Registered with R.R. Bowker, N.Y., N.Y.
LIBRARY OF CONGRESS CATALOG CARD NO. 88-80829
Includes Index and Bibliography

Printed by Braun-Brumfield, Inc., Ann Arbor, Michigan, U.S.A.
First Edition 1988
ISBN 0-9619349-2-1 (hard cover) 1987

Logo by Barbara Preece
Cover design by Randy Crawford: Omnigraphics, San Diego, California

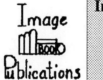

Image Book Publications
9974 Scripps Ranch Blvd.
Suite 304
San Diego, Calif. 92131
Telephone: (619))578-0587

And gladly would he learn and gladly teach.
Chaucer, Canterbury Tales

ACKNOWLEDGMENTS

If I didn't express my appreciation for the years of rewarding personal relationships with hundreds of teachers and thousands of secondary students, some of whom still correspond with me, I would do a disservice to too many fine people.

To the multitudes who have entered my classroom doors, I say that our country should be thankful for you who have done your best under many trying conditions during years of social change and turmoil.

What's wrong with public school teachers and students? Very little. Classroom teachers are mostly good, competent people working hard for little recognition, status, or pay. The students are basically well-meaning youngsters often exposed to the bewildering demands imposed upon them by modern society. To them I bow.

Thanks also to my wife, Barbara Preece, whose good nature and encouragement never took a day off.

Finally, thanks to Miss Lillian—wherever you are.

PREFACE

This book is intended for classroom teachers whose pride is in the classroom, not merely using teaching as a means to more prestigious jobs. Its purpose is to deal with daily problems in today's public schools. Yet, basics of successful teaching apply to private schools and special programs as well. This book provides a perspective for teachers that transcends classroom walls.

In spite of, or because of, thirty years' experience on the front lines of secondary schools, teaching in fine and not-so-fine public schools, having taken most of the maligned education courses and, (heavens!) earning a master's degree from a teachers college, I left teaching with optimism about mostly fine teachers, many good administrators (heresy!), and mostly good young people—all of whom were doing the best they could under trying circumstances.

There is no evidence yet of any system proposed or enacted in the public schools which works best for most teachers, with most students, in most schools. Too many idealistic proposals have been made which could work only in Utopia, not in the daily give and take of public school education. There is no one personality nor any one method for successful teaching.

There are many critics who could not stand the heat and bolted from the classroom. Several became best selling authors. Others paid their dues by earning Ph.D.'s, thus acquiring the mantle of infallibility. Neither psychiatrists nor politicians feel any compunction about advising classroom teachers how to teach even though few were ever school teachers. College grads gainfully employed in administration or college teaching feel free to criticize an area in which they have had no personal experience.

Many things are right with public schools. Given proper school environment with competent administrators, teachers can effect positive changes. But change must begin on the front lines.

• TABLE OF CONTENTS •

> *Tears, idle tears, I know not what they mean,*
> *Tears from the depth of some divine despair*
> *Rise in the heart, and gather to the eyes,*
> *In looking on the happy autumn-fields,*
> *And thinking of the days that are no more.*
>
> Tennyson, The Princess

CHAPTER ONE

DISCIPLINE: A DIRTY WORD

Gallup polls of recent years concerning the public's attitudes toward schools showed discipline as the major concern. Campaigns initiate "get tough" policies; people in and out of education, far removed from the daily struggle, create solutions and theories for teachers to practice. But beginning or even experienced teachers are left swinging in the wind when practical help is desperately needed.

Without effective discipline there is no effective teaching. In classrooms where students are legally required to attend, where students have extreme difficulty in transferring, where teacher/pupil conflicts must be dealt with on a continuous basis, where poor home and school conditions exist, teachers will always have problems with discipline.

Virtually any public school system has identical built-in disciplinary problems. Yet, a special teacher and a willing group of students can make things work, regardless of poor environment and lack of support. However, instead of discussing how it could be, let's look at how it is.

Teacher burnout, career changes, early retirement, and many physical and emotional problems are directly traceable to frustration and stress created from struggles to maintain discipline. Even with experienced, understanding, and unflappable instructors, maintaining classroom control has first priority. Teachers not maintaining reasonable classroom control cannot expect to impart effective learning. Students are unlikely to be willingly obedient for a person they meet for less than one hour per day. Teenagers who oppose discipline at home are unlikely to accept control at school.

Some instructors maintain discipline by a strong personality, coercion, intimidation, surprise quizzes, grades, and massive parental contacts. Who has not entered a classroom where there is deadly silence for the full period, where pupils file in and out like zombies? Some might consider that effective discipline. It is not.

No saints or robots make teaching a career. If we minimize the teacher's personal qualities and downplay the infinite mathematical mixtures of personalities of each class, what remains which would be basic for classroom control even before any teacher faced a class? Where does discipline actually begin? Does it start when teachers and students first meet eyeball to eyeball? By then, it is too late.

Several factors precondition students to effective discipline: the room's appearance; the clothing and personal qualities of the teacher; lessons plans, organization, use of texts, lighting, ventilation, and seating arrangements make important contributions to effective classroom discipline.

Discipline: a Life Support System

For teachers, mental and physical discipline is a matter of professional survival. Discipline should not be a dirty word. It is a fragile concept that assumes a physical form. It is a tool which must be utilized immediately and consistently or it becomes worthless.

Discipline depends upon the imposer's will, character, and the receivers of that discipline. Too much discipline and it evaporates; too little and it becomes chaos. Inconsistent discipline is as bad as none at all. Young people feel more secure knowing guidelines for acceptable behavior. Rebelling against norms and knowing the consequences is different from being confused by inconsistent norms. While right or wrong may be in the eyes of the beholder, it is vital not to be confused about acceptable behavior.

Teachers may lose control because of their own aversion toward discipline; some may want children to develop "naturally"; others make an honest effort to maintain control and lose. The results are the same—effective learning disappears.

Where teachers run from the classroom in tears, are fearful to face classes or individual students, where constant aid is sought from supervisors, or where vice principals appear to warn classes, there is a serious control problem. Teachers quit, administrators are miserable, and students are shortchanged. Learning cannot take place under such conditions. No discipline—no teaching—no teacher. Even the best teachers are not always backed up by the counselors or principals who, in turn, are not supported by the education center. Teachers are expected to handle their own problems.

One of the few perks left to teachers today, and perhaps a major reason for teachers to stick with the profession, is their independence— boss of a four-walled environment. Stepping outside the classroom in some schools is entering the asphalt jungle. Once that jungle is allowed to encroach upon the learning environment, the classroom itself becomes a blackboard jungle. Only the teacher's freedom and will to make it work can keep the jungles away from the classroom.

Students should want to be in your classroom, accept normal restrictions for dealing with groups, and expect to be admonished or punished for disregarding norms. Yet this must not direct resentment toward the instructor. Whether it's called soft, gentle, sub-conscious, silent, or fragile discipline, many factors contribute to student control long before the teacher faces the first class. Here are the building blocks for workable discipline.

Who Says?

Dictionary definitions of discipline include "branch of knowledge," training which develops self-control and character," and "strict control to enforce obedience". The public and educators can't agree on what discipline means, either. "Disciple" is the source of "discipline" and is defined as a pupil of any teacher of learning. Disciples, then, should accept the definition of discipline interpreted by the teacher, right? No agreement here, either.

Bad Example

One type of discipline is painfully illustrated by Steve Stecklow's article, "Undercover Schoolboy", (Philadelphia *Bulletin,* Nov. 9, 1980). The reporter, having enrolled as a high school student, found restrooms locked between the first and last ten minutes of each period; widespread cheating; almost no homework; high absenteeism; excessive regulations; indifference on the part of students and teachers; boring lessons; and wide ranges of teacher competence.

Gainful Employment

Effective instructors are aware that students must be kept gainfully employed. Crowds that are bored at rock concerts often end up rioting;

police in their daily activity break up groups of loungers at street corners. Teachers having groups of youngsters in class with little to do can expect pent up energies to find non-academic outlets. Careful, constructive planning is critical. Always have more planned than you expect to accomplish. Constant lecturing, unlike in colleges, will not work.

Pick Your Seat

Seating students is one of the most important tasks a teacher can do to forestall problems. This is discussed more fully later on. Be aware that if malcontents or disruptive students are removed from their turf, they are deprived of their ammunition and peer encouragement.

Don't

Corporal punishment in public schools is a legal minefield, even if the psychological and social factors are disregarded. Short of being physically assaulted first, the teacher has no defense in the eyes of the law or the public. You may be a 100 pound weakling against a 200 pound defensive lineman, but if you hit such a "kid" you will likely lose your job and, for dessert, get sued.

Ground Rules

"Classroom regulations" (euphemism for "discipline") must be discussed with each class during the first few days of school. Identical rules should be posted also. Periodically, the class should be reminded of infractions, especially during grading periods. Transfer students should always be given handouts of class regulations.

It is unwise to beat upon the same theme, however. If the class behaves reasonably well, works well, although maybe too exuberant at times, you have control. Some classes are happy and high spirited and, although tiring for the teacher, are to be treasured. If classes are raucous and always ready for a fight or a frolic, whipping out regulations will have no effect. When rules are unenforced or unforceable, start enforcing what you have neglected or make the rules more realistic. Students are likely to respond positively when explanations are given and cooperation is requested. Threats are counter-productive and merely create a barrier.

Minor Adjustments

There comes a time not to act or react. Rules must be practical. If pupils are constantly late to class from a gym across campus, adjustments must be made. Either you adjust, or arrange with the staff for an earlier dismissal. If assignments (classified as a discipline problem by some teachers) are not done because of unusual problems, be flexible. Don't take offense at every infraction you see. Not only will you wear yourself out as an enforcer, pupils may pay more attention to rules than to learning. On school grounds, the same caution applies. If a simple finger wag doesn't stop a "public display of affection", keep moving. A kiss is a kiss is a kiss.

No school rules are valid or enforceable if teachers disobey them. If teachers forbid gum chewing, they have no justification for chewing gum. If teachers are late for class, students must be given an explanation. They will get a big kick out of teachers being late, but will appreciate being worthy of an explanation.

There is no arguing with state law or board of education mandates, but dress and other codes are negotiable. However, codes are difficult to enforce unless students take part in the process. Anything deemed "too far out" can usually be resolved with compromise and common sense.

Pride Factor

Most pupils seek pride in their schools and in their classes. Studies have shown that vandalism, graffiti, and behavior problems are greatly reduced when students are proud of their schools. Sometimes that pride flowers with a good sports team. Pride also comes with acquiring a good education. Pride is found in unexpected places. Develop it.

The Extra Step

Good teachers can handle 95% of the problems as they occur without recourse to outside authority, and they do it without confrontations. When teachers know students, work hard at meaningful instruction, and function as allies, discipline won't be a problem.

Contacting parents may be a good idea as long as it is not overdone. Parents may feel that a criticism of their child is a complaint against them. Others are upset when teachers don't warn them in time to take action. Parents often want to know of their child's misbehavior. However, some parents should not be notified because the teacher could very well be putting the child in danger. Brutality may be the result of a teacher's call to the home. Some teachers make it a policy to contact homes right away, especially in elementary school. In secondary schools, counselors may assume that responsibility. As long as it is routine, parents need not feel they are being blamed for their child's misbehavior.

Body Language

Once classes accept behavior norms, verbal reminders could become redundant and tiresome. Enter body language. A serious or even half-smiling eye contact alerts offenders that big brother is watching; a menacing finger or a slight head movement works wonders. A stroll down the aisle while the class if working can remove potential for wrongdoing. During instruction, silently interrupting the lesson until the inattentive or the talkers are transfixed is more effective than verbal gymnastics. However, if your students are not yet playing by the rules, get back to basics.

A Principal Role

At an elementary school where I was an integration monitor, the principal was living evidence of discipline conditioning. He arranged his schedule so that whenever students were outside for lunch or other activities, he would be there. He teased and talked; he hugged everybody in sight, including female teachers. Handouts and booklets were generously distributed. Parents and other community members had very strong participation; rewards abounded in the form of stickers, plaques, certificates, and bonus points to be redeemed in the school store.

Disciplinary problems were minimal; parents were contacted fast, and children received a set punishment for a set offense. Moreover, children who got into difficulty were not regarded with any admiration by others. The principal visited classrooms often and casually, maybe staying only a couple of minutes to praise the class. Even though the school was under serious scrutiny covering many different areas during the two days, teachers and pupils were always calm and friendly. There was no feeling of insecurity, suspicion, or anxiety from anybody.

This school illustrates how good parent contact, praises and rewards, unemotional and effective punishment, and excellent leadership which sets the tone for the staff can combine effective learning with effective student control.

Teacher Machine

When the teacher's nerves are ragged and it is one of those days when everything goes wrong, everybody demands that teachers be calm, impartial, non-judgmental, bear no animosity, ignore previous incidents and still impose just punishment. Teaching is tough. Teachers are not trained to be enforcers. Their psyche is foreign to any type of police action. I found it mildly amusing when police officers addressed my seniors fully equipped with guns, nightsticks, and handcuffs.

When emotion affects discipline, discipline suffers. Teachers know they can handle 175 teenagers a day in school better than they can handle one teenager at home—the emotion factor. When things go seriously wrong in class, teachers must be seriously calm.

Aggression Forever

A report presented to the American Psychological Association in 1984 revealed that a study began in 1960 of 875 rural third graders in New York State showed continued aggression through the current years. Ten years after the study began, there was a definite correlation between what peers said about the subjects when they were 8 and how the peers rated them at 19. In 1984 the correlation still held up.

In 1987, researchers reported that a follow-up study of aggression and intelligence of 300 adults involved in the 1960 third grade group showed that the former third grade bullies had weaker intellectual and professional achievement than their non-aggressive classmates having the same IQ's. "Aggression in childhood actually interfered with the development of intellectual functioning." A previous analysis found that childhood bullies had about a one in four chance of having a criminal record by the age of 30. The researchers concluded that the traditional view that assertiveness and aggression lead to high achievement and success does not hold up.

Pity the poor unsuspecting teachers who, when dealing with aggressive behavior, assume that such behavior is temporary. Yet the above study stated that negative aggression is continually rewarded with material items as well as attention—good for coaches but not exactly a thrill for classroom teachers. Follow-up research showed that aggressive behavior learned early in life resulted in adults who committed more crimes, received more traffic violations, and were more aggressive toward their spouses. (Nothing was mentioned about drivers of little red sports cars.)

As of 1985, the Los Angeles School District automatically expels anyone found with a knife, gun, or any other lethal weapon. Until then, a student often got preferential treatment if a lawyer or parents fought the expulsion.

The 1985 Gallup Poll repeated the public's feeling that discipline was the most important problem in public schools. The 1984 Gallup Poll also showed the public felt teachers were at fault, but only ⅓ of the teachers thought so. They, in turn, blamed lack of discipline in the home (94%), lack of respect for authority, courts, and especially the lack of parental support. Surprisingly, only a small percentage of teachers polled said that criminal activity in school occurred most of the time, or even fairly often.

Other causes contribute to disciplinary problems which teachers face every day which result in the loss of teachers who, otherwise, had been able to control unruly students. These include: a general lack of proper child raising as found in one parent families, with fewer than half of the minors living with both parents by 1985; a 12 year old can expect 14½ minutes of communication with parents, most of that time being spent in reprimands; watching more television than for any other waking activity, contributing to inadequate sleep time and a distorted view of life; acceptance of drugs as a way of life; and an accumulation of poor attitudes and habits from both home life and passing from one grade level to another.

The task of teachers, schooled in books and college backgrounds, is monumental when faced with controlling a group of youngsters with so many negative backgrounds. Teachers are neither physically nor emotionally equipped to deal with this type of trauma. What's left unsaid is that schools are the repository of future mass murderers, psychopaths, pyromaniacs, abusers, and other threats to society. How many teachers can separate normal from abnormal behavior? Yet teachers must assume that everyone in class is a rational human being.

Conflicting reports on crime in public schools pour out daily. Police and security guards give a gloomy picture, while teachers and administrators wonder what all the fuss is about. *The Safe School Study* says that the crime rate of a school correlates with that of the community. Everyone has difficulty defining what a school crime is. In a high crime area, an offense committed on school grounds, such as shakedowns or intimidation, may seem to be nothing but a part of daily outside activity.

The litany of what is wrong with society and how to handle the breakdown of discipline in public schools needs no further cataloging, but it does need workable techniques to be used by all teachers. Granted, not all practices will work for all teachers nor all students in all circumstances. However, since the classroom can be a battleground it can also be a laboratory where various ideas can be tried and, if need be, discarded. Whatever works for you and results in a productive, satisfied class, use it.

The following chapters will help make your lions love you (without losing your head).

CHAPTER 2

CLASSROOM LIVING

Although teachers have no control over the construction of classrooms, they can make the best of what they have. But what effect does the physical layout have on conditioning for discipline?

A Room Without Windows

Make adjustments to minimize unsatisfactory window locations. Either the teacher's desk or the pupils' desks can be relocated for outside lighting conditions. Unfortunately, many modern schools are built like fortresses. This simplifies window problems negatively by making windows unavailable to make problems. Reasons advanced for solid walls include security, elimination of outside distractions (which are many) and, more likely, saving money on glass breakage and heat loss.

Confining youngsters without retaining some sense of freedom is a mistake. Being under control is a necessary evil but being in a windowless classroom is an unnecessary evil. Windows do encourage distractions as well as occasional daydreaming as the school year draws to a close (teachers not being immune), but seeing a small, detached portion of the outside world is a small price to pay for a bit of contentment.

Windows must be under the teacher's control; otherwise, a game starts when half the class is "too cold" and the other half is "too hot". Hyperactive students are thwarted from leaping up at the least whim to adjust the temperature. Old friendships are not renewed.

Having taught in a school located in a frigid zone where broken windows were replaced strictly by the budget or, worse, by the custodian's good will, I had often wondered whether windows should

11

be outlawed. However, my better nature prevailed and I still believe that windowed classrooms are much more humane than fortresses.

A positive trend was illustrated by the San Diego Unified School District. It "changed its design emphasis from the windowless and security-conscious schools". In 1976, local architects had bestowed the Onion Award to the school district for the opposite reason. A new team comprised of design professionals and school administrators are responsible for the design of more comfortable and appealing schools. Significant, though not surprising, was that teachers were not mentioned. Has there ever been a commercial building designed without business people being consulted?

Open Door Policy

Doors should be open whenever possible unless your class noise level is a threat to the environment. This minimizes feelings of confinement; allows easier entrance and exit; permits the steady stream of messengers, support staff, late arrivals and early departures. Excessive doorknob grabbing breaks the fragile attention span of young people, and who can believe that the teacher's train of thought can't be derailed almost as easily? Besides, your open door policy is evidence you have nothing to hide. Principals love it.

Let There be Light

Fluorescent lighting is the optician's friend, but since it is cheaper energy, instructors must live with it. Ever sit in a night class under fluorescent lights? It's bad enough for the class to look ghastly without also looking like part of a nightmare. Some teachers turn on lights in the morning and ignore them the rest of the day, even though natural light is preferred by students. A few teachers keep their rooms as dark as possible, hoping that darkness will have a quieting effect on the pupils. It certainly helps them sleep better.

Educators discovered the hard way that students should not be left in the dark (literally). When lights are turned off for an audio-visual presentation or for an assembly program, watch out! Dim lights are fine but be careful of blackouts. Light up your life with natural light whenever possible.

Bulletin Boards

Bull boards—bane of elementary school teachers and repository for secondary teachers of publishers' flyers and time lines. These are posted in September and chiseled off the cork in June.

Ideally, information should apply to your subject matter, be timely, and be a reference source for instructors who can remember it's there. Items may be morally uplifting, humorous, or even educational. When a teacher is being evaluated, a bulletin board could be the key to a superintendent's job. Bulletin boards should either be changed or destroyed regularly. You never know when you'll be featured on your own display!

Chalkboards

In days beyond recall, these were blackboards. Now they are greenboards. When useable wall space is scarce, foot for foot the chalkboards can be your best aid in discipline. They should record course schedules, room number (students have been known to sit in the wrong room for a whole period, you know), and the teacher's name— unless the teaching is so bad that the teacher wants to remain anonymous. The chalkboard is also a great place to hang a calendar so that students will know when they've done their time. Be sure a bell schedule is posted nearby, preferably on a large cardboard. This comforts students by comparing the schedule to the clock, and relieves the harried teacher who may have reached the stage of not knowing what day it is.

Chalkboards are great in handling exam dates, test items, assignments, and due dates of official forms. During instruction, writing key words, phrases, or grabber questions like "Can you really own a cat?" helps maintain concentration. This technique also allows instructors to follow logical sequences without consulting texts or notes.

A chalkboard is an excellent way to keep the class's attention, especially during the latter part of the day, Mondays and Fridays. Moreover, it aids greatly in overcoming nervousness or anxiety of teachers beginning a school year or when treading unfamiliar ground. It is also a valuable supplement when the instructor is being officially "observed". Once you know your class, you can paralyze pesky pupils by telling Mike to knock it off, while your back is to the class. This confirms the terrifying certainty that teachers do indeed have eyes in the back of their heads.

An unforgettable college professor (seldom described this way) I once had, would have a complete outline and drawings on the chalkboard when the class entered, then followed up with handouts. I don't recall ever learning more or retaining more than I did during those courses.

Using the chalkboard will minimize confusion, let students know where they are, where they're going, and furnish aid and comfort. When a pupil says during a test, "When did we have that?", it is so comforting for the teacher to say, "Well, it was on the board!".

Litterbugging

Make it easy for litter disposal. This removes signs of bondage and incriminating evidence like poor test grades, romantic notes, gum wrappers, apple cores, and caricatures of teachers. Teachers should be humble enough to pick up litter. This simple act, like good manners, can be contagious. A polite "Is this yours?" alerts both the unthinking and also the deliberate litterer to unacceptable behavior. Asking the above question inevitably produces a negative response.

Wastebaskets next to doors are always popular. In more affluent school districts like Beverly Hills, instructors may have a second wastebasket by the desk. Remove graffiti and doodling regularly. Don't depend upon anyone else to do this or acute embarrassment may occur during Open House Night.

If the above chores seem picky picky, remember that evidence of excessive litter and graffiti indicates little effective teaching is going on—motivation and production are lacking. Unless an uncluttered environment welcomes pupils, the image of a productive class suffers. Students should like entering a class even though they might prefer torture before admitting it.

Sitdowns

Seating seems a minor part of a new semester, yet it is a critical element in discipline.

Don't be premature in assigning seats the first few days. Schedule changes and unstable class sizes will occur. However, immediate identification of students is vital for establishing effective class control. Normally, groups first sitting together are ones to watch when permanent seating is assigned. The rear of the room is a good place to clear out, but priority for front seats first goes to those with physical disabilities, and known disciplinary problems. The relatively few students who desire front seats could be some of your brightest pupils. Visibly older and shy students may be more comfortable at the rear.

Alphabetical order, which can be modified later, is a good place to start. This aids greatly in promptly identifying your expected daily secondary school load of 175 students. With two weeks of concerted effort you should have paired names with faces. Cliques having a strong work ethic can be kept together, since their enthusiasm is contagious. Splitting them may dilute the unity needed in a class made up of indifferent students.

An open secret of professionals is that an unmanageable class can become manageable by reseating certain individuals. If one arrangement doesn't work, try another. If you have continuing problems with certain pupils after seat changes, reseating is not the answer. Students who enter your room as a boisterous group must be separated quickly. Some problem pupils straighten out when removed from their peers. Conversely, this could backfire if problems are dispersed throughout the class. Motor mouths and those who regard school work as "Mickey Mouse" feed on each other. However, it's better to work on a single problem child than to challenge the herd.

There is no formula in this lab. Every class is different. Your best class one semester may return virtually intact except for a few additions who destroy the class's morale and work attitude. Experienced teachers watch transfer students carefully, suspecting there is a negative reason for the change. Seating is your first line of defense. Here are a few seating arrangements you might want to try.

Traditional

The teacher's desk is at the front and the pupils face the teacher—a big advantage. While your alphabetical order may be imperfect when you begin teaching, you now know students who are either very good or very bad. The middle group, the backbone of any class, takes longer to know. They easily survive a whole semester working and behaving in virtual anonymity when instructors don't make the effort at recognition. When pupils greet you on campus and you don't know them, re-study your seating plans. Alphabetical order simplifies roll taking, makes it easier to return assignments, and call on pupils by name.

The advantage of the traditional arrangement is that teachers are the focal point of the room and can oversee the class easily. Pupils are surprised at what an instructor can see from the front of the room! Critics object to the formality of the arrangement, the dominating presence of teachers, and the artificial barrier separating teachers from students. Yet virtually all college classes, including teaching methods courses, are set up in the traditional way.

Choose Your Partner

If your class is like an old friend and has voluntarily enrolled because of previous courses, your reputation, or sibling ties and has proven to be a well-behaved group, you could permit them to select their own seats. This might work out well.

Circle Time

This arrangement depends upon instructor and class personality, subject, and the teaching method. *Advantages:* the circle is good for discussions, and also the inquiry method whereby pupils deduce answers from readings and the teacher is primarily a discussion leader. Shy students and other regular onlookers feel freer to contribute. When a few groups work as units, the instructor can give equal credit for group members, allowing peer pressure to stimulate non-workers to shape up. *Disadvantages:* the teacher has no place to hide; must handle questions and justify answers without relying on lecterns or notes; and be able to handle close personal give and take. Without expertise and a good memory, it can be difficult. Moreover, everything needed for backup is at the desk; it is difficult to collect or return assignments. When messengers or support staff want to see you, they can't find you. (That could be an advantage.)

Three Sided

While similar to the circle in purpose, it is another alternative to traditional seating. Each side may contain three rows and be designated as working groups. No grouping is to be based upon scholastic achievement. Whenever the A Group or Bluebirds are regarded as the "brains", others make little effort to participate. Advantages and disadvantages are similar to the circle. Disciplinary problems are minimal because of high pupil visibility.

Seating the Teacher

The traditional position of the teacher's desk is here to stay. Professors crying for educational reform do so from a desk at the front of the room. This marks the communications center.

Some instructors have placed their desks at the rear. Locating desks here may have an advantage only in the minds of the teachers. Although there is an initial unsettling effect on students who feel investigative eyes behind them, they gradually become unaware of the difference and conduct business as usual. An outrageous example is the 1984 movie, *Teachers,* in which classes filed in and out all day without knowing the teacher had died at the rear of the room. Excluding that example, my brief takeover of a rear desk proved that all legitimate business takes place up front.

Today's schools are inundated with paperwork, staff contacts with students, messengers, and late arrivals—all of whom must thread the minefields of the aisles. Getting tripped on the way to the teacher's inner sanctum is an assumed risk. Another disadvantage is that the instructor must reach the front to use the chalkboard, or talk to parents or graduates at the door. If the teacher prefers to use the chalkboard at the rear of the room, the class is in danger of whiplash. Further chaos occurs during a fire drill when the class rushes out, being chased by their fearless leader.

On a more positive note, there is no more humbling an experience for a principal than to enter a room to find the desk missing, the teacher missing, and thirty-five pairs of eyes amusedly enjoying the whole unnerving tableau.

However, it is more lasting fun to select any seating arrangement in which you and your students find most efficient and comfortable. Class, be seated.

CHAPTER 3

TEACHER QUALITIES AND INEQUALITIES

"And making a special appearance today is—YOU!" Another ingredient of effective discipline is the quality of the teacher. What qualities should a teacher have which strengthen classroom management? A string of adjectives would do nicely: mentally tough, self-confident, honest, fair, knowledgeable, and presentable. This "best" list, like all others, is flexible, debatable, and personal.

The Look

In appearance, teachers should set the example and not follow the lowest common denominator. "Casual" is not a synonym for "sloppy". Being one of the guys might indicate that you may be less secure about yourself than you think. Are T shirts, sandals, scruffy dungarees, unkempt hair or beards the professional images you want to promote? You can be sure that if you present a super cool and laid back image, you'll have imitators.

Student dress codes were relaxed years ago and became ridiculous. Equally ridiculous were old codes requiring male teachers to wear suits and female teachers to wear nothing attracting undue attention. Male students had to wear dress shirts and ties. Long hair or beards were cause for suspension. Today, upgraded personal appearance is making a long awaited return, but not through school boards. Students themselves decided to improve their looks. Fashion was in for girls, and boys got the message. The clean, neat look is back.

The Groom

Since faculty members work in close proximity with each other and hundreds of students daily, personal grooming is important. Stress may take its toll during the day but starting out from home well-prepared should aid your professional image.

The Attitude

Self-confidence in the classroom develops with knowing you are in charge, can handle close relationships in quantity, and have techniques plus knowledge to be an authority in your subject. Ego weakening events are never absent during normal work days, from both peers and students. Your expertise, grading, methods, and personal qualities may be subject to question. At faculty meetings the form might be "Certain teachers are—". Perhaps you are criticized by parents or challenged by pupils. These types of negative reactions can erode a teacher's self-confidence. After a while, many instructors start looking for other occupations or early retirement. To maintain credibility in the classroom and a sense of personal worth, you will need all the confidence you can store in your reservoir.

The Head

Being 6'5", weighing 250 pounds, and being a retired professional athlete doesn't hurt when you are facing teenagers, but it won't do you much good either. Physical intimidation is not a substitute for mental toughness. Size is seldom a factor in effective discipline. Discipline is a prime example of mind over matter. As kids say, "I don't mind and you don't matter". Self-confidence and an internal toughness count much more than physical strength. Any teacher who has confronted a 200 pound teenager knows this. Teachers must stand before groups which resent being there, tolerate incessant interruptions, deal with parents, administrators, or other faculty members. They may feel that few people really care about education yet, like Willy Loman, they put on a smile and a shoeshine and make believe everything is just fine.

The Honest and the Fair

Honesty and fairness are like Siamese twins. Students have heard so much double talk during their young lives that everything taught in class is subject to skepticism. Can you honestly say you never met a kid you didn't like? Can you honestly encourage college degrees for all your students? Textbooks and tests contain errors. Your assignments may be the pits. Your choice is to either admit you are wrong or cover up. If you cover up, students clam up. But they will know—and there goes your credibility.

Fairness involves treating everyone as alike as you can, including students who are troublesome and unfair themselves. This does not imply that a teacher be a doormat. Moreover, applying democratic principles itself may result in unfairness. Deserved rewards are withheld, all in the name of fairness.

The Smarts

If you don't know your subject, get out of teaching. Basic competency tests for teachers are the result of years of sloppy preparation and sloppier thinking. Many teachers came fortified with methods but not with knowledge. The idea that anyone can teach is nonsense. It is no longer acceptable to discuss whatever strikes the teacher's fancy. "Rapping" is out. Planning is in. Whatever your subject area, you had better know the right stuff.

The Stage

The teacher's personal qualities are there to read every day. If you really want to know a teacher, make a couple of routine classroom visits. There you will find the teacher's character, personality, qualifications, and idiosyncrasies—warts and all.

Warts and All

Poor souls, like teachers, who make a living speaking to audiences, acquire subtle coverups to nervousness or self-consciousness. Since teachers talk under duress all day, not just for the six o'clock news, they develop many irritating habits. Idiosyncrasies include talking with hand over mouth (sometimes a blessing to the audience); clearing the throat; focusing on cheerleaders outside the window; finger on or up one's nasal passages; playing with eyeglasses; ballet dancing; imitating a rocking horse, doing a Rodney Dangerfield with tie; using Okay? and other oddities.

To test your own foibles, listen carefully to your students doing a takeoff on you. Too bad you can't hide in a closet. Also, the faculty lounge is an excellent place to hear theatrical renditions of absent teachers. Being fresh from Boston I thought everybody in California had accents. Very shortly, I was dismayed to discover a friendly teacher was acting out a benign scene involving me. But on returning to Boston later, everyone remarked how I had lost my accent. Like all figures of great authority I knew I never had one.

Popularity

"Popularity" represents a quality that people admire. It is often used as a synonym for good teaching by educators and public alike. There is a connection, but not necessarily a valid one. Some teachers are unpopular even with their mothers, but are outstanding in their jobs. They may not give high grades or be darlings of administrators, parents, students, or faculty, but teachers know good teachers even if they don't like them. They may never visit the faculty lounge nor lift a beer with teachers on Friday afternoon, but they perform in class as few teachers are capable of doing.

No Golden Apple or Teacher of the Month awards are given to them nor expected, maybe not even accepted. They do not engage in school politics. They are not considered for department head nor put on committees. Often they are in trouble with principals and parents for being obsessed with tough standards. Some end up being transferred.

Other teachers may possess qualities combining great teaching with great popularity. It's nice to have, but not required to do the job well. It is often the unpopular teachers who are vocal and adamant opponents of cracks in discipline. They take the flak off the Golden Apple Pickers. Strive for popularity, but not at the expense of discipline or good teaching.

The Good, Bad, and Ugly

Teachers must deal with emotional events with an absence of emotion. Yet normal interaction with students requires teachers be demonstrative, although too much emotion or affection could cause teachers grief. Emotional teachers are not identical with feeling teachers; those who reveal too much of themselves crack the veneer, the invisible line. By opening the door to excessive familiarity, discipline evaporates. A breakdown of teacher effectiveness often occurs as a result of emotional confusion. Teachers must know when to relax and when to crack the whip without alienating students.

Poor teachers are inconsistent in handling pupils; sometimes the class is allowed to be rowdy and sometimes it is expected to maintain deathly silence. The work may be simple or impossibly difficult. There are teachers who cry in class, rush out of the room, scream at students, and expect perfection from youngsters. Such teachers know it all, listen to no one, and become irate when students hint that they don't know their business.

Whether teachers read newspapers during class, use the same text and tests for ten years, or teach the same subject every year makes no difference in financial benefits. If poor teachers are loud and obstinate enough, most principals will turn to more cooperative teachers to handle the load. Good classes end up with atrocious teachers—all in the name of democracy. Everyone must be treated alike. Knowing that good teachers get the same pay as the bad is strong justification for leaving the profession. Democracy regarding teachers has been carried to insane lengths. The Director of the Council of Basic Education stated that about 40% of these teachers can't do their jobs because of their own illiteracy. Their paychecks are not affected.

Statistics show that it was bad enough that education majors, historically, were at the bottom one/third of college grads, but even worse to find that between 1973 and 1982 the ed majors scored even lower on the S.A.T., A.C.T., G.R.E., and National Teacher Exams than other university students. To discourage low quality students from getting started, states are now requiring admission tests for education majors. Indiana requires 23 of 40 accredited colleges and departments of education to give written admissions tests. They feel that high quality teachers are needed for high levels of achievement. Reformers point out that no standard program is utilized for the training of education majors. A college grad can get a credential without attending a school of education and may be a better teacher for it. Novices who never spent a day as a sub or student teacher may develop into crackerjack instructors. Enter the personal quality factors.

Teaching as a Life Sentence

The quality teacher who can handle career teaching must be prepared to accept a low status job with little recognition. For this, pay is inadequate for standards and performances demanded of teachers. For those who aspire to nothing more than classroom teaching, a dead end promotion prospect awaits.

Teaching skills are largely ignored by business, since teachers deal with young people and not adults. Government forms always ask how many people the applicant has directly supervised. Class numbers don't count because young people don't count by federal standards for hiring in non-teaching jobs. The attitude also prevails at the college level where nothing done at the high school level matters. Although you can teach 18 year olds you can't teach 19 year olds since they are college students and are smarter than you are. Government and business stress "leadership" for resumés; a vice principal with two years "leadership" wins hands down over a first class teacher having twenty years' experience.

An M.Ed. is virtually useless for community colleges in some states, regardless of a non-education bachelor's degree. Applying for a college teaching credential is an exercise in frustration. Ten years of instructing high school seniors does not impress college personnel departments. One year teaching college classes is more important. Trying to teach outside of your major field is almost impossible. The educational bureaucracy is said to have no peers; one wonders about "academic freedom". Having an academic major translates into having inadequate knowledge to teach anything else.

College grads who assume that teaching jobs are always available as a last resort will discover that departments of education are requiring more courses for the ever-critical credential. A secondary teacher wanting to switch to elementary school also must return for additional college courses. Even though there are obvious differences between the two levels, the requirements and expense involved are so ridiculous that they preclude much transferring.

Any valid evaluation of teacher qualities should acknowledge that a good teacher is as valuable as an administrator, and the salary should be commensurate. Teachers are punished in pay and prestige for remaining in the classroom. In a society where titles and high salaries determine worth, teachers stand low on the worth scale. Someone commented, "Either we are martyrs or we are fools". A career teacher has to live with these attitudes.

To establish an accepted level of teacher quality is estimated to take from five to ten years. But those who evaluate teachers for promotions, job retention, or merit pay are often ones who bolted from the classroom after the required five years' experience before becoming administrators. Teachers should rate teachers. The system doesn't allow teachers to evaluate administrators. Granted, determining teacher quality is not easy; the characteristics are mainly subjective: getting along with people, being effective in educating others, and willingness to work under difficult conditions.

College classes or student teaching never prepares new teachers for what happens in a classroom. New teachers receive inadequate help and encouragement. The job requires working alone. Other teachers are knee deep in daily survival themselves, and principals do not look kindly upon instructors who cannot work independently. Coupled with demands of the present, teachers must deal with administrators who are always planning for the future. While teachers deal with young minds, the rest of education deals with mainly impersonal concerns. Whatever intangible quality a teacher needs to deal with, the second world of education could be a necessity for an extended career.

Leadership, setting the tone, and being a role model are recognized qualities necessary for good teachers. Yet none of these can be taught to a good teacher. Verbalizing and courses just won't do it. A good teacher is unique, yet the only true recognition of talent must be seen onstage. This is similar to meeting an actor who may seem unimpressive yet transforms immediately when facing an audience. Having the tools of the trade is fundamental. The difference comes when a teacher inserts numerous yet separate traits to create a consistent mosaic.

How can you recognize a good teacher? Teachers and students know the good ones. Walk into any school and ask.

CHAPTER 4

ON YOUR OWN

With your head full of "how to" and your room ready for occupancy it's now time to take your first steps—time to face your first classes. Set up ground rules immediately so students know rules before they can break them. Handouts are good, especially for transfer students. Post class procedures on your famous bulletin board. No new rules should be added unless discussed with classes first. No surprises.

Pupils appreciate knowing the teacher's background; keep it brief; you are not running for office. Give an overview of daily and weekly schedules and semester requirements. Inform classes about types of tests you give, when to expect them, homework, reports, and other requirements affecting grades. Issue texts as soon as you are reasonably sure classes are 90% stabilized. This initiates the business end of the course.

This is the ideal time to impose the orderly environment you are striving for. Expect to inherit residual disciplinary problems. Having a black belt in karate or having a voice of a bull moose is inconsequential when your adversary is a wisp of a girl with a gutter mouth. Here are ways to strengthen your first steps.

Name Calling

Know your students! Make a temporary class roll during the first meeting and begin by using names. Go through the official class list pronouncing each name and looking at each person. Use first names only; this establishes a more humane bond which students appreciate. Some instructors call all pupils by their last names. This may be acceptable for macho purposes but this raises an unnecessary barrier. Teachers must never be addressed by their first names nor last names only, without the accepted social titles. Students will test this. With 5–7 pupils in virtually every class likely to be troublesome, they must realize they are not anonymous. If these pupils are not controlled right away, you have already lost control. When the dam breaks, you can't repair it.

Using Audio

Don't be a motor mouth; talking too much is a turnoff. Before staring eyes become glazing eyes—stop! Incessant talking, reiterating information for inattentive pupils, or repetition of empty warnings breaks down your control. If you give a warning and do not follow through, your words will have little future effect. Speak loud enough to be heard in the rear row; it is unnecessary to bellow or project your voice in a normal size room. Keeping your voice raised constantly and showing exasperation not only causes your class to ignore you but also may result in a shaky or non-existent voice. Speaking above the normal bustle of a class, roar of jet planes, or Friday band practice outside your window during 25 hours of class time per week, you learn quickly that your voice is your living.

Raising your voice must mean something. In a well-disciplined class, the effect of a teacher's voice being raised should be silence. Directing your attention to the culprit accomplishes this purpose. This is very effective during class discussions. Accept no surliness or discourtesy. Having established norms of mutual respect, you will have the class silently on your side. If you leave an opening by saying, "Are you talking to me?" and the answer is "Yes!" then the battle lines are drawn. You take it from there.

Using Video

Body language is very effective once you establish a good working relationship. Careers have been prolonged by preserving voices through wise use of silent communication. Pupils are talked at all day and hear the same things so often that even the best pupils sometimes get turned off. A cocked eyebrow, a casually pointed finger, a pause in the discussion while looking at a pupil are effective. Wandering to the location of the distraction while continuing your lecture will normally stop dialogue. Don't betray undue annoyance. At this point, you are trying to indicate a variation in the norm. Calmness is catching.

Using appropriate body language assumes your classes are trained to accept normal classroom behavior. When instruction is not in progress, it is counter-productive to maintain the same level of control. Young people need time to unwind. Their attention span is limited but, unlike adults, youngsters are not so successful at concealing theirs.

Teachers can develop a positive, easy-going attitude and have productive classes with high morale if they make the effort to know their students, material, and use necessary organizational skills. If you are defensive or hostile, your classes know it and there will always be someone ready to push your buttons.

How to Self-Destruct

1. Ask questions inviting undesired responses: "Do you think I'm a fool?" "What do you think I'm here for?" "If you want to talk why don't you come up here and take over the class?" I did that once in summer school and a boy accepted. Luckily, he ran out of gas in two minutes and became embarrassed all by himself. Teacher also learned a lesson that day.

2. Back a student into a corner. His choices are to be humbled or pull out all stops. If the teacher forces the issue, he is in a no-win situation. Yet in any confrontation with a student, the teacher must prevail; but in an unjustifiable situation, the teacher loses, no matter what. No disruptive pupil can remain in a classroom. If you have a reputation for respect and fairness, you can have such students dropped or suspended from class. If the problem is a serious personality conflict you must make a strong stand on refusing to keep a disruptive student. If it's "him or me", force the issue.

3. Allow the "invisible line" to be crossed. Let yourself be called by your first name, last name, or nickname. Come on strong on a personal basis with your students. Tell risque jokes, use obscenities, criticize administrators, agree with students that Mr. Johnson is a lousy instructor.

4. To avoid conflicts and ingratiate yourself (who doesn't want to be liked?) be sure not to offend the small group that doesn't give a damn about school or anybody in it.

5. Don't accept excuses for being late or why assignments are not done. Assume every student is unreliable and untruthful. Don't consider that if you are honest and trusting that your students might knock themselves out making sure you don't lose respect for them.

6. Be omniscient and omnipotent. Use tests and pop quizzes as a means of discipline; constantly threaten everyone with poor grades, suspension, or expulsion.

Following those guidelines is an excellent way to create immediate misery and a spot in the unemployment line.

✓ Book Learning

In most classes, instruction begins with textbooks in the students' hands. Texts are not made equal. If textbook committees do their job right, your books will be around for at least five years. (A teacher's expertise includes knowing which portions of a text should be omitted, clarified, or corrected. It is not a bible, only a tool. In most texts, the Preface, Chapter 1, and the last chapters can be omitted.) Pupils rarely read these for assignments, knowing from experience that exams do not contain items from such chapters. Don't be a slave to chapter sequence. Related chapters are often found separated by other chapters. Some chapters are little more than padding.

Factual errors or slanted material is usually present. An instructor must be so well-versed in the class text that a glance at a page during the class lesson should be enough to trigger enough memory for the next five minutes. If you use three texts for three different subjects, the same requirement applies. You are the expert. You are dealing with pupils who may be more knowledgeable than you were at the same age. If you give wrong information, admit your error and thank the student who brought it to your attention. You are not expected to be perfect, but you can be perfectly accepted as a flawed expert. When you can lend your teacher's edition to a pupil and not break stride in your presentation, you've got it made.

Insist that students bring books to class daily unless told otherwise. To make this work, your discussions, assignments, and exams must be based upon the text. Discussing world hunger, saving whales, and pollution may be more interesting and relevant than the 1929 stock market crash, but if that is not what your course calls for, you're off base. If you are sidetracked, return to square 1 fast. Since you will go slowly insane keeping track of books lent to chronic "forgetters", don't establish a lending library. With public school books quite costly, you could be responsible for the loss of hundreds of dollars from just one class. Once the pupil has signed a book receipt, pupils are responsible. Textbooks contribute a common bond of belonging (or peonage to some) and credence to the subject. The presence of texts gives evidence that pupils are not merely visiting just before the p.e. class. A good idea for the instructor is to annotate the text. If you have to pay for the "destruction", it is well worth it. Be sure to mark errors and notify the students, who should not mark up their own books, however.

Reading to students verbatim is a bad idea for secondary students. However, the instructor should feel free to read excerpts which prove a point: "Let's see what the Constitution really does say". Some students enjoy reading aloud since it is a rare activity today. Silent reading in class is not effective from junior high on. Students figure it's a good time for makeup work, finishing off last night's assignment, note passing, bull sessions, and dozing off last evening's tv programs. Occasionally, your ego will be destroyed when all of the above occurs during your most scintillating lesson.

Keeping Classes Awake

Don't expect to put on a model lesson every day nor have a class of ten students for five minutes once a week as seen on television. What a delight to give your punch line at the dismissal bell as your class files out marveling at your wit! There is hope. If you can master the timing of a class period and use variety, you can be a pretty good, popular instructor. Be careful with timing. Both student and teacher interest and motivation will remain at high levels in classes where the clock is respected and monotony is not. The instructor must be always mindful of the amount and quality of daily work, yet keep a wary eye on the end of the semester. This is somewhere between the tortoise and the hare.

Lectures, a word in disfavor in public schools, should be kept to 20 minutes or less. Remember that students are talked at all day. Constant talk wears thin fast. To tie into the current lesson, a brief review of the previous lesson is a good technique and an icebreaker. The use of worksheets, homework discussion, group work, audio-visual presentations, test reviews and previews, and introduction of new material are activities which supply variety to daily lessons. A caution: when assigning homework started in class, plan it for the last 20 minutes. Anything less, and the end of the period falls apart. Whatever the activity, don't permit a letdown. The usual result is for pupils to kill time by talking, wandering, or discovering that it is a matter of life and death to visit the restrooms.

Seeing is Believing

Select audio-visual aids for your subject, not for entertainment. Refer to them before and after presentations. While films are more inclusive, soundstrips are more flexible. Most are specifically designed for a topic and short enough to be good supplements to daily lessons. Filmstrips are good if the instructor donates running comments and has interaction with the class during the presentation. Overhead transparencies are excellent. These can be shown and discussed from the front with no need to darken rooms or lose sight of classes. Transparencies are a salvation for nervous or beginning teachers.

Publishers' Packages

Many courses today are anchored by modules or kits costing $200–300 as a supplement to new textbooks. They often accompany inquiry method courses and are closely correlated with text material objectives. Contents include ditto masters for tests, worksheets, quizzes, information handouts, discussion booklets, soundstrips, filmstrips, and overhead transparencies. Such kits provide a unique course which allows teachers to contribute much of themselves, their ideas, and materials. Moreover, such packages give direction and unification as well as automatic variety.

The inquiry method departs from usual teaching methods in that specific information is given from seemingly unrelated information leading to general conclusions. The teacher is then a guide to knowledge, not a dispenser. Teachers trained to be the fountain of learning and the final judge of acceptable conclusions must relegate themselves to sifters and listeners, biting their tongues until students figure out answers. There are no expected conclusions, no "wrong" answers. Even right answers do not end the discussion. Sessions are introduced by the teacher summarizing previous discoveries, right and wrong, but not designated as such. To make the inquiry method work requires teachers be part of the class by sitting with each learning group in turn. With the teacher scheduling the final twenty minutes for correlating individual groups' findings, students know they have made progress and have made contributions to their classmates.

Drawbacks are: teachers and students are playing unfamiliar roles; some pupils find it difficult to assume small group responsibility; they are confused at first because there are no visible, correct answers. Also, teachers get worried that a visiting principal may assume the class is goofing off. However, with patience and organization, the inquiry method can make instruction a learning adventure.

Teaching Theories

For teachers, this usually means "read them and weep". More the norm than the exception is the awareness that proponents of how and what to teach are invariably people who have had little experience in the daily struggle of "them versus us". If, as many educators believe, it takes several years in the classroom to know what makes instruction effective, then many people who write books, articles, and make speeches at conventions are proposing theories not backed by experience. It is true that many instructional theories have worked at one time or another—but often with model classes or within confines of campus schools. Also true is that most of the great movements in education have gone full circle to where instruction basics began in the first place.

No experienced teacher claims that changes are not necessary nor will they defend their method of instruction as the best since Socrates. However, many proposals flooding education have seldom been tested in the daily survival world of teachers choking on chalk dust.

Suggestions include having teachers teach subjects out of their assigned areas. Nothing wrong with that, but it is a dead proposal. Secondary teachers are routinely assigned from two to four subjects out of their field. Yet when teachers attempt to transfer from their major field, administrators fight tooth and nail to keep the status quo. Perhaps having high school, junior high, and elementary teachers teach for a year at each level so each would be aware of the others' problems might work, but only at their request. Some teachers would be out of their element and others, after a year in junior high, might just quit entirely.

Some reformers want grades abolished to avoid fear of failure, learn for the sake of learning. Teachers would love that arrangement, great but idealistic. What brave soul aware of unemployment lines would effect that system in September? Those advocating teachers undergo psychoanalysis as part of their training would be pleased to see the above teachers seeking psychiatric help the following June. There would be plenty of justification for the therapy. Can we assume that those who advocate psychoanalysis for teachers also would include everyone involved with education at all levels?

When criticism of public school teachers includes "not knowing the real world" then criticism should really be directed at most college professors and administrators. If we accept surveys showing colleges of education draw their enrollment from the bottom third of the population, then we must assume that this bottom third got to know much about the real world before becoming teachers.

We are constantly reminded how important is higher education. Yet secondary teachers place more importance on the role elementary teachers play in the eventual academic success of children. Psychologists tell us that our traits are pretty well established by the first few years of life. In education we find that the first few school years are equally critical in the child's success. Success is within the grasp of most children at this time, given home support and good teaching. By ten, it becomes more difficult, and by the time junior high arrives there is much less chance for change. Primary teachers can invariably predict that new students in junior high will remain true to form. High school teachers can accurately predict success of new students in college, regardless of high school transcripts. Kids catch on fast when discovering what is important. Teachers seem to know what is important for the child, but in the world of the young are such things as other kids, other families, other values, and other interests—many of which are in direct conflict with school values.

Also, schools vary widely regarding courses, activities, and time spent on hard courses. Some districts make sure that teachers instruct mainly on passing a state achievement or a competency test. Teachers going on an independent path could very well find themselves in deep trouble.

Caught up in this potpourri of instability, the elementary student is understandably confused, once arriving in the junior high or the middle school. Many a parent and many a teacher have shed tears, saddened by the child's transfer to the real world of education, buffeted by more untested educational theories. The result is that elementary students are aware from this point on that the goal of all courses is graduation, not necessarily knowledge. What happened to learning for its own sake?

Zoo Annex

Junior highs have a well-deserved reputation for raucous, rowdy student behavior. Faced with unpredictable responses and erratic academic achievement, teachers acquire a strong sense of futility with gradual lowering of expectations. If students can leave the ninth grade achieving controlled behavior, then junior high years have been successful. Many teachers transfer to high school where, although having its own singular problems, is much more predictable than anything at the junior high level.

Many teachers claim that the worst grade to teach at elementary schools is the sixth grade; at the junior high level it's the eighth grade; at the high school level it's the tenth grade. The rationale for this is the sixth graders are kings of the hill and no amount of legalisms will expel them from school short of armed robbery. In the eighth and tenth grades, problem pupils feel they have little to lose. Here, many behavior problems of the non-learners may even be designed for eventual expulsion. However, both the ninth and twelfth grades have a graduation on the horizon and few students are willing to risk non-graduation. It is difficult to find teachers for junior highs, therefore many of the first teaching assignments are made to that level. Meanwhile, elementary teachers are wondering what those monsters in junior high school are doing to their prize students.

Teacher "Power"

Teachers are not helped much by famous people like Mencken who said that the main thing children learn in school is to lie; or George Bernard Shaw who claimed the only time his education was interrupted was when he was in school. Yet it is difficult to argue with cartoonist Al Capp who told a Princeton audience in the 1960's that any professor who thinks his students are intellectually equal with him is probably right. When Hemingway maintained that a great writer must have a shockproof, built-in crap detector, we can readily see how this can readily apply to certain people in education.

English teachers, to whose club I belonged, have had special blame heaped upon them for student performances in the basics of our native tongue. But when did English teachers ever establish courses of study or determine how English should be taught? They have always been aware of the trivia, inanities, and stupidities inherent in what they were teaching. Almost any spelling or pronunciation is acceptable. When can teachers justify something being incorrect? Punctuation is a minefield. There are several ways to punctuate any sentence correctly. Authors with English major Ph.D's find that either their editors or recent college grads decide what punctuation or manuscript style is "correct". Pity English teachers saying to students wanting to know the right way, "It is better to do it this way but it is not wrong to do it your way". Pupils wonder if teachers really know their business. Authors critical of the lack of basic skills lay the blame on teachers who are then accused of poor instruction.

It is a revelation to see research studies showing teachers have so much influence and downright power in establishing curricula, imposing teaching methods, creating educational philosophy, and determining disciplinary standards. It is also revealing to see research studies showing teachers to be ill-prepared, timid, non-assertive, and academically inferior to graduates of non-teacher colleges. Classroom teachers would feel very smug if they truly believed that professors, school boards, state and national boards of education, and literary critics had only a minor effect on the state of education in the past twenty-five years. Who is really at fault? Carl Rogers in his "On Becoming a Person" concluded that he could not teach another person to teach; that anything taught to another is not only inconsequential but it also has little effect on behavior; that the only learning influencing behavior is self-discovered and self-taught and, as such, can't be transmitted. His blockbusting conclusion was that he lost all interest in being a teacher. Our loss, but pity the professionals who still keep trying to teach the unteachable. Teachers have the ridiculous idea that schools are for learning and that schools exist for students. They instruct with the idea that knowledge is vital for survival, if not success, in our society. They innocently fight to instruct all things to all people willing to learn. Teachers rave and rant against constant interruptions, needless paperwork, apathy, lack of support at all levels—and teach anyway. Surely, teachers need therapy.

Whose Relevance?

Since elementary schools are responsible for the grounding in learning essentials and attitudes, then it is the responsibility of secondary schools to expand those essentials and add relevance. Young people, actively involved with daily events, want meaningful education. But "relevant" means relevant to whom? A few instructors have hangups on their "relevancies" and impose them upon their captive audiences.

At one high school where I taught, a massive classroom was divided by a folding vinyl wall. Because this "wall" was not soundproof, my classes were subjected to daily harangues on a young teacher's favorite hangup—sex. His classes were always in an uproar, undisciplined, and rude. His assigned subject was American Government. Many pupils thought him a great teacher because he was "relevant". Students attending college in September had a different concept of him when college instructors expected them to know something about their own government. No one knows what, if any, exams on government were given, but grades appeared on report cards. After a constant barrage of complaints from parents to the principal, (a flexible man trying to cope with the turmoil of the 1960's), and eventually to the Board of Education, the teacher returned to his home state rather than face dismissal.

Putting personal pet peeves and crusades aside in the classroom is the obligation of all teachers. However, no teacher should evade questions which legitimately arise during class discussions. If students want more information, teachers should make every effort to answer students' concerns honestly. Sometimes, parents complain to the principal hearing that abortion was discussed in an English class. However, as long as the topic was brought up by a student or discussed as a text topic, the teacher has a clear obligation to discuss the topic to the point of a clear explanation, but no further.

While still a probationary teacher, I assigned a student to support the use of animals for research since I had to fill in a spot on a panel discussion. The next day I was summoned by the principal to explain my action. The student's mother was an avid anti-vivisectionist. However, since this was at Boston Latin School, it was an easy job convincing the principal and the irate parent that the boy's academic development should include researching the other side of an emotional topic.

As battle-scarred classroom teachers readily acknowledge, there are some days that no matter what you do, what you say, how much time you spend, or how much effort you make—nothing works. Your lesson is going to be a dismal failure, relevant or not. Don't take the gas pipe. The next day you may be awarded the Golden Apple.

Memorize, Memorize

After teaching ten years in the Boston School System, I moved to San Diego, similar to moving from the North Pole to the equator. In 1961,

Boston educators believed that California schools were better at student freedom and sports than they were in academics. Stories were rampant on how California pupils transferring to Boston schools were far behind in achievement or how Boston pupils transferring to California schools were immediately promoted. Whether these stories resulted from wishful thinking, no one really knew. I did know this: the Boston school system stressed rote memory of literature, and grammar and spelling rules. Discipline was firm, sometimes unfair and arbitrary. Corporal punishment was permitted under proper supervision. Administrators had authority and autonomy.

Memorization was mandated by the courses of study. This method of learning has had few supporters, yet it had the effect of imprinting lifetime information, negating the constant use of reference books. For example, would-be teachers studying for the mandatory teaching exams had to memorize a multitude of seemingly trivial information in various subject areas. Pupils had to memorize selections like the Preamble to the Constitution, the Foreword to the Declaration of Independence, The American's Creed, Lincoln's Gettysburg Address, excerpts from Washington's Farewell Address, and poems like "The Midnight Ride of Paul Revere". Memory was not a factor in the San Diego public school system, but there were factors of cultural and educational shock.

Eastern schools had their plusses and minuses and so did the western, where courses were not so demanding, formal memorization was not required, class control was easier, and teacher-student relationships were a refreshing change from Boston. Because of various activities available, school and outside life were very much in harmony. In Boston it was standard practice to call all students by their last names. In San Diego, first names of students were used. Male teachers were not required to wear business suits; boys were not worried about demerits for not wearing ties. To some, examples from both systems provide a good example of how not to teach, how not to learn, and how to turn off students from real learning. To these critics, none of the above is really worthwhile, especially memorization.

Yet how can anybody learn how to spell without rote memory? Most spelling and grammar rules have so many exceptions they are almost worthless. No one has yet devised any effective method of learning how to spell except to do it the hard way—bald memory. Teachers know enough to instruct from real life situations, and to use compositions and speech as a springboard for proper spelling and grammar usage. They are painfully aware of the morass that passes for accepted "standard" or "proper" English. Consulting a dictionary for acceptable spelling alternatives gives the impression that anything goes.

However objectionable it may seem to some, rote memory has an important place in education. Little learning occurs through osmosis. Much of what we retain today has been through memorization. Memorization is tough. Anyone learning a language can attest to that. True, you can certainly teach without rules, or slugging it out with memory, but there comes a time when students ask "Why?". "How do we tell one part of speech from another?" "What are the rules for algebraic equations?" Memorize, memorize.

What should be the role of rote memory in modern schools? It certainly can't be rejected just because it is tough. To learn by doing is not good enough. Furthermore, we can no longer recommend that pupils use the media for role models of our native language. We are on our own, no matter what school system we are in.

Principal Effects on Instruction

Principals have a strong impact on teaching, especially at the elementary level. Secondary teachers are more ornery when following administrative directives. Principals consider good teaching and learning are taking place when class noise is under 80 decibels and teachers are not armed. They are impressed when rooms are attractive and bulletin boards show evidence that students have been accomplishing something.

However, teachers get upset when administrators forget the purpose of education; many times the administrator's idea of educational progress is planning for next September. If the PTA is satisfied, sports teams are doing well, and a minimum of yelling is going on in the classrooms, then all is right with the world. When competency tests or SAT's look adequate, it matters little to many administrators how those scores were attained. In short, don't rock the boat.

Principals must recognize that teachers require autonomy. They must be left alone unless they show they can't handle a class of normal human beings. Teachers must have the authority to decide whether gum chewing is acceptable; the dress code is being obeyed; textbooks are to be brought to class; cheating is not to be tolerated; accepted rules of common courtesy are to be obeyed; a learning atmosphere is the norm; disruptive students or any other distractions to learning are not to be tolerated. If a principal insists that disruptive students remain in class, the teacher must take a stand and make big waves.

Teachers must earn respect to be allowed to teach; this is what they are being paid for. Teachers are not policemen, psychiatrists, mediators, fighters, lawyers, or parents—though their job calls for them to be all these.

A 1979 survey in Texas showed that one half of every school day was devoted to non-instructional matters; in Delaware, up to one third of the school day was spent on management tasks; a six year study by the National Institute of Educational Research revealed that the amount of time on task varied as much as 100% in classes of the same grade level. The total time on task for reading and math combined was less than 100 hours per year in many classes. Numerous studies have shown a definite correlation between time on task and academic achievement. Yet because of a variety of pressures from outside groups to offer non-academic activities, there is tremendous waste of the teacher's time when academic achievement is the main goal.

Although state boards of education state specifically that a certain minimum of hours be spent on basic subjects, it is often beyond the teacher's control to adhere to the requirements. When time on task is achieved, it is mandatory that it is quality time; however, failure to achieve required hours need not be an indictment of the quality of teaching. Administrative burdens should not interfere with the primary duty of teachers, which is to teach. Administrators at all levels need to place themselves, mentally and physically, in the classroom to re-establish instructional priorities. By tying the teachers' hands, effective teaching cannot take place. And if instruction is not allowed to be effective, merely adding to the school year is not the answer.

Good Times

In March 1985 the Association for Supervision and Curriculum Development released results of a survey of 4000 public elementary school principals. This revealed that the average fourth grader spends only 60% of the class day learning science, social studies and the 3 R's, with 100 minutes per day being spent on reading and language arts. Math classes averaged 52 minutes, social studies 34, and science 28. An average of 22 minutes is spent in health, 15 for p.e., 14 for music, and 13 for art. Ninety-two minutes each day is consumed by recess, lunch, special programs, and activities other than regular classroom instruction.

A typical school day runs 5½ hours for 180 days per year. School districts are under pressure to increase the school day to devote more time to basics, yet not decrease non-academic studies or activities. An extra half hour in class results in 16.4 extra school days in a year and 114 extra school days from kindergarten through the sixth grade. The longer day results in ⅔ of an extra year before the seventh grade. Down the road, what effect will this have on student burnout at the high school level? Will possible extra learning during this time be offset by student apathy later?

Without good teaching accompanied by consistent motivation, more hours or days may not accomplish what is expected. Being bombarded with constant information wearies the body and the brain. We all get turned off after listening, writing, or doing anything beyond our capacity to absorb. Yet by the age of 18 we are expected to know most of our essential learning. Brain weary students who claim they can turn it on in college are seldom successful. Lifelong habits are not turned on and off like faucets. A longer school year is not the answer.

The role of a teacher is to organize, be creative, demonstrate persistent enthusiasm, keep students alert with pertinent questions, and assign meaningful work. Teachers need not and should not attempt to make every lesson or discussion of equal importance. Some things are vital to know in life while others are useful to know but don't make dummies out of those who don't know everything. Trivia is part of learning but learning is not trivia. Unless isolated facts can be assimilated into logical, coherent information, then real learning does not exist. Good classroom teachers must impart the idea that classroom activities are worthwhile. If something must be memorized, classes should be informed of the reason. "Training the brain" is not a good reason. If teachers feel a mandated assignment borders on trivia, then negative editorial comments will do nothing to motivate pupils. Maybe rethinking of one's values will help. Weekly test giving may gall teachers, but the other alternative is to expect pupils to learn for the sake of learning. If so, forget it.

Perceptive teachers know what is relevant in life and what is not; they question facts, surveys, and authorities—which include their peers; they acknowledge they don't know all the answers; they are willing to see other sides of problems and, above all, have enough self-confidence to trust their own judgments.

Teaching Without Tears

Computers are proposed as one method of making instruction more effective. So now the rush is for computers, calculators, word processors, and spelling checkers. Certainly, they can perform many functions better than humans. It is easier and faster to do math with a calculator than with one's brain; it is a blessing to use a word processor rather than a typewriter; a spelling checker can make anyone competitive with the state spelling champ. Why learn to tell time the old way when you can use a digital clock? Computer use, although worthwhile, has limited application in classrooms. Moreover, personal qualities and expertise of teachers cannot be replaced by electronic devices. If brain power had to depend upon battery power, perhaps Einstein might have been replaced by Eveready batteries.

We like to say that the computer will never supplant the human brain. We also dream about brain transplants being available for certain people we may not be too crazy about. Not that we would ever need one, of course. Although classroom teachers are required to be of major league quality and of infinite patience, they fall far short when it comes to head to head competition with the computer.

Yet, the passionate love affair with computers is dissipating rapidly. Thousands of buyers and advocates of computer learning are either no longer interested or are expressing no-frills action by simply throwing the computers out the window. It has happened. Few computer courses are available for public school pupils. Even when generous corporations donate machines, few instructors are available to handle the classes. Moreover, in a class of 35 pupils, how effective is the use of two computers? However, it is estimated that about 350,000 computers are currently to be found in schools below the college level. Another estimate is that about 550,000 computers are in schools, no indication if the figure includes colleges. But there are many times more computers in homes than there are in schools. It is quite likely that the home computers being used by young people are being used mainly for games. With the desertion of the public arcades using computerized games, this might indicate that home computer games have also had their day.

Computer learning, like other learning, requires study. The mystique of computers fades rapidly when school subjects are being learned and the computer itself has to be studied. Some school districts are putting their funds into computers because it is the wave of the future—or is it because computers don't go out on strike as math and science teachers do? Computers do not require qualities that society demand of teachers but they are excellent in perseverance, repetition, patience, and staying on the job 24 hours a day. They are quite unsatisfactory, however, in brushing away tears or explaining "why?"

Computers do open up new worlds of techniques and new approaches to old subjects. While computers rely on the much maligned rote memory method, it is less painful than having human beings insist that students keep doing it until it is right. Teachers claim that home computers give pupils an unfair advantage over those who don't have them; parents feel that as long as they can afford it that their child be given the most help possible in today's competitive atmosphere. Since most software is being used on home computers, however, software manufacturers are paying less attention to the schools as a source of business.

Eventually, computers may be found in most schools where new teachers are assigned. Computer knowledge may be required as a condition of employment some day, and the teacher with that jump may have a foot in the door. It is also likely that this could turn out to be another useless teacher training requirement. It should also be a condition of employment for that same teacher come equipped with a heart.

CHAPTER 5

GRADING WITHOUT GRIPING

Evaluating students is one of the most wrenching of a teacher's responsibilities. Grading time is emotional time. Whether grading standards are set by school boards, schools, or teachers makes no difference. Yet students throughout history have rarely felt that grades received were indicative of grades deserved. As in life, most of us seldom get what we deserve, and perhaps it is just as well.

When it's time to reach for grade sheets and the calculator, it is also time to reach for the aspirin. It is time to remember overachievers, underachievers, foreign born, accident and illness victims, and truants. Then the class favorites flash into your mind—ones who made the class catch fire, who set the work habits and the disciplinary levels by responding to the teacher's leadership, yet the grade book shows these students earned (not deserved) only C's. There are makeups never made up; the accident victim who lost the final month of school; shy ones who did excellent work but never participated in class; the ones who tried and tried yet never could quite make it. In what ways can you justify failing certain pupils?

Many causes contribute to school failure, but undoubtedly the biggest reason stems from the types of grading systems being used. Failure expectation usually begins in elementary schools where letter grades are given. Some use a subjective evaluation or a pass/fail system at different grade levels. While these decrease the chances of failure, colleges, employers, and the community insist on knowing the students' level of achievement and, indirectly, their smarts. Yet an A in a course or a PASS may not indicate mastery of a course in either case. Teachers are quite good at predicting C students' success in college and also A students' probable difficulty in college. Studies show that while grades are a good barometer of future success, don't bet the family jewels on it. But there seem to be no other practical alternatives to current grading practices. Teachers must determine a final, fair grade. A report from the American Medical Association stated that there was almost no correlation between medical school grades and success either in the practice of medicine or competence. These do not necessarily go together, as we all know. We also know where demand is greater than supply or when applying for the second job, school transcripts are redundant.

Parents feel that discipline is wedded to good grades, and they are pretty close to the truth. Pupils with disciplinary problems are not likely to be good students. Also, since image in our society is all-important, grades are correlated with learning, diplomas, degrees, and status type courses.

Another puzzle is confusion of what ''grade'' really means. Students and parents seem to believe that C's indicate students or teachers are mediocre, and A's indicate students are brilliant, the teachers skilled, and the schools excellent. Ironically, the last bastion having the utmost faith in grades as a criterion of ability is the institution which should be the most cynical—the colleges. If you are 60 years old and have been a nuclear physicist for 40 years, you'd better show your transcripts or forget about enrolling in a math course.

Adults returning to class develop an attitude similar to the youngsters'—do whatever you can in course and teacher selection to increase odds of getting good grades. Where good grades are possible with the least amount of effort will be found a popular instructor. An expected result of stressing grades is that students work for grades, not knowledge. Maybe that is being a bit naive. Today, at least in non-college classes, grades are not ''posted'' nor listed by rank nor read to the class. That embarrassment, we hope, is gone. Too many pluggers have been humiliated and too many unearned A students have been praised as a result of these practices. The emphasis on grades too often has caused unhealthy pressure, cheating, dislike of school, and conflict at home.

Whatever shortcomings the traditional grading system has, it does provide a reliable evaluation of a student's performance. It furnishes pertinent information and a standard of achievement. The teacher determines a standard based upon a variety of intangible and tangible criteria. Teachers teaching identical subjects must vary the instructional quality and quantity according to each class, time of day, day of week, and time of year. All classes are not equal and teacher grading is not engraved on marble. Teachers walk a fine line between expected pupil achievement and realistic achievement. While a class may work to its maximum level, it may do poorly on standardized or competency tests.

In the same subject, an A or a D in one class could very well be a B or a C in another. Some teachers are more affected by behavior problems than others; girls may be favored over boys; articulate students may be assumed smarter than they are, even though their assignments don't bear out that assumption. Experienced instructors size up students the first couple of days, give assignments, and casually categorize which pupils will probably get certain grades. However, teachers do make an effort not to allow emotions to influence their grades. Here are some ways they use to evaluate students:

Pass/Fail

This appears to have fallen into disfavor after its popularity during the 1970's. Institutions still using the pass-fail system have begun offering the letter grade option as well. The pass-fail method does not help employers since the system does not give much information that employers need to know. Moreover, personnel departments do not want to spend time reading performance evaluations, wrestle with educational terminology and clichés, or wade through the double speak of instructors' comments. Parents are not satisfied knowing their kids merely "passed" English or physics. Parents and students alike realize that in the practical world of competition, most academic colleges, occupational colleges, scholarship agencies, and employment offices base their decisions upon objective letter grades, rather than guessing whether PASS means an A or a D−.

Using the Alphabet

Most teachers start out with traditional letter grades and stick with them. Why? They work. Biases, usually subconscious, may still appear. It is just as easy and justifiable to give a C+ instead of a B− to a kid who pushed your button once too often. There is the fine but critical threshold between a D− or an F. This is the teacher's ultimate power that can easily be abused. Weighing a whole semester of steady work against a one shot super report or test, or deciding whether homework is worth the same, double, or less than someone else's facility at creaming tests but little else, is a worrisome decision. If teachers grant a separate grade for class participation, should shy students be penalized?

2 Winning on Points

This method has been gaining in popularity because it is more objective than letter grades yet allows for adjustments. Every test or assignment has a definite number of points assigned to it. Whatever the student earns is based upon the possible that could be earned if perfect. No need to worry about even numbers or the basic grading scale of 70 out of 100 = C, for example. The number of points earned is marked on a returned test as a fraction, e.g., $51/75$. The letter grade C is also marked on the paper, but only for the student's peace of mind. Entered in the grade book, however, is a numerical score but no letter grade. At the bottom of the grade book is entered the number of points which could have been earned, and the assignment. At grade time, each student's score is tallied, as is the number of possible points. A pupil earning 400 points of 500 possible would earn a B, since 400 is 80% of 500.

The point system minimizes subjectivity, drastically decreases students' complaints, and allows teachers to include any assignment. Homework can be equal in value to several tests or quizzes, depending upon the number given. The advantage here is that it compensates for hard workers who do well in everything except tests and does not penalize those who do. Also, it adjusts to students who do well in tests, yet seldom do other assignments. ("Got a B without cracking a book.")

Using the point system places the responsibility for good attendance upon the student. Not allowing makeup work for truancies can materially aid in better attendance. When makeup work does not count so much as the original work, then it is up to the student to be present for regular class activities. Bonus points announced in advance is a good motivational device as long as teachers keep the overall value in proportion to normal assignments. The point system is good mainly because the final letter grade is under the control of the students. No work, no pay.

Making the Grade

In education, we are successes or failures mainly because of tests. Yet the type of tests often has more of a bearing on the results than the content itself. In some classes, especially in college, our future may depend upon only a midterm and a final test. That's it. Secondary education allows more chances to succeed as well as to fail. While everyone has equal opportunity, instructors can easily control grades or even class discipline simply by the test chosen, such as essay tests.

Essay Tests

To incite a universal groan, announce an essay test. It is extremely difficult to include all pertinent facts, write coherently and concisely, discuss each 2, 3, 4 part question adequately, and complete the test in the allotted time. When test results generate complaints, it is difficult to justify grades a few days later. Re-reading the test is time consuming; what the grader was looking for at the time may now be hazy; emotion may have played a part; poor handwriting, grammar, or sloppiness may have influenced the grade. Sometimes merely glancing at the student's name is enough to influence a grade. Teachers partial to essay tests may assign them in order to develop critical thinking and encourage better writing skills. Even though it is commendable and also recommended for improvement of basic skills, teachers simply do not have the time nor endurance to make this type of test a habit. At best, one or two essay questions may be included in objective tests to separate or even validate students deserving A's, or perhaps use for bonus credit. Secondary teachers having to correct 175 essay tests from their daily pupil load will switch fast to the much criticized objective tests.

Objective Tests

Virtually every student who ever lived would take an objective test over an essay test if given a choice. Instructors have maintained a semblance of sanity thanks to multiple choice, matching, or fill-in items. While college entrance exams now include essay questions as tiebreakers, the rest of the exams are still objective. Computers are not yet capable of supplanting the human brain in evaluating essay questions, and even if they were, rest assured that teachers would not have the computers to do it with. Computers will not outlive objective tests. The harried classroom teacher can cope with 150-175 objective tests, even though nobody said it was going to be easy. By using test keys, the job is manageable. The rap against objective tests, of course is: ''They do not stimulate real thinking''. Then again, in the heat of battle, test takers are not too choked up about stimulating thinking, either. Critics advocating essay tests don't have to correct them.

Objective tests do require facts as well as some superficial learning. Like weekly spelling lists, there may not be much effective carryover. Another complaint is that not much room for ideas is available during this type of test. However, a good classroom teacher has already put together a package of thoughts during the teaching process. Terminology and connections have been put into focus and discussed. While these ideas may not be included in the test, this does not necessarily mean that students taking the test are not putting these ideas together during this time.

Open Book Tests

While not a common practice, the use of open book tests has merit as a variation and as a motivational device. It does help sharpen perception, word recognition, following directions, and paragraph comprehension. Students feverishly look up answers, and cheating is not a problem. Negatives include pupils not studying for the exam, spending time searching for each answer and running out of time, and teachers faced with either lending books or giving absent-minded pupils an F. Also, open book tests do not help poor readers. One danger is using this type of test to keep classes frantically occupied for the whole period. Oddly enough, students appear to have the same test results as they would with closed books tests, provided the open book test is used sparingly.

Making the Curve

Yes, some secondary and many college instructors grade on a curve. Unfortunately, the wrong people suffer. Why should there be only 5–7 A's and a majority of C's? Classes vary tremendously in ability and even during a time span. There is nothing wrong with giving mostly A's to a class if they have done A work. Conversely, it should be equally permissible to fail most of a class for the same reason, although it would be a brave or defiant teacher to make a habit of it. Since the theory is based upon a ''normal'' class, the normal curve would have reason to be applied if there ever were such a thing as a normal class. However, using the curve entails more mathematical work and generates unnecessary class hostility.

In Hollister, California, high school students rioted in 1987 when the superintendent ordered grading on a curve. This was to prevent too many high or low grades and to review performance of teachers who deviated from the grade expectancy range set by the school district. Teachers complained that the new system would give good students lower grades and give poorer students higher grades than they would otherwise have gotten. Another example of administrative action without consulting people who know better. Teachers don't need any more trauma than they are now getting for free.

Homework

The only ones who like homework are the ones who don't have to do it. Alas! The emphasis now is on more homework. Newly required mandatory basic skills standards, especially for writing, puts more stress on home assignments than ever before.

In a practical sense, it is not only a burden but also a mind bending chore for teachers to assign homework to five classes even three times per week. Figuring out the basic math of 5 classes $\times$ 35 pupils $\times$ 3 days $= 525$ papers to check, assuming each pupil does only one sheet each. Some pupils turn in two or three sheets every time an assignment is made. For a teacher to evaluate and record this assignment takes much time. Good teachers have never abandoned the benefits of home assignments, mainly because of the need for expanding lessons as well as instilling beneficial work habits.

If the community and administrators demand instructors assign regular homework, all well and good. But to impose a set quantity or make English and social studies teachers bear the brunt of a heightened interest in basic skills is unfair and unenforceable. No additional compensation is given for extra work but, even if it were, those teachers would be hard pressed to add to their already overwhelming responsibilities. Also, some subjects by their nature make homework impractical. Moreover, a few teachers in any subject won't assign homework, regardless of administrative directives. If assignments are made, they must be pertinent, and important enough to be counted as part of the student's grade. Papers are occasionally seen tumbling into the "round file" as soon as the last pupil exits. Students catch on fast, and the result is self-evident. Timing is important for assignments. Don't expect to be overwhelmed with papers if you have assigned work over a weekend, holiday, or a vacation.

Record keeping depends upon the teacher's option. A scale of 4, 3, 2, 1 or letter grades, or +, −, check mark might be used. A separate grade should be given for homework. This is especially helpful for student and parent information as well as serving notice that such assignments are required for passing grades. Collect homework when due and set up a penalty system for late work and unexcused absences. Conversely, give extra credit for superior work and make the class aware of good papers. It is also good practice to remark upon certain questions that the class did well or poorly on in order to make them aware that you are reading their work. Another good practice is to return work either at the beginning of the class period or, if time does not permit, to set them upon the table before each class enters. Some pupils avidly retrieve the homework, while others don't bother. Returning homework during class time cuts into your instruction time.

Teachers can easily determine course grades simply by the number and difficulty of homework assignments. Conscientious teachers don't do this, but it does happen. Even though it is done with the best of intentions, daily homework assignments can have the same unplanned effect, devasting the grades of some students. There are pupils who willingly sacrifice a letter grade rather than do homework. This is their choice, but they have the opportunity to affect their grade positively as well. Nothing upsets parents more at Open House than hearing their child is not doing homework. Poor tests they can cope with, but not doing homework is "irrefutable evidence" that the child is not making an effort. Yet there is a prevalent attitude that homework is merely another name for busywork. When teachers assign work to be done at home then correct and record it religiously, they would have to be masochistic to keep homework at the level of a Mickey Mouse assignment.

Administrators, counselors, and parents regard teachers who consistently assign homework as "good teachers". Whether children in the lower grades get much out of homework is debatable. How much this contributes to frustration with school or the need for parents to do the work for their children, we don't really know. Homework gets a bad name in the early school years either because it cuts into the child's free time, bothers the parents, or reaches the point eventually where the parents can't keep up with the kids. Secondary students are in a better position to understand the need for homework and are expected to do the work themselves. Teachers are able to cover additional material through reports, readings, projects, and home study. Elementary pupils, being with the same teachers all day, have more chance at classwork and are less subject to the tyranny of the bell schedule found at the secondary level.

Complaints about homework include reinforcing wrong answers; excessively long assignments; several teachers giving assignments on the same night; and teachers paying little attention to submitted work. Also, poorer students won't do much homework anyway while better students are always under pressure to complete assignments without knowing why they are doing them. Students in large families or those without a satisfactory place to work will always have trouble completing assignments. Also, in some circles doing homework can mark a kid as a "brownie" or worse. Some teachers feel that they could do more real teaching if they didn't have to assign homework. Since the public is now demanding more and more regular homework, it's unlikely that these teachers will be successful in bucking the tide.

On the brighter side, reading homework has saved many a teacher's sanity. Although there are several books already published covering humor in the classroom, a few of mine would not be amiss at this point. From my psychology classes such gems as: "duckless glands", "rabbit eye movement", "acute halitosis" (hallucinogen), and "A stimulus is what activates an orgasm" (organism). In American Government, "The penalty for bigamy is having two wives". I never could fathom how teachers had the time to stop and record the publishable jewels of classroom humor, but power to those who can—perhaps a good argument for assigning homework.

Other Headaches

Who has not quaked at the teacher's pronouncement of a book report due next month? Or even worse, an oral report. Assignments vary, of course, according to the subject. Term papers in high school are not that rare anymore. In some classes diaries or notebooks must be kept as a major part of a semester grade. Newspapers clippings or special television program reports may be required.

No matter what the choice, the assignment must be capable of being done and must be worthwhile. Is there a valid reason to assign a report on the Teapot Dome scandal or one on the life of John Whitcomb Riley? The rate of forgetting being what it is, what students are expected to retain from your assignment must be the primary consideration. When assignments are given without good guidelines, instructors end up grading Tolstoy, Hemingway, book jackets, or last year's graduate. The wise teacher thinks carefully before assigning work that merely perpetuates an image of deep teaching. No matter what the assignment, it should have a definite, understandable, fully explained worth to exist. If it cannot be justified in terms of valid learning, don't assign it.

Something For Nothing

Handling cheating and cheaters is a delicate matter having far reaching implications. School exams, SAT scores, scholarships, letters of recommendation, parental and community pressures affect young people as perhaps never before. When teachers stress tests unduly, or teach only for the test, panic may result. If it means getting caught, then chances must be taken.

There are people in this world who cannot take tests successfully. Many persons work diligently and succeed in everything in a course except testing. Some accept that fact and take their lumps; others cheat. To forestall prevalent cheating, some teachers have turned to essay tests. These are the most difficult test to do well in; grading strongly depends upon the subjectivity of the grader. A standard practice in education is having English teachers exchange student essays and grade them. Teachers seldom agree on one grade because they are looking for different things.

The alternative, objective tests, are easier to correct but make cheating easier. Who among you out there never asked for or gave out answers during a difficult objective test? How to handle? Each instructor has methods—some severe, some lenient. Catching wigwag signals, holding up two or three fingers, or tapping the person in front can usually be handled covertly by an alert teacher using body language. During exam time, teachers should not try to squeeze in desk work, no matter how pressed for time. When cheating becomes blatant, more drastic measures must be taken, such as confiscating the test paper and tearing it up with a flourish. A better way would be to speak privately to the culprit, showing that person a failed test paper. Much depends upon the teacher's upbringing when reacting to cheating. Referrals to counselors and phone calls to parents are other alternatives.

When successive classes appear for the test, be alert for paper passing, paper left on desks, and answers written on desks. Whether you are using publishers' tests or your own, they should be changed regularly. While easy to say, it is very time consuming. Having Tests A and B, or changing the order of questions are very useful for makeup exams or for exposing classes or individuals you suspect of cheating. You may discover that certain pupils are always absent on test day then score well on makeups.

If you lead by example, build an atmosphere of trust and confidence, and prepare carefully for tests, students will be less likely to cheat. "Pop" or unannounced quizzes don't help. Tests must be expected at regular times, such as the end of a chapter or unit. Notify classes of test dates and general content at least a week in advance. Also, don't overstress the importance of one test over another. Having the semester grade depend on two or three tests places an extremely heavy burden upon the pupils and could lead to desperation cheating. A balanced evaluation program of tests, homework, special assignments, class participation, and attendance minimizes the possiblity of getting grades dishonestly. When you hear someone from your class bragging about getting a B and never studying, you can be reasonably sure that your student was a better cheater at his job than you were in catching him at it.

Handling Cheating

Cheating is a familiar topic to everyone who has attended school. Techniques are well known. The problem is trying to combat it. Since even our military colleges are not immune, maybe we have not been using the proper weapons. Knowing how to handle cheating is rarely covered in education courses. The trust of students is of paramount importance to teachers. It is not a trust to be gained lightly and it can be lost very easily. An erroneous judgment on apparent cheating can result in not only a loss of confidence in your good sense but also a loss in class morale. One wrong call is not so damaging but a second chance may be the last chance. Much depends upon how the instructor handles the situation. If the teacher has had previously pleasant working and personal relationships with students, a questionable accusation of the class might result in strained relationships for the balance of the semester. A bitter-sweet memory will always remain with me of catching three senior cheerleaders passing around a crib sheet. The girls were very close friends in class and on campus, a mutual admiration society. I quietly confiscated their tests and gave F's. The girls apologized and were greatly embarrassed, but the cloud of cheating was never dissipated even though the incident never left the classroom.

At Stanford University exams are not proctored; students not only support the honor code but most said they would report any cheating they saw. Little change was noted from the 1961 and 1976 surveys. Prestigious academies such as West Point, Air Force Academy, Annapolis, and numerous other colleges have been wracked with cheating scandals. Also, negative cheating has occurred in which students give each other wrongs answers in order to lower the grading curve and allow students to pass with lower test scores.

One survey showed that at least 55% of college students cheat for better grades. A 1965 survey of 99 colleges by William Bowers in which he interviewed 600 deans and 6000 students over a two year period showed cheating at all 99 colleges. The extent of cheating was three times what the deans thought and twice what the students themselves thought. Stress of grades is the main reason for dishonesty. Students learn the expected material and virtually nothing else. However, many students wouldn't listen at all if they thought lessons were not to be tested. Do students want to learn more about less and less or do they want to learn less about more and more?

Cheating begins slowly in elementary grades and becomes common in junior high. Surveys show cheating increases with higher grade levels; from Grades 5–9, girls cheated more than boys. Teachers are aware that cheating is more widespread in some classes than others. Why do some pupils cheat and others don't? Perhaps it is the teacher's apathy, stress on grades, or difficulty of the subject. In some classes, rooms are crowded; the teacher has not discussed the possibility of cheating nor its penalties; the teacher has not taken a stand or acted positively when noticing cheating, and either has not taught well or has stressed grades beyond reason. Coupled with a lack of ethics at home and belonging to the wrong peer group, some students will cheat routinely.

Some suggest eliminating grades would eliminate cheating; some suggest that there should be no closed book exams because in the professional world knowledge comes from looking up information, not memorizing it. Mechanics, lawyers, surgeons, engineers use books or manuals daily. Students can't. Punishment should be a swift consequence of cheating. Otherwise, cheating continues to the point where cheaters make better grades than the good guys. Prompt and effective action by the teacher will make for a better class with a much better image of itself.

Crime Without Punishment

Regardless of grades, non-working students have, for years, been automatically promoted. Some cases involved principals overruling teachers. Teachers noted for their tough grading standards, flunking an excessive number of students, have been special targets of administrators. Affluent communities having articulate, vocal parents have had a strong influence on undeserved promotions.

Non-professional reasons allow social promotions to occur simply because teachers and principals don't want disruptive children around. This policy can be clearly seen in advancing elementary pupils to junior high and especially from junior high to high school. Even though troublesome children in the elementary schools can be controlled reasonably well, the same is not true for junior highs. Junior highs have no really effective punishment except for the most serious of crimes against society, not necessarily crimes against schools. These students are aware of their rights and special status as juveniles. They are aware that being disruptive or poor students is no barrier to promotion.

Administrative procedures allow troublemakers or drug users to be transferred to schools either in the same district or through arrangements with other contiguous school districts on a reciprocal basis. "You take our problems and we'll take yours." The major punishment in this situation is mostly an inconvenience in transportation. For continuous unacceptable behavior, students can be expelled. However, especially in large city schools, the process takes a horrendous amount of time. Voluminous records must be submitted covering many months of student violations of acceptable school behavior. Some cases may start in September and not be resolved until the next semester. Meanwhile, the time of teachers, counselors, administrators, and juvenile authorities is tied up. Junior high students have more leverage in this area than high school students mainly because of age and the awareness of school personnel that these teenagers are undergoing many physical and emotional changes. Therefore, school personnel find it difficult to separate growing pains from anti-social behavior. As a result, suspension or expulsion is used as a last resort. Yet in some cases the very students who are being suspended or expelled are receiving exactly what they want. Such students get to milk the system for all it's worth.

Children in the sixth grade automatically plan promotion to junior high in September. Children in junior high know they'll be in high school in the fall. In September they buy T shirts proclaiming they belong to the graduating class three years later, regardless of their academic or disciplinary problems. And they are right. High school grads know they must be accepted in most states to the local community college. While students work for decent grades because of peer or parental pressure, athletics, cheerleading, or scholarships, there is very little incentive for students to do any more work than necessary to avoid getting into trouble. Promotion is automatic and every student knows it. High school graduates enrolling in college hearing college profs repeat the cliche of "Look to your left then look to your right because two of you will not be around at graduation" assume the other two won't be around. After 12 years of routine advancement, they are unlikely to exert effort necessary for college success. Senior high teachers are familiar with the litany of underachieving students who claim they will work hard when it really counts. It seldom happens.

If the purpose of automatic promotion is other than preventing failure being implanted in the psyche or keeping young people off the street, what is the point? A situation which is a crime in itself occurs on high school graduation day. Regardless of grade point averages or not fulfilling state mandated course requirements, every pupil still in class in June will mount the podium to be handed a diploma folder by some local dignitary.

Preceding this scenario long before this memorable rite of passage, students have been able to attend the senior prom, mail out graduation announcements, and see their names printed on the graduation list. Upon receiving the coveted folders, and graduation caps having been thrown into the air, new grads return quickly to the school to receive diplomas. Instead, they may be handed a slip of paper informing them that a diploma will be issued when more course requirements are completed. A cruel hoax has been perpetrated by the adult world at a time when it hurts the most. Some might dismiss this as a just punishment, reaping what was being sowed for 12 years. To lay the blame solely on the teenager is perhaps not fair, but projecting what follows is even less fair.

The adolescent is out of day school because his class has graduated.

The alternative is evening school. Long suffering parents usually have no intention of housing and feeding a newly designated unemployed guest. If a job is available, evening classes are difficult to attend and the high school diploma fades away. Paychecks become difficult to give up. He may maintain the illusion of someday earning a diploma or a degree, but it seldom happens. How much more humane it would have been to repeat a class in the early years.

States and local school districts have taken a hard look at automatic promotions and have instituted some firm policies regarding the practice. If competency tests are the solution, it will be a long time before a meaningful effect can be evaluated. As with all testing, results depend upon factors such as validity of tests and integrity of the personnel involved.

School districts are now attempting to establish a coherent policy regarding non-promotions instead of placing the full responsibility upon teachers. To forestall cumulative problems in later grades, proposals are being made to identify educational problems in the early grades, especially the 6th and the 8th. Having a principal, parent, and teacher discuss the probability of non-promotion is one method. If the parent objects, then the student is moved ahead, the parent taking the responsibility. In such cases, the problem is pushed to other actors in the scenario for an ultimate solution. Whether holding a child back is dooming him to failure in future schooling, will cause a sense of inadequacy, or will create social pressures by not being part of the former peer group are all serious considerations concerning promotion at any cost.

A Washington *Post* account of November 2, 1984 reported that the retention of 900 students in a Virginia school district had cost $4.5 million in one year. This fact alone should stimulate routine promotions. Other studies have shown that students who have been held back, especially during the early grades, later drop out. Given the conditions where class enrollment is correlated with a progressing course of study, the system does not allow space for students not grasping material the first or even the second time around. If a child is kept back once, maybe not too much lasting damage occurs. If twice, however, it becomes more unlikely the child will ever recover in the academic world.

In San Diego, about 2200 of over 111,000 students were not promoted during the 1982–1983 school year. The feeling is that it is less traumatic for children to be retained at the elementary level than at the secondary level. Under a more unified policy being considered, the child is put "at risk" if, in elementary school, that child falls behind two years at the expected reading level for a particular grade. Also, promotion may be allowed but only on probation. A pupil not responding is returned to the previous grade. The purpose behind the move to set up guidelines for teachers regarding promotions is to make possible beneficial effects from denying automatic promotions. These would include allowing more time for maturity as well as more time to master the skills necessary for academic success.

On a more massive scale, the Los Angeles City Schools held back more than 11,000 children in the first three grades from 1980–1982, including 3200 who failed to pass kindergarten. The reason? Lack of basic skills. Teachers there stated that the reason for retention is that kindergarteners are not ready for reading in the first grade. Nobody was happy with keeping back so many, so young. The school board was given a report which said that only one in five who fail the first or second grade will ever graduate from high school. When children are held back at this level, it is because they are not expected to succeed at the next higher grade level. If a child cannot follow instructions, cannot cope with classroom environment, or attain the skills required for success the following year, then there is no promotion.

Back in San Diego, a major revision was made in preparing for competency tests for high school graduation. In 1982–83 only 21 of one graduating class of 6569 pupils were not awarded diplomas. Under new procedures, normal classroom tests in English, math, and other basic skills will be the basis for determining qualifications for graduation. Previously, special weeks were set aside for competency test reviews. With the tests now being an integral part of classroom instruction, students should pay more attention to daily lessons than ever before. Even though new guidelines will result in tougher tests and more pupils are expected to fail the competency tests, the tradeoff is for higher expected educational standards.

Automatic promotion leading to automatic graduation is an educational travesty. Let us hope that most of the current remedies being proposed will cure a very sick patient. Behind it all is the classroom teacher, red pen in hand, trying to write the prescription.

CHAPTER 6

I HAVE AN ATTENDANCE HEADACHE!

Effective class discipline is wedded to stable attendance. Pupils are expected to be present whenever possible and teachers must insist upon their presence. Being there for instruction is similar to having a job to go to. No work, no pay. In this case—no knowledge.

Dissenters point out that in secondary schools you are only one teacher of several others your pupils have each day, so why get hard nosed about it? By insisting your pupils make your class, you cause them to miss other appointments and not able to make up tests in other classes. Besides, what's the difference if a p.e. class is missed as long as a chemistry lab isn't? However, should any faculty member or student decide which classes are expendable? Is art less important than algebra? That depends. While teachers have little to say when passes summon students to the office, they can express their feelings when a pattern develops. Counselors may wait until pupils are in a nearby class until they are sent for. Sometimes, only cooperative teachers are interrupted; grouches who make a fuss about excessive passes are left alone. Be a grouch. Justify this by knowing that not all appointments are equal, on or off school grounds; makeup tests or conferences with other teachers are not your responsibility.

Being There

Students may run breathlessly to one teacher's class yet stroll casually late to a second one. Is the first teacher a strict disciplinarian and the second too liberal? Maybe. Perhaps the difference is in the value system. It isn't wrong to insist students be punctual and have good attendance. Punctuality and dependability are transferable qualities for adult life. Instructors must set the example. "Do as I say but not as I do" does not work well with young people. They should not be exposed to a double standard from a role model. "If you can't trust a teacher, whom can you trust?" is a valid assumption. Television scripts freely portray doctors, lawyers, businessmen, police, and politicians as dishonest and untrustworthy. Teachers have been immune to tarnished images. Whether this will continue depends upon teachers continuing to be worthy role models.

In addition to the legal assumption that you are responsible for knowing where your students are, an ethical obligation exists in insisting that everyone has a chance to succeed as well as to fail. Many students undergo a tough period when parents are getting divorced, personal relationships are strained, and school seems to be unimportant. Some students respond well later on and should not be written off too soon. But they can't be helped if they are not there.

Absent Without Leave

Reasons for truancy range from "Surf's up!" to "School is boring". The daily concern of the teacher is handling, not researching it. Keeping track of truancies is a burdensome but mandatory procedure with legal implications. Pupils flunk classes because of excessive absenteeism; "excessive" is determined by the school district, school policy, or by instructors who combine attendance credit into the grading system. Some educators argue that students cannot be failed for absence alone but can be suspended or expelled for habitual truancy. The results are the same. If a student cuts classes, tests can't be passed, and failure is the result. One theory is not to search too hard for habitual truants. Professionals justify this attitude by knowing that classes learn and behave better without those who have no interest in learning.

In Fitchburg, Mass. a fourth of the freshman high school class was failed for truancy and had to repeat the school year. School district policy stated that missing the same class more than 15 times is cause for administrative F's. Parents supported the action. About the same time, Massachusetts instituted a statewide crackdown on truancies, trying to reverse a ten year trend. A Wisconsin judge sentenced a 14 year old boy to 30 days in jail for a past record of truancies and a new binge of missing 18 out of the first 38 days of school.

Regardless how a teacher feels about maintaining mind-deadening records, reports, counselor plus parent consultations, and personal phone calls, failure to maintain records could result in more trouble. The law requires detailed evidence before a school district can expel a student. The process usually takes months. Meanwhile, neither the police nor the community want teenagers wandering the streets. Elementary students who can't accept schooling can be managed only through their parents since the very young are highly unlikely to be expelled. Regardless, teachers always must keep a separate file for the ghost people.

One of Our Teachers is Missing

A day arrives when old reliable is ailing and a substitute must take over. The career teacher winces at the thought, regarding subs as the penalty for being ill. The fault lies not with most subs, but in the system that uses them. Subs get phoned early in the morning not knowing exactly how to get where they're going or what subjects they will handle. (I didn't say "teach".) Arriving at their destination an hour late, they receive expected useless information. Regular teachers are supposed to leave lesson plans with the main office or on their desks but they often don't. Also, sudden illnesses can't be planned, so teachers do not have the chance to prepare for takeovers of their classes.

Subs don't know the pupils and the pupils know it, so some take advantage. Classes seldom work for substitutes even having the regular teacher's lesson plans. Students are convinced that the regular teacher won't use any assignments from the sub anyhow—and they're right. Regulars returning after absences view the sub's presence as a highjacking. They gripe about lost books, lost records, breakdown of class control, and lack of progress. But sometimes the regular teacher defends the indefensibility of some subs, if only to support the image of teachers.

Teachers who are rarely absent from class feel quite defensive about their classes and are concerned that any foreign body at their desk is going to victimize the students and destroy a whole year's work. These are attitudes based upon feelings which may not be valid, but they exist because they may be true.

For all it's worth, subs have everybody's sympathy. It is a losing proposition no matter how good they are. Anybody who has subbed in a public school has really earned money about the toughest way possible.

Student Burnout

While teacher burnout is currently a hot topic in education, little consideration is directed at student burnout. Shortening the school year, or eliminating non-essential courses gets little space in educational publications. Yet, after 12–16 years in various learning groups, modern students are glassy-eyed to the point of zombieism.

Some diapered toddlers begin the long road through education taking almost their first steps in nursery school. This is usually the first group experience away from family life. These toddlers may remain in day care facilities anywhere from 2½ to 8 hours. They could also be placed in Day Care Centers for working parents, private family day care, or franchised day care centers. Next could be pre-kindergarten, then kindergarten around five, approximately one year behind the first grade. Kindergartens may admit at four and the child will have two years in kindergarten and be in school five half days per week. Kindergartens are operated by public school systems, churches, university lab or campus schools, research centers, or private schools.

Meanwhile, children are exposed to rudiments of reading, language, social studies, art, music, math, and science. This begins the adventure to a long, frustrating journey through the wilderness called education. Such an early start culminates with a normal expectation of high school graduation by 18. Yet high school is not enough. Vocational or college training lies ahead, possibly four years or more at the college level. Meanwhile, the motivation, energy, excitement of discovery, and sense of accomplishment, erodes.

During a period spanning about one-fourth of normal life expectancy, students are experiencing overkill. Virtually all subjects taught to children from the beginning of comprehension are repetitious. Identical English, math, and social studies courses have been taught repeatedly in alternating years in junior high and high school. Only the course names are changed, but not to protect the innocent. Most college courses are segments of survey courses learned in secondary schools. How much difference is there between English 7 in junior high and English 101 in college? The information in Civics, American Government, and Political Science are basically the same. The differences are in details, the quality of work, and the maturity of the students. After a while, students get little new information.

Nobody wants to listen to the same information year after year. When most of us can't stand television reruns, perhaps subconsciously we remember how new teachers taught excitedly about the Battle of Bull Run as though classes had never heard of it before. Maybe the assumption is that nobody learned anything the first or second time and eventually the pupils will catch on. Courses of study must be streamlined to eliminate repetitious and irrelevant courses. Who decides what is repetitious and irrelevant opens up more ceaseless arguments. Psychology of learning requires repetition and review for the memory, and overcoming the loss rate of learned material. Many teachers feel, however, that if the basic skills and study techniques have not been learned by the beginning of high school, little change will occur later. Late bloomers are not common enough to make repetitious courses worthwhile.

A current trend is the growing breakdown of elementary schools classes. Students have begun to change classes as in secondary schools. This means that students will have less contact with peer groups or with familiar teachers. Also, handles must be attached to separate courses, alerting pupils to identical courses in higher grades. In addition, years are added to the routine of changing rooms between classes.

Some educators advocate a school year extension, and elementary education being more tailored to the upper grades. The sharp contrast between an orderly, safe, environment with enthusiastic children and few disciplinary problems, and the generally haphazard, unstable realm of secondary education has triggered a word jam. How can a kitten be compared to a tiger? Having sent two of my children from pleasant elementary schools to the public junior high schools thirteen years apart left no confusion in my mind about the disparity between elementary and secondary education. Some assume that secondary education is only a little different. Not so. Promoting an extension of the secondary concept merely creates more problems which add to eventual student burnout.

I was a volunteer guidance counselor for one semester in a marvelous new elementary school located in an upper middle class suburban area. Computers, closed circuit television programs operated by the pupils, school newspaper, carpeted classrooms, media center, heavy parental involvement, and highly trained teachers characterized this school. In short, an educator's dream. Having taught in an ancient, run down, brick junior high in a blue collar working class neighborhood in Boston for seven years, I imagined how much all children's attitudes and achievements could be changed by transferring values developed in a fine elementary school to secondary schools. Shootdown time arrived when I asked the district counselor with whom I was working what the carryover effect was from elementary to junior high. The answer was, "Almost none".

At what point student burnout occurs is difficult to determine. Junior high teachers are convinced it happens with them. Teachers of high school or college freshmen wonder why many students are apathetic or candidly admit working merely for grades. Similarly, after twenty years at the same job, adults may wonder at what point in school they decided they stayed too long. School boards and government leaders believe that answers to the lack of basic learning and mediocre standardized test scores can be solved by a longer school day and/or a longer school year. It would make more sense to keep little children at home longer, eliminate kindergarten, maybe shorten junior high or high school by one year, thereby shortening the journey to a high school diploma. We luxuriate in the expression "Quality time is better than quantity time". Why shouldn't this work in education?

Undoubtedly, consistent attendance throughout the school years is necessary to a decent education; however, we are now seeing the results of law of diminishing returns. Less is better.

CHAPTER 7

TRAUMA UNIT

Teaching school during normal school days is traumatic enough to cause widespread burnouts and dropouts from the profession. What accelerates admission to the Teachers' Trauma Unit is a number of unwanted and unplanned occurrences, including but not restricted to the following:

Unappreciated Rewards

Celebrities (not to be confused with classroom teachers) and well-known business executives have revealed that their recurring nightmare is opening a door to find Mike Wallace and his television crew waiting on the threshold. Lacking name recognition does not shield teachers from requests allowing local TV news crews to film "background material" in their classrooms. Requests usually arrive on the day you wear your Mexican peon shirt and/or your distressed Levis—leading to further distress. The best way to avoid this trauma is to be a miserable teacher. Some teachers come by this condition naturally; others have to work at it. But I digress. Having a reputation as a good classroom manager and never having been run out of a classroom by your students qualifies you for additional rewards.

Besides unexpected television debuts, other benefits include: working with student teachers from local colleges, field-testing instructional materials, and performing for community members, the Board of Education, or even other teachers who wonder how you got away with it so long. This inflates one's ego and status, but it plays havoc with carefully planned instruction.

Anticipating the arrival of observers, you conjure up a "worst case" scenario. But the worst rarely occurs, because students try to look like scholars, trying not to fuel the public's already poor image of American youth. Yet, when it is over, you always feel that someone else should have been given the honor.

Rally Days

Anxiety levels peak for teachers who must face classes after a lunchtime sports rally. Their nerves are already frayed from having the band practice outside the classroom all morning. An occasional view of cheerleaders eases, but does not wholly quiet the symptoms. When the class settles down, ten minutes into the period, several athletes swarm through the doorway. The calmest among them is three feet off the ground. Whatever tenuous control the teacher had, now disappears. Teachers are not exactly enamored with rally days.

Rock and All That Jazz

Guitars, radios, and cassette players are fine in a suitable environment, but a classroom does not qualify as suitable. Most administrators have finally outlawed the musical enhancement of mundane school life. Prior to this brave stand, many teachers voluntarily banned such distractions from the classroom. Confiscation was the consequence of possession. But repercussions from students or parents found the teacher searching for a backup group in vain. Nonetheless, teachers still battle to keep learning the top priority.

The Eyes Have It

Murphy's Laws apply to everyone, but most people do not have to worry about things going wrong under the anticipating gaze of thirty-five pairs of eyes. On test days, the duplicating machine breaks down. If not, there's either no fluid or no paper. And, if you took the precaution of duplicating your test materials before the duplicating machine broke down, the fluid dried up, the paper was used up, the filing cabinet where you stored the tests will jam. Having what's left of your brain stored in a temperamental file must be avoided at all costs. Keeping thirty-five teenagers gainfully employed, well-behaved, and quiet every minute does not rank among life's greatest pleasures.

Unassembled Assemblies

Not forgotten are instant assemblies magically occupying empty seats which would be facing unannounced visitors from the Board of Education. Fire drills, either principal-planned twenty minutes into the period or inspired by a public spirited student citizen, do nothing to further the absorption of learning. Fire drills are always scheduled in the middle of a test upon which the future of the world depends. By this time, the class has had a surge of camaraderie and an unabashed thirst for knowledge. Upon returning to the classroom, the only pupils not receiving A's or B's on the test are the absentees.

Bad, Worse, Worst

Certain days are more difficult than others. Mondays are deservedly labeled "blue" because everyone in the classroom, including the teacher, would rather be anywhere else. Fridays are the hype days, test days, TGIF celebrations, and hot date nights. Various other sporting events occur on Fridays also (many of which the parents thankfully never find out about).

Jolly fun is available just before any major vacation. Freud himself would have found it challenging to explain student behavior during this time. Administering therapy rather than explaining it would be more beneficial to all concerned. Two weeks before summer vacation can convince teachers to make a career change by September. Yet teachers are eccentric enough to attempt meaningful instruction during this time, knowing full well that pupils need not be Rhodes Scholars to know that grades are already recorded in the office.

Yanks and Pullouts

Administrators, counselors, faculty advisors, and coaches benignly pull athletes, student government leaders, and other doers from class in the name of public good. You may be highly upset with this practice, until you are forced to remove students from classes to carry out your own assigned activities. When this practice is carried to an extreme, instructors have only two alternatives: scrub a super lesson plan or face massive makeups.

Coaches are generally good about keeping athletes in class. They may be sincere about the value of academics, or may simply be aware of the risk of terminal ineligibility for a superstar. But athletes, cheerleaders, and student technicians must be excused for the two or three lunch periods during which rallies are held. Once teachers have accepted that situation, they find that on certain Fridays athletes must suit up during the last period of the day to catch the team bus. This is one of the facts of interrupted education. To those who say "Education can also be found outside the classroom," teachers respond with a stare that only teachers, mothers, and cats can give.

The Camel's Back

"Since you're such a great teacher, I'm sure you won't mind accepting five more non-English speaking refugees and two more students who graduated magna cum laude from reform school." Protesting such assignments does no good. You can't argue that you can't handle the extra load, nor can you admit you are incapable of the challenge.

I once had a principal who was asked why a certain English teacher always taught advanced classes. He said the teacher couldn't handle the discipline needed for regular classes. Moreover, some less-than-dedicated teachers pound on the vice principal's desk and say, "Hell no! I'll be damned if I'll accept anybody else! I don't have time to finish my crossword puzzles in class as it is!" Just reach for another bottle of aspirin.

Hostile Forces

"Hurry, Mr. Chips! There's a fight outside!" Words like these can make a grown teacher cry. Rushing to carry out your obligation, you know full well that you will be the only one in the mob who wants the fight stopped (except, perhaps, the loser). Moreover, you will be the first one on the scene. Timid, and many experienced teachers have learned that discretion is the better part of valor, and they have developed a slow gait or a tin ear. Given a choice, occupy a room some distance from hallways, the lunch area, and especially near student lockers.

When arriving on the scene of the hostilities, remain cool. Don't scream unless you get hit and for goodness sake don't step between the disputants. If you recognize the combatants, using their names and telling them to knock it off is language they will usually respond to. Enlisting the aid of recognizable athletes is a capital idea. (Athletes seldom get into fights on campus). When the fighters separate enough for you to spread your arms and still stay out of reach, you can safely become vocally forceful. Hope that help has arrived. More specifically, hope that the fight didn't coincide with the security guard's coffee break. Such coffee breaks often last all day.

After the cease fire is in effect, your duties are to get the names of the unfriendlies and send the damaged ones to the school nurse. Notify the office. If a security guard, administrator, or counselor is at the scene of the crime, return to your room and pick up the pieces. Wait for your pulse to decrease to 200 beats per minute, however. During the day, rest assured you'll be asked for a full report. Since fighting on school grounds is regarded as a capital offense, be accurate even though your memory of the whole event has become markedly blurred. You may be required to make a deposition.

Fights inside the classroom are less prevalent. When one occurs, however, you must handle it alone. Don't overreact. Walk both fighters to the office, walking between them, not allowing them to talk with each other. If a scuffle occurs without damage being done, you may not want to make a big deal of it. This could help build your image with the class. However, legal realities require you cover your flank by mentioning the incident to a friendly counselor.

Laughs, tears, frustrations, and satisfactions abound and overlap in the classroom. It would be idealistic to expect teachers could teach without extra burdens, maddening interruptions, countless distractions, glitches, fights, and indifference toward learning from surprising sources. But one quality common to all successful teachers is mental toughness. Coupled with that toughness must be a special space for the teacher's very personal trauma unit.

CHAPTER 8

ADMINISTRATORS AND OTHER PROBLEMS

Teachers must be idealists in order to teach. Classroom control depends upon the skill of teachers, yet administrators have an important role, either by active support or lack of it. Since administrators are basically in the business of business, their practicality often shatters the idealism of teachers. An awareness of the administrators' approach to teachers' problems is necessary for teachers to realize that the only front line help they can expect in managing classes will come from themselves.

School board members, like politicians, need to meet no educational qualifications to become experts in their field. Once elected, they are instant experts. By reason of their office, they are rarely challenged on their specific knowledge. Perhaps no other field is so controlled by people who have so little experience in what they are controlling. New school board members absorb expertise by osmosis in budgets, integration, curricula, architecture, teaching, and administration just as newly elected politicians are assumed to know all about nuclear weapons, social security, foreign policy, space, and high finance.

School boards, like legislators, have a legal right to give themselves raises in many states. Five San Diego school board members unanimously granted themselves a 100% raise in thirty seconds, reaching the new maximum allowed under state law. The president of the classified employees' union (which was trying to get raises) noted that it takes her workers twenty years to double their salaries while the school board can do it in less than a minute.

Board members have pretty much of a free rein in their dealings with schools, although the media portrays a different view. In spite of teacher unions, strikes, protests, or arbitration, teachers can do little

73

except make noise and negative headlines. It got so bad in Cleveland, a superintendent went to a high school office and wrote: "Use this event to rid yourselves of petty politics, racial politics, greed, hate and corruption. This city deserves better. The children deserve better . . . my last piece of dignity is being stripped. The fighting among school board members and what petty politicians are doing to the system has sickened me." He then killed himself.

At the site level, principals transfer excellent teachers as a routine movement of bodies. Body count has high priority. Being good is no protection when the principal decides that pupil numbers show that one less teacher is needed. Rarely is thought given to the quality of the teacher—just another body to be disposed of. Continuity of education, familiar faces which had been a comfort both to students and parents alike, are shuffled off sometimes to a school where excellent teachers spend more time on chores and discipline than in teaching.

Moreover, administrators have recognized the financial advantages of encouraging parents and other volunteers to assist in the classroom. Large classes can be justified because classroom teachers have more help—a lower pupil/teacher ratio. Fewer teachers, fewer problems, fewer changes, less tenure, and more bottom line money for school districts. So much for academic standards and "giving our kids a good education".

Brain Operations

Teachers realize, with good reason, that too many administrators have forgotten what schools are really for. Few principals have ever taught a class of juveniles from the day they were appointed from the classrooms. To them, it makes little difference if good teachers are assigned to classes not in the area of the teacher's subject mastery or whose main responsibility is to babysit disciplinary problems. There is a tremendous waste of teaching talent when pupils who never cared to learn and are resolved never to learn are given proven effective teachers. Nobody can make them learn. This holds true even if such classes are taught by psychiatrists or Harvard professors. We hear how all normal children can learn and how their test scores can be improved by using new techniques and better approaches or equipment. Maybe so, if they want to learn. But what answers do many administrators have for students who simply will not learn? One answer is the practice to randomly assign teachers to any class for mere expediency and nothing more; whether teachers want to or have the ability to handle non-learners is unimportant. It may be called democracy or unbiased administration but, in practice, administrators are more concerned about the ratio of placing one warm teaching body before 35 warm student bodies.

A glaring example of this is in school systems using computer registration, with first priority assigned to the upper grades, and segments of the alphabetical roster alternated each semester. On the surface it seems a fair method. However, classes of known good teachers are filled within a few hours of the first morning of registration. Less popular classes may take two days to meet the quota. This has the advantage of being a natural selection based upon choice and ability. But administrators, knowing full well what will happen, set a quota of perhaps twenty-five registrations of a potential class of thirty-five. This closes class registration. It also forces students whose only offense was being at the wrong end of the alphabet or being #28 in line to enroll with unsatisfactory teachers. The usual rejoinder for a complaint of this nature is to observe that in life one must learn to adjust to all people.

What happens after all classes are filled with the twenty-five pupil limit? As expected, the limit is raised to whatever the eventual class size must be to accommodate the total school enrollment compared to the teachers available. Simple arithmetic. The kicker here is that students interested in classes offering valuable learning and good classroom control have been shunted off to an environment they don't want to be in. Now with a possible ten seats open in each class, the door opens for truants, those who don't care about school, and those with a cavalier attitude of showing up at their own convenience. During the next two weeks or more there occurs a revolving door syndrome where teachers expect transfers in, transfers out.

The resulting paperwork involves many changes in attendance forms, issuing and collecting textbooks, makeup work, and several conferences with counselors, administrators, and parents. Teachers, by necessity, go easy on instruction the first two weeks, knowing much of what they do will be wasted, that transferring pupils cannot be expected to take tests on instruction given while they weren't there.

No doubt, some students will benefit from teachers they just happened to be assigned to, but teachers are not magicians. On the other side, good students forced to register with ineffective teachers or those with personality problems are quite likely to do what is expected of them and not much else. By the end of the first semester, whatever spark of learning they had is extinguished. These students feel they've been had by the system. Non-achievers end up with good teachers and achievers end up with the poor teachers. The nucleus of an effective class is shattered.

Teachers know that in every class there are five to seven students whose departure would improve class learning and control immeasurably. Having these types of students in any class creates continual problems for both the class and the teacher. Such students are contantly being summoned to the counseling office. Door hinges groan from constant action. Meanwhile, teachers attempt to maintain the day's scheduled lesson. The only immediate chance to unload occurs when teachers are requested to send students from oversized classes to undersized classes. Survival takes precedence over ethics and the worst students are sent out. Later replacements, however, are usually the same caliber as the ones just departed. For this reason, teachers willingly accept overloads as long as they know they have a cushion of good students.

So much for having good teachers paired with good students. This is just one situation where the policy of matching body numbers of teachers to body count of pupils illustrates the difference between the minds of the classroom teachers and those of the administrators.

Charges of elitism arise whenever proposals suggest that the unteachables and uncontrollables be separated from serious students. The situation today promotes a type of democracy which is anti-intellectual. In a majority of classes, effective teachers are not matched with effective students. The A.M.A., state bar associations, business groups, and other professional associations are organized to maintain quality in their respective fields. When it comes to schools, many school board members and administrators are willing to settle for the lowest common denominator. Gung ho teachers finally get the message.

It is no surprise that our society does not place the same status on teachers as it does administrators, nor does it accept the idea that teachers should earn as much as principals or college professors. The present system has no rewards, only punishment, for teachers wanting to remain in the classrooms. Yet teachers establish quality in classrooms, not administrators or school boards. Forget about new curricula and outstanding administrators, money, equipment, and environment— teachers make it all work.

Teaching is an altruistic profession in a materialistic society, and teaching as a career is a dead end if teachers choose to remain in the classroom. Teaching is one of the toughest jobs in the country, having low status and little financial satisfaction. School administrators and the rest of our society are not expected to be "dedicated" to the point of surrendering their pay checks for the benefit of others. Yet, in teaching, it comes with the territory.

In our society the money, titles, and promotions go together like bridesmaids. Teachers as a group have a history of being left at the altar. Nothing on the horizon appears to give this marriage a chance. Teachers feel now that if you can't beat administration, join it. Those who don't, must believe that teaching is worthwhile enough for a career, regardless of the influences of administrators.

Coping with Strikes

Part of developing a mind set which aids in keeping professional control is coping with strikes. This is another area where teachers are dealing with problems alien to their training and their psyche. Teachers can expect, sooner or later, to hit the pavement. This is true in both urban and rural areas. The mere mention of "strike" causes stomach churning for most teachers, who tend toward conservatism and moderation in all things. A profession that demands so much effort for so little financial reward does not attract many movers and shakers.

Teachers' decisions on whether to strike are affected by ethics; relationships with other faculty members, students and parents; loyalty; public image; and family responsibilities. Thus the inevitable outcome of strikes is emotional scars. Strikes create hard feelings that persist long after the settlement. Strikers never forget which colleagues walked picket lines and which ones didn't. There is camaraderie with those who joined and disdain for those who benefited without risking their purse or their professional files.

When strikes begin, superintendents immediately announce schools will remain open and instruction will continue. That is a contradiction in terms. Strikes preclude any semblance of genuine teaching and learning. Teachers must struggle to keep control and teach even on normal school days. Administrators summon substitute teachers for employment at higher than normal pay rates; this act displays utter disregard for experience, training, or personal qualities.

On the best of days, subs are no substitute for regular teachers.

During strikes, conditions are worse because there are no lesson plans. Striking teachers do not give aid and comfort to the "enemy". Lacking lesson plans and familiarity with students and schools, subs count their day a success if they can cross the morning picket line without having the strikers question their parentage. Subs are difficult to obtain during strikes; many support teachers by refusing to cross picket lines; some are college students earning extra money; others are housewives with college degrees; notably absent in the sub pool are retired teachers. In large city school systems, subs can work steadily because of inadequate labor pools, but during strikes the labor supply is depleted. Moreover, as strikes drag on, more teachers may join the picketers, creating more need for subs.

Students having subs during strikes who are asked by parents the age-old question "What did you do in school today?" and give the answer "Nothing", are absolutely right. Young people are not fools. They recognize that even having the same sub assigned to their classes for the duration of the strike won't make any difference. Subs assure them that all work will count, and that all disciplinary problems will be reported to the regular teacher. Students exchange knowing looks and understand that this is another adult head game.

In addition to emotional assaults and ruptured relationships, other losses become evident over a period of time. There is a pay loss, a loss of cash reserves from the school system for substitutes, court fees, and a poor public image for everyone. Effective instruction is lost, only to be replaced by a longer school year as compensation for education time lost. Whatever prestige, status, or good will the teachers had been able to build up is now replaced by words such as "unprofessional", "betrayal", "disloyalty", "greed", and "callousness".

Class sizes increase over a period of time even when it was a strike issue to begin with. Administrators trade off increases in teachers salaries with increases in class size. Often the administration decreases the number of teachers as a further adjustment. Hence the concept of a "half teacher" assigned to schools. An elementary school or two may be closed down, justified by figures showing a population shift.

Counselors' work loads can be expected to increase, since the non-replacement of only one counselor makes it even more remotely possible for them to make contact with anyone but students requiring obvious help. As it is, many excellent students go through school not having seen counselors individually even once before graduation.

Overall, teachers' strikes always lose because nothing ever changes.

This is not an argument against teacher strikes, but an observation of practical results. Moreover, teachers as a group have almost no political clout. Their only drastic recourse is to strike, but discover they can't fight the system. School boards listen to parents, not teachers. Perhaps that is the role that teachers should play in order to be more effective.

Having walked the picket lines during the first teacher strike in San Diego, I received a rude awakening as well as disillusionment regarding teacher power. Teachers facing the prospect of a strike should be prepared for the same. Yet, it is all part of teaching—to work at maintaining personal and professional control over circumstances difficult to cope with.

CHAPTER 9

TRACKS AND TRENDS

Classroom teachers are involved in some type of tracking system during their careers. Most teachers look forward to instructing the very bright in what used to be called advanced classes, now called gifted, college prep, or whatever euphemism catches on. When the highly motivated and achievers are assigned the same classes it follows that the less motivated and the under or average achievers are grouped together also.

In the 1960's the charge leveled at magnet schools today was the same—elitism. As a result of changes of that era, accelerated or gifted classes were absorbed into regular classes, adding the term "mainstreaming" to the already confusing educationalese. The anticipated result was to raise the standards of learning by having brighter students share quality work and interest with other students. Handicapped children were introduced into the often rough and tumble regular classrooms. Most became rapidly overwhelmed and returned to special classes with an additional sense of frustration.

What contribution did gifted students make to the regular classes? Since teachers must teach to the middle of each class, brighter students did not have to work too hard to get good grades. The bottom of each class discovered that passing standards were just high enough to create a failing situation that did not exist before. Many critics agree that emphasis on democracy of class assignments resulted in an unacceptable level of academic standards to the point of perpetuating failure. A corollary to academic failure was behavioral failure as well. Teachers are unlikely to have disciplinary problems with academically successful students. What has always caused fits for teachers is having many pupils at both the high and low extremes.

A 1985 report, "The Unfinished Agenda" by the National Commission on Secondary Vocational Education, came out flatly against separate tracks that lead to distinct diplomas for academic and vocational students. It also questioned the stress made on more academic courses. ''The assumption is that more academics, which may be the best preparation for college, is also the best preparation for life. This assumption is wrong.'' Another recommendation against tracking was that vocational training take place primarily in regular high schools and not regional vocational centers. It was also suggested that vocational courses be substituted for some academic courses when the difficulty of the courses was comparable. Since the great experiment with non-tracking has run its course, there is now a resurgence in tracking systems—complete with additional emotional controversy.

The practice of placing students in tracks is making a strong comeback in the '80's. Many school districts responded to demands of the previous two decades for abolishing what were classified as undemocratic practices. These school districts discovered eventually that non-tracking did not solve many problems. Most pupils placed in classes with the gifted realized they could not compete, and their academic shortcomings were publicly emphasized. Dropouts, absenteeism, and failures increased for average students while movers and shakers had little challenge to do their best and, as a consequence, got bored with learning.

Most teachers feel that classes organized according to ability are much more efficient. Teachers can adapt lessons to the academic level of students; the less academically inclined need not be lost in the shuffle or ask endless questions on routine assignments. When students in low achieving or regular classes show evidence of consistently better scholarship than their peers, teachers can recommend such students to a higher track. Critics claim that tracking locks in children as a result of invalid tests or a background of poor achievement. However, this assumes that teachers of track classes don't know or care what they are doing or, worse, they can't discern real academic achievement from an image of achievement.

If teachers equate A's as meaning the same for all classes or assume an A based upon extra credit work, makeup work, or articulate students who seldom do assignments is a worthy grade, then critics have some ammunition. My experience revealed that virtually all teachers I have known are extremely aware people and know their pupils often better than their parents do. Teachers are quite capable of winnowing out the really good pupils from public relations types. Students who may not speak up much in class or try to slip past the teacher without making personal contact can be the brightest of all. Some students who make easy A's in regular classes while decrying "Mickey Mouse" assignments are not likely to do much in college. Some claim that this is the sign of the superbright, the misunderstood, cloaked genius. Hardly likely. A really intelligent student has more than just brains. There is a constancy, a persistence, a desire to get things done, to do them right, and a desire to learn more about subjects beyond the classroom. Experienced teachers are not conned into believing that a straight A report card indicates a necessarily brilliant student.

Tracking can work as long as teachers are given the confidence in their professionalism they deserve. Students can be and should be moved to lower tracks regardless of grades if their level of achievement, although high, is not high enough for their present class. Conversely, if grades in a lower track class do not measure up to the qualifications of an upper track, there is no reason why students cannot be moved up as long as other observable criteria indicate a more challenging class will warm the dormant buds into late bloomers. Tracks should lead to success.

June Cox, head of Pyramid Project at Gifted Students Institute, concluded after a four year study that 90% of bright students remain in an inappropriate classroom situation. Even though 63% of 1600 schools surveyed indicated enrichment activities for the gifted, only 16% were found to have legitimate enrichment activities. Recommendations were that the "gifted" label be avoided and graded classrooms be downplayed; different measures be used to identify the gifted, not using standardized tests at all; a comprehensive plan be developed covering kindergarten through the 12th grade to identify the more talented pupils.

Advanced Placement exams, in which high school students are given college credit before entering college, has increased nearly 200% in the last decade, according to a study by the College Board. 70% of the 177,406 high schoolers taking the exam in 1984 earned college credit. In 1974 there were 60,863 students who took the exam. More than ¼ of the secondary schools in the U.S. or 6,273 schools now offer college level courses and the Advanced Placement exam. Moreover, the percentage of women taking the exam itself, the math exams, the science exams, increased over the past fifteen years. Minority students taking the exam showed a small increase while white students showed a small decrease.

The National Education Association's annual survey of public schools showed that from the 1974–5 school year (last year that baby boom children were in school) that six million fewer children are now in school while the number of teachers and administrators decreased very little. In spite of the projected teacher shortage and expected "boom" in new students, public school classrooms are losing students faster than they are teachers.

A new grouping could result from a proposal by the president of the National Community College Association who has called for a new type of associate degree spanning the last two years of high school with the regular two year community college degree. The purpose behind this proposal is to involve the middle 50% of students in a meaningful degree program. Dale Parnell hopes that such a program will stem the current 27% dropout rate of those who see no reason to complete high school. He noted that only 17% have baccalaureate or higher degrees while 87% of Americans have either no academic qualifications, a high school graduation, or have some type of community college work.

In order to motivate high school students to enroll in this proposed new A.A. degree program, Parnell has asked the cooperation of four year colleges, states, and especially from employers. If employers insist on an A.A. degree as a condition for employment, then employers would benefit from better trained and better educated employees. Currently, high school grads can take a couple of community college courses and pass themselves off as community college students, giving employers less than they thought they had. Parnell hopes that by conducting dialogue between 1000 high schools and community colleges, the bridge between them that has widened in the past several years can be shortened for the benefit of all concerned. Perhaps high schoolers would have a much higher motivation to bridge the gap to an associate degree, knowing that the job possibilities would be much greater with, than without.

Another innovative concept is taking place with the blessing from the Department of Education and the Modern Language Association in using international television as a teaching tool for language instruction. So far, five universities have accepted an initial federal grant plus contributing their own money to further language teaching. Other universities will be asked to attend a national conference in 1988 after two years of study are done. The idea behind the use of international programs involving news, cassettes, commercials, debates, or drama is to make language a practical course. Supporters claim than many language teachers cannot speak the language they teach, while many students lose interest after a year of a foreign language when they can't even speak simple, useful sentences.

Another variation of tracking takes place in private schools which, as a result of strong but often unjustified criticisms of public schools nationwide, have gained greatly in their enrollments. A major program established by Accelerated Christian Education, Inc. involving 5000 church schools and 350,000 students from K-12, is a good example of innovative and sometimes controversial teaching. Some labels applied to the A.C.E. system include "God in a box", "Christian Correspondence School", and "revolutionary learning technique". It has had steady growth for fourteen years and has accounted for $25 million in sales of books and other materials. What is different is that students almost do without teachers.

Individual schools decide whether certified teachers are necessary. Supervisors take a one week crash course and exert a minimum of discipline and guidance. The only requirements for supervisors are to be of high moral character and be church members. Even though many studies have shown that classrooms with qualified, skilled teachers are clearly superior to those without skilled teachers in acquired basic skills, the A.C.E. schools can point to impressive results.

Teaching procedures include setting up daily individual learning goals, using progressively difficult 40–50 page workbooks with five basic subjects of math, social science, English, literature, and science. Pupils grade their own work which is checked for accuracy by the adult supervisors. When errors are found, pupils must re-do the entire page. Scoring violations are regarded as a form of cheating and results in demerits. Excessive demerits not only result in academic problems but could also require parents being summoned to school to administer corporal punishment. Any upper grade student violating these rules can expect expulsion.

During study periods, students are not allowed to talk, but if they want to talk to the supervisor, a flag is placed on top of the pupil's work cubicle. One hour of physical education is assigned and work breaks are given each hour. The dress code requires wearing of conservative uniforms: the boys must wear white shirts, ties, and blue slacks; girls wear blue jumpers.

Despite misgivings on the effectiveness of the A.C.E. methods, state officials in California acknowledge that the program is perfectly legal under state law. An annual report on the number of students, instructors, and administrators is required, as well as a form certifying that basic subjects are offered as mandated by state law.

In California, the education code does not require state testing of private school students nor do teachers have to meet any minimum standard of educational qualifications. It is conceivable that an entire school could be run without a certified teacher present. Yet A.C.E. officials claim that their students excel in achievement in all subjects at a rate far superior to that of the most gifted public school students. They point to the California Achievement Test (CAT), a standardized test covering basic subjects and administered annually in public as well as many private schools.

The average ACE student is consistently 1½ to 2 grade levels above the average public school student. In defense of the public schools, however, it is no secret that they do not have the luxury of pupil selection nor can they depend upon more highly motivated pupils or parents paying tuition who want their children to make their school attendance worthwhile.

Educators know that when one group does better on a test than another, it does not always indicate more effective teaching. It is also a truism that test scores are not necessarily an accurate indicator of success in teaching methods. Even so, in the math segment of the CAT tests the A.C.E. students in some grades have not done as well as the average public school scores as of 1984. The vice president of A.C.E. explained the unfavorable CAT math results by stating that at the levels of the 4th, 5th and 6th grades, the scope and sequence in teaching math is different from that of public schools.

Whether schools without teachers are as good as their supporters claim is debatable. Nebraska challenged the lack of certified teacher concept and lost in the courts. Parents strongly supported the system; other states realized that no challenge could be effective as long as scholastic achievement of A.C.E. students in standardized tests such as CAT, and the number of successful A.C.E. students who pass the state administered high school diploma exam remained at current levels.

Moreover, many other parents are looking at this type of education system with more awareness. For those observing the emphasis on basics, discipline, working at one's own pace, selective admission standards, and economics, private schools look very good. With the A.C.E. schools having no mandate to hire certified teachers and having low overhead, administrators can charge low tuition. One official claimed that some schools buy a complete year of school supplies for only $2000. However, the parishes usually have to subsidize the operation of schools since the low tuition does not cover all expenses. No matter. This is a movement to watch. For certified teachers wanting to deviate from standard teaching methods, the Christian schools could provide the change.

Another departure from the norm ended up in the Supreme Court in 1984 when the Grand Rapids, Michigan school system was challenged for using public school teachers in private schools. Title I federal funds were used to teach remedial and enrichment classes to disadvantaged children. The Justice Department supported the school system. A Manhattan appeals court had struck down the program in New York, basing its decision on four previous Supreme Court decisions which had said that public school teachers could not offer instruction on premises of church affiliated schools.

In Grand Rapids, one-third of the city's school age children attend private schools. However, when public school teachers taught classes on church property all religious symbols were removed, the classroom was rented, and signs announcing the Grand Rapids City Schools were posted. The shared time program involved 11,000 students, 470 teachers, and six million dollars in state money. Taxpayers, however, objected that the program directly benefited the religious mission of the schools by allowing more time for religious instruction, time that would otherwise be spent on teaching remedial reading.

In July 1985 the Supreme Court in a 5–4 vote decided that public school teachers could no longer teach remedial classes inside parochial schools. But the 1965 law was not changed. Public school teachers now have the dilemma of teaching parochial students outside of parochial schools. A method under consideration is to use mobile classrooms parked outside of the parochial schools. Another way to get away from the classroom. Another way to assemble pupils of similar abilities.

CHAPTER 10

WHAT'S UP?

Stanley Wellborn, in an article in the *U.S. News and World Report,* stated that about 23 million Americans or one in five adults lack the minimum abilities in reading and writing to handle daily living. It is estimated there are one million dropouts each year even though publishers "dumb down" texts by using large print, many illustrations, and simplified language. About half of U.C. Berkeley freshmen, who are drawn from the top eighth of high school graduating classes, have to be placed in remedial reading classes. About 55% of adults read daily newspapers; of people in their 20's only 40% read newspapers.

Yet, conventional illiteracy, defined as the inability to read or write a simple passage in any language, has virtually disappeared in the U.S. The government's definition of illiterate is someone at least 14 years old not completing 5th grade. By that standard, only 1% of the U.S. population is affected, making the U.S. one of most literate nations in the world. Educators use "functional illiteracy" to gauge ability to perform productively as a citizen, worker, or consumer. A person now needs to read at the 6th grade level to understand the driver's license manual; 8th grade level to prepare a tv dinner or read IRS forms (?); 10th grade level to understand directions on aspirin bottles; 12th grade to understand insurance policies (or pass the state bar exam); college level to figure out the meaning of an apartment lease. By application, half the adult population of the U.S. could be judged as functional illiterates. To assume that an 8th grade education enables a person to understand an IRS form or a 12th grade education will help to understand insurance policies is quite optimistic, if not ridiculous. A major study at the University of Texas found that 20% of adults nationwide could not read bus schedules, understand written finance charges, or address a letter so it would reach its destination. Also, 56% of Hispanics, and 44% of blacks were functionally illiterate. Women were more likely than men to be functional illiterates, especially in rural areas. To no one's surprise, poverty was a companion of illiteracy.

The same year that the devastating report on the status of education in America came out under the banner of the National Commission on Excellence in Education, six other reports were released. As expected, all that was bad and nothing good in American education were there. However, U.S. Census Bureau figures show that the average American is better educated, more literate, more exposed to math, literature, and science than a generation ago. The former Director of the National Institute of Education stated that schools are in pretty good shape. What is changed is people's expectations. The 1983 Teacher of the Year said current criticisms and recommendations are responses to what used to be. Decline in test scores were used as evidence of failure of the system, not as an indicator of success of a social experiment of an incredible adjustment period under desegregation guidelines. Former Secretary of Education Bell said even though a 1982 report showed a very small number of 12,000 high school transcripts checked had met the National Commission on Excellence recommendations, the good news was a national movement underway that will change the picture.

What hurt education was the segment of the 1960's "me generation" that had more freedom at home and expected it at school. They demanded relevancy and were allowed to design their own school curricula. Lost were extra language, math, and science, but more "how to", driver education, and guitar classes. These values were absorbed by schools because parents didn't know their own values anymore. The burden for education was now on the students.

Isaac Asimov in "A Cult of Ignorance" in *Newsweek* posed a thesis that is probably all too true. In spite of our paying lip service to the future depending upon the education of our children, he stated that there has always been a cult of ignorance in America. Teachers hear about high standards demanded of teachers, schools, and students but also hear cries of elitism, irrelevant courses such as Latin and algebra, and mainstreaming special class pupils into regular classrooms where they have no realistic chances of succeeding. Coupled with the demand for excellence is the demand from the public that real estate taxes are not to be used for schools. Asimov stated that the strain of anti-intellectualism winds through our political and cultural life. "My ignorance is as good as your knowledge." Politicians are careful not to show too much education for fear of offending audiences. "Elitist" is the buzzword for anyone who admires competence, knowledge, skill, and wishes to spread it around. People have a right to know providing they can read; reading is an elitist subject. Asimov also said that the slogan "America's right to know" is meaningless when we have an ignorant population and the function of a free press is zero when hardly anyone can really read. Does it make sense to denounce elitism?

Albert Shanker, President of the A.F.T. claims that schools pass unqualified students from grade to grade because the public demands it. He says: "The country stores its misfits in schools because there is no other place to put them. At one time, misfits and failures had a place to go. The economy absorbed them. Schools weren't blamed for the failures. Now there is no place to go for the uneducated or untrained. Also, while basics might be mastered by some graduates, there is not necessarily a carryover to more complicated applications of those same basic skills. Society is either unable or unwilling to go beyond." Shanker has crystallized the thinking of many people in education when he says we make kids read but parents don't give a damn about literature. Do we want a more civilized, better educated society or do we just want to shape up the kids next door? We have begun to turn public school teaching into dirty work. To many school teachers it becomes more and more apparent that they are all working for the least common denominator.

Public schools have always been unfavorably compared with private schools whenever academic achievement is discussed. In a comparison study among private, Catholic, and public schools in 1981, John Coleman claimed that Catholic high schools outperformed public schools even when differences in family background were discounted. Not all critics agreed. However, it was pointed out that non-public schools produced better cognitive outcomes, discipline was better, and more homework was being done.

However, Coleman also stated in the 1982 edition that differences between public and non-public schools weren't really that great. The variation of six or seven points in math achievement of a non-public school child in the 50th percentile would result in only a modest gain in the standard deviation. There was no real evidence that the small increase in scores resulted from better schools, better teaching, or from higher levels of abilities of students whose parents could afford the tuition. When public schools can draw students voluntarily because of reputation or because parents are willing to pay the economic penalty, there is no reason why public schools couldn't exert firmer discipline, form smaller classes and demand higher academic standards along with more significant curricula.

The Catholic schools, in particular, took their lumps down through the years as having a second class image. A March 1985 report "The Catholic High School: A National Portrait", a study by the National Catholic Educational Association, shows that the Catholic school system has made tremendous strides since the 1960's. In 1962, 69% of their teachers were priests, brothers, or nuns. Today there are only 23%. Now 83% of Catholic high school graduates go on to college compared to 52% of all graduates. Yet tuition covers only ⅓ of expenses, there is a high teacher turnover rate, and educating the handicapped is not a high priority in Catholic high schools.

Overall, public schools are looking better and better when one considers the pressures placed upon public schools to educate anybody who can make it through the door.

Magnet schools have become the answer to many problems besetting public schools. Because of voluntary enrollment, flexibility, screened teachers, a more offbeat curriculum, serious students are attracted to these magnets. Bright, creative, some undisciplined but not rowdy students have found a place to fly.

Even though the basic organization of magnets is similar to that of other public schools, it is evident there is more quality teaching going on. Students are volunteers, parents supportive, administrators more liberal, and the curriculum more tailored to pupils' individual differences. Teachers must apply for magnet schools and undergo a selection process. Moreover, unlike neighborhood public schools, magnets reflect more of the community as a whole, and are more natural in its makeup of race and socio-economic factors.

Negatively, magnets have discouraged equally bright but untraditional teachers and pupils because of reported excessive freedom allowed the intelligent but often spoiled pupil. Teachers looking forward to a new style of school and teaching have declined to get bogged down with hairy discussions on popular topics of world hunger, saving the whales, or Central American repressive regimes when the curriculum has little to do with what students might rather spend time on, however admirable the motives. College entrance exams and achievement tests pay scant attention to the applicant's feelings toward apartheid in South Africa or human rights in Russia. Scholastic Aptitude Tests, American College

Tests, and College Achievement Tests are hardnosed concerning what applicants know about English, composition, math, science, and history.

Critics of magnet schools complain of elitism—undemocratic because not all students are qualified to attend. They also state that in siphoning off more able students, not only do neighborhood schools suffer academically, but also seriously dilute the cultural heritage of neighborhoods. Critics also comment that magnet teachers are not necessarily better for their students than the neighborhood school teachers are for theirs.

Yet we are all aware that no matter what schools or teachers we had, not all teachers were equally good for all of us. However, studies of magnets show their students do achieve more, discipline is much better, there is almost automatic racial integration, and dress codes are much more successful in their observance.

A 1981–2 Department of Education study showed there were 1018 magnet schools: 601 elementary, 173 middle or junior high, and 244 high schools. With the positive records of magnets we might assume expansion to the point of eliminating their reason for existing, but school districts have made few of their schools magnets simply because it is self-regulating. Some like it hot; some do not.

Wouldn't it be great for public education if all schools had motivated students, little absenteeism or truancy, little vandalism, supportive parents, well-trained teachers, and a humane learning environment? Magnet schools have accomplished this. Unfortunately, the more magnets expand, the less likely that the above standards would remain very long. A good example of less is more.

Secretary of Education William Bennett's speech to the National Press Club in 1985 revealed a frank and unpolitical philosophy on education which would not have been tolerated in a cabinet member a few years ago.

Regarding controversy over teacher competency tests, Bennett stated that if teachers fail the exam, so be it. If teachers are to be professionals then they must subject themselves to exams the same as doctors, lawyers, or plumbers. He observed that for a national teacher exam to be administered it would be very difficult to decide whose test would be used, whose standards would be used, and also whether a practical application of the test should be included. Apparently, each state would have to decide upon what standards it wanted to impose upon its own teachers. In this way the colleges within each state would tailor their courses of study to the state standards, thereby creating a new era of educational upheaval.

Regarding excellence in education, Bennett said that if excellence in education is to be the goal then some students and teachers will have to fail; if low standards are to be maintained then the deprived student will suffer the most. With higher standards, it follows that some students will have to be held back so that graduation will mean something. Again, if some have to fail in order to achieve higher standards, let it happen.

Bennett also was quite definitely against forced busing, especially if it was compulsory by race. He cited Dallas where minority groups were on record as opposing compulsory busing. Nine major studies disagreed on what effect busing had on academic achievement. Studies were inconclusive. He claimed that if pupils have their choice to bus to certain schools, then schools being avoided would be forced to change. His philosophy was that a voucher plan, magnet schools, and voluntary integration might be the answer to many of the problems with schools which, so far, have had little success with solutions.

Another sign of change came in the form of an open letter to parents and students published in the San Diego *Union* in December 1984 by the University of California at San Diego: "The best course of study for all students, whether or not they plan to attend college, is one which encourages reading, writing and reasoning skills, and good study habits; these skills require regular practice as with athletics or music".

U.C.S.D. recommended that students enroll in English classes requiring regular written compositions, and also math courses every semester during junior and senior high school. Subject to the students' career choices, additional courses were recommended for high school subject requirements for the Fall 1986 admission to U.C.S.D.: one year of history (or one semester of Civics or American Government), four years of college prep English, three years of math (elementary and intermediate algebra plus geometry), one year of lab science, two years of a foreign language, and college prep electives pertaining to the above subject requirements.

This is in dramatic contrast to the U.S. Education Department's disclosure that only 2.6% of the high school graduates of 1982 qualified under the academic standards recommended by the National Commission on Education. The commission had recommended four years of English, three years each of math, science and social studies, and a semester of computer studies as the "new basics". Almost simultaneously, the Carnegie Foundation for the Advancement of Teaching called for a core curriculum for all students in which non-electives filled two-thirds of the load instead of the then current half load. English mastery again had top priority. Signals have come constantly from Ex-Secretary of Education Bell, the National Association of Secondary Principals, and the New York Commissioner of Education that students all over the country will feel the pressure to shape up academically. With the support of politicians and business people, educators are now being aided in emphasizing the link between good schools and jobs, which also became an issue in the 1984 presidential campaign.

Learning all over the country is on the rebound. Even before devastating reports began shocking the public, big city schools, which had usually received most of the flak had begun re-writing curricula and had set tougher teacher certification standards several years before. Atlanta's 90% black student population had only one-third of its pupils score above the national average in reading and math in 1980; in three years 48% were above average in reading and 54% in math. College entrance scores by the end of 1984 showed an upturn in 31 states, reversing a decline in every state from 1972–1982. The federal survey, "State Education Statistics," also found that there was no correlation between cost per pupil and improvement in student scores. No clear meaning was apparent in why some states do better than others in college entrance exams. In other words, pouring more money into education does not guarantee better results. The answer lies elsewhere. Classroom teachers would agree with the observation that classroom atmosphere, homework, and fair disciplinary codes along with adequate funding is important in educational achievement. However, no one really knows why college entrance scores based upon the A.C.T. rose in 16 of the 28 states and in 15 of the 22 states where the SAT is used. It would be invaluable to determine the formula for its success, but for now it is most satisfying not to ask the reason why—just enjoy.

A March 1987 report on the results of the California Assessment Program showed high school seniors breaking two 10 year old records: achieving the highest 12th grade academic test results with the largest increase in scores. Seniors in the San Diego City School District in the second largest city in the state did even better than the rest of the state in the testing of the CAP areas of reading, writing, spelling, and math skills. Three other major high school districts in San Diego County also surpassed the statewide averages. What happened? The class of 1987 is the first of the seniors to have passed through California's 4 year old education reform legislation of 1983, mandating basic subjects to have high priority. Bill Honig, Superintendent of Instruction, said, "Legislation has proven that higher standards and more rigorous courses make a difference." School superintendents were informed that schools were to be held accountable. In 4 years, the schools exceeded the goals set in 1983. Thirty of the lowest performing schools made great progress; scores of minority students improved at an even faster rate than the average. When the most heavily populated state in the country with such a diverse mix of students encompassing a sprawling educational system can do it, can nation-wide improvement be far behind? Again, enjoy.

CHAPTER 11

FREE LANCE TEACHING: ALTERNATIVES

Some hardy souls find classrooms quite confining, yet their talents and pleasures are geared toward teaching everyone who wants to learn in any place they can be found. Instructing captive audiences using formal courses of study in classic environments is not for them. While school systems, of necessity, mandate rather inflexible programs, teachers do have interesting alternatives. After leaving a teaching career with big city high schools, I assumed I would be alone in sailing unfamiliar waters. Not so. One journey into the unknown proved that other instructors had lives beyond the confines of the familiar. This was my alternative.

Afloat with the Navy

Few teachers have sailed with the U.S. Navy as civilians. Those who have, recognize the disguised envy of others hearing about it but are reluctant to discuss this unique job for fear of ruining a good thing. A few accredited coast colleges periodically submit bids to the U.S. Government to administer the PACE program (Program Afloat for College Education). My experience was with the U.S. Navy, although other military branches participate. High school basic skills courses are offered under a different program but commonly identified under the PACE banner.

High School Courses: These are available for self-improvement or diploma credit. Personnel may volunteer or may be assigned by department heads if a sailor's basic skills are inadequate. During the course, students are excused from most duty. Classes are held five days per week, six hours per day. The length of courses varies according to the needs of individual students. Work is done at the student's pace and grade level; assignments are organized according to difficulty, based upon initial test results. Students must pass tests to progress to the next lesson.

Subjects include reading, writing, grammar, vocabulary, spelling, and may include math through algebra. Because of wide ranges in grade levels and abilities, the instructor acts mainly as a coordinator and counselor. For this reason, lecturing, discussion, group testing, and outside assignments are seldom done. Basic skills classes likely will attract lower ranking personnel since successful completion of classes could result in promotion. Another factor is that high ranking enlisted men are unlikely to give out signals indicating lack of basic skills.

Because of the shift in military requirements plus an upgrading of salary, the Navy has been able to weed out undereducated personnel and require higher educational standards for enlistment. This change already has made a deep dent in basic skills classes aboard U.S. Navy ships.

College Courses: Classes run for 2½ hours twice a week for eight weeks, or 40 hours' class instruction, as in standard college courses. Mid-terms and finals are given; assignments and class discussions are handled as on a college campus. Term papers are seldom assigned, due to the nature of shipboard life and lack of facilities. A set maximum of college credits can be applied for college admission without residency requirements. The contracting college accepts credits with no problem. Other colleges may negotiate.

A PACE classroom on U.S. Navy ships is the only place aboard where rank does not have its privileges. Higher ranking enlisted personnel and officers enroll mainly in second career courses such as police or fire science, cooking, or real estate. On one occasion, the ship's captain had enrolled in a real estate course but his duties often prevented him from attending classes. Academic integrity was assured in this case when the captain received a C for the course because of his poor attendance.

Shipboard Living

Facilities: Classes are held in the evening during the crew's off-duty time. Classes may be in the library, in a ship's conference room, or in the ship's hold. On smaller ships like destroyers, the lounge may be used. Classroom amenities are sparse. A portable or a wall chalkboard may be available, but audio-visual equipment is locked up by evening. Any chalk the instructor has, must be scooped up after class or it disappears.

Classrooms are subject to constant noise and distractions, as in public schools. Incessant public address announcements, fire and flooding drills (occasionally for real), "man overboard" drills, whistles, and "abandon ship" drills punctuate the 24 hour activities. I still remember painfully the welding and hammering of steel walls and pipes while my voice was changing to soprano. However, a public school teacher would call that part of a normal workday.

Keeping House: A frustrating occurrence is having a security check imprison you when class has just ended. This consists of a sudden blockage of all exits for an unspecified time. No one is allowed to move anywhere until the security is lifted.

Whether your Spartan quarters are shared or private depends upon the type of ship and the number of crew aboard. Civilian instructors have officer status. This includes berthing in the officers' section, use of the officers' gangway when boarding or leaving ship, and eating in the officers' wardroom. However, civilian instructors quickly discover that the best food is found in the Chief Petty Officers' mess. The catch is that entrance is gained by invitation only. Civilians make friends with CPO's very rapidly—a survival tactic.

Getting back to the rack, as sailors call it, may mean you return to a renovated closet as aboard a destroyer, a cramped room with three decker bunks as in an aircraft carrier, or in a private "stateroom" as on a destroyer tender.

A destroyer tender is a huge ship, rivalling old battleships in size. It is a mother ship to destroyers, and is a floating factory capable of handling virtually all repair problems. It has shoe repair, optical, welding, pipefitting, refrigeration, and other departments and is capable of absorbing temporary berthing and meals for other ships' crew members. The destroyer tender is the ship that the contract colleges prefer for instructor assignments, although it will honor requests for shipboard classes on any ship furnishing adequate facilities.

Aircraft carriers, in spite of their small city image, have a difficult time absorbing civilians. A good friend of mine who joined an aircraft carrier in the Indian Ocean was literally given a broom closet. He watched while the brooms were removed. My first assignment was the carrier U.S.S. Midway, home-ported in Japan. The night I arrived at Yokosuka Naval Base, a seaman led me to a very small dark room.

There were two 3 decker bunks, and luggage strewn over the deck amidst swirling water recently released by a broken pipe. These were instructors' quarters. I sensed that I was about to serve hard time in the brig. Luckily, there was no more room at the inn. I found a niche near the bow in a pilot's stateroom. He was in the Philippines for training exercises, and never knew what a pampered life he was missing.

Having unheated quarters and only one blanket did little to warm my heart to a new adventure. Adding to the cold welcome, toilets at that end of the ship had been clogged for days. Education didn't seem too important that night. In all fairness, it was January in Japan and the Midway was undergoing a major overhaul. Moreover, I didn't have too much to gripe about because a contract dispute between the Navy and the college caused me to return to the U.S. after one week.

Navalese as a Second Language: While not a job requirement, you need either a seagoing background or you bone up on the lingo. Calling the galley a "kitchen", the ladder "stairs", the deck a "floor", the bulkhead a "wall", or similar offenses to the naval ear will further enhance the crew's negative opinion of civilians. Knowing the hull number of your assigned ship, be it CVN-65 for a nuclear carrier, or AD-37 for a destroyer tender, is important when trying to find your ship at a naval base. Finding a ship by name is not easy. Within the ship, a landlubber should know that deck 0 is the main deck, that 01 is above it and 1 is below it. Coupled with deck numbers are compartment numbers which indicate whether you are forward, aft, port, starboard, and the main use of that compartment.

Knowing Your Place: Instructors must understand and accept ship priorities. Safety and security mandates knowing standard operating procedures (s.o.p. in navalese), and the layout of the ship. Civilians have no responsibility for any duty except teach classes. Your time is your own after that. But you need enough common sense to remain in designated areas during drills or ship's work. Discussing politics, criticizing the government, especially the President, is off limits. Commenting on officers or handling of the ship are also breaches of ship etiquette.

Crew Relationships: You may beware of built-in animosity toward civilians. On deployment to Diego Garcia in the Indian Ocean, our ship had the largest group of civilian instructors ever aboard a Navy ship. Breakfast and lunch had informal seating, so everyone mingled rather easily. However, dinner seating was more formal; personnel were seated according to rank; civilians, having no rank, barely qualified for a table. Like kids on vacation from home, we had an enjoyable time and close camaraderie. In the wardroom, this seemed unprofessional. Warrant officers showed the most resentment. Several ignored instructors entirely. Common social graces disappeared. Once, in a foreign port where absences caused instructors and warrant officers to sit together, a loud complaint echoed throughout the wardroom that the table was reserved for warrant officers only. So much for the doctrine of civilians ruling the military! When I returned to the same ship many months later, much of the crew had shipped out and the atmosphere was much friendlier. However, instructors must realize that shipboard life for the crew is very demanding, that civilians are guests, and act accordingly.

Absence with Leave: An area where toleration is required is classroom attendance. Requirements are established by the contracting college whose rule of thumb sets three cuts as maximum. However, on navy ships the crew must stand watch 24 hours a day. This requires a great turnover in personnel. Students are not excused from standing watch. Sometimes crew members receive almost consecutive watch duty. The instructor must make adjustments for this as with all shipboard drills. Navy business always takes precedence over educational activities.

Educational Services Officers: The designated contact for instructors is the Educational Services Officer (ESO) who takes care of problems, fills classes, makes arrangements for classrooms, supplies, keeps records, and apprises instructors of precautions or procedures to obtain ID's or special passes in foreign ports. These are the good ESO's.

You may find aboard some Navy ships that only one officer wants PACE classes. Because of an officer's rank, classes are arranged but nobody wants to be the ESO. On my last assignment, the designated ESO wanted no part of classes and bucked the job to an enlisted crew member who had no knowledge of what was going on and was never available. In such a situation you do the best you can, never miss a class, and deposit your class records with whoever happens to have an office open at night.

Job Prospects:

Physical fitness and an adjustable mental attitude is required for shipboard teaching. You need not be single, but being gone from two to six months (if you opt to remain as long as the crew), puts a severe strain on personal relationships and, if you are married, you may end up single. During the three years I worked by contract aboard Navy ships, only male instructors were assigned to ships at sea. Women teachers had teaching assignments in port. The nature of shipboard life and lack of facilities make it difficult for women in a masculine dominated world. Moreover, since military women are not assigned to combat units, the chance of civilian female instructors being assigned to combat ships is non-existent.

Still interested? If you are flexible, can adjust to uncomfortable conditions and personalities, it is worth the experience to teach aboard a U.S. Navy ship. But don't expect to make a career out of it. Contracts are not automatic and not many people can live at sea for months at a time. Happily, besides officer status you have commissary privileges in foreign ports. Transportation and meal expenses are reimbursed by your contract college. You really can join the Navy and see the world for free, and get paid well. For example, going on deployment from the West Coast can take you to Hawaii, Guam, the Philippines, Hong Kong, Singapore, Thailand, Diego Garcia, Africa, Australia, and New Zealand. Shorter trips may include coastal cruises to San Francisco, Catalina, or Seattle. Upon completion of your contract, you may fly home on civilian and/or military aircraft with high priority from any part of the world.

Run, do not walk, to your nearest civilian recruiter. Anchors away!

IN THE SLAMMER!

Another alternative to standard schools is prisons. Some people go kicking and screaming while others regard it as just another work day. Most teachers will never go to prison either way, although as a unique work experience little can top it. If one has taught in certain public high schools, dealing with hard core criminals is different only in location.

Just Like Home

The physical environment in a federal prison is much better than in most public schools. Colorful posters, color painted walls and bookcases, personal computers with appropriate software, stacks of duplicated, disposable material for reading, grammar, and math are available.

Books and manuals range from lowest grade levels to high school equivalency. Scholastic Aptitude Test preparation and Advanced Placement manuals for college are also available. Foreign language texts and tapes, first class encyclopedias, and a law library rivalling a judge's chambers complete the picture.

Student Selection

Adult Basic Education (A.B.E.) classes are mandated by the Federal Bureau of Prisons, although optional students are allowed. An initial modified Scholastic Aptitude Test (SAT) is administered upon arrival. Inmates scoring below the 6th grade level in reading, spelling, vocabulary, comprehension, or math skills are assigned to the ABE class. Enrollment is limited to 8 pupils. Inmates, mostly reluctantly, attend class twice a week, up to five hours per day. Men and women attend on different days. Fraternization is not permitted.

Teacher Qualifications

Contrary to public opinion, a criminal record is not a qualification to be a prison instructor. For some abstract reason, the instructor must possess a master's degree. Being bilingual and having a strong teaching background makes more sense. Personal qualities are more important than college degrees. Looking like a criminal does help.

Who's The Boss?

A prison teacher has a unique position in being a daily, non-adversary link with the outside world. Another difference is that the only authority for classroom control comes from acceptance by the prisoners. The Bureau of Prisons makes rules for inmate behavior and standards. Smoking is not permitted on the floor. Time and length of breaks are set. Little flexibility in teaching is allowed. No guards loiter outside, and even if emergency procedures were enacted, they would be too late. Entering the restroom to insist the break is over is not covered under your standard insurance policy.

Inmates relax after a while and discuss their own families and future. Prisoners feel free to discuss their crimes, attitudes toward guards, and talk, usually idly, about breaking out. A successful prison teacher speaks no evil, sees no evil, and hears no evil. During one break, inmates were discussing "breaking out". Though I made a studied effort not to pay attention, one inmate said, "Don't worry, Mr. Preece. If we break out, we'll take care of you!" At the time I took it as a compliment, but since then I've often wondered what he meant.

Why Are We Here?

One common denominator with prisoners, including some with high school diplomas, is being unable to read at the primary level. Without reading skills equal to elementary school graduates, these inmates never had a chance at job survival. Convicts often repeat, "What am I doing here?" Being close to prisoners creates an awareness between law and justice. Attorneys have said, "I'm not talking about justice. I'm talking about the law!"

An example concerns an attractive 27 year old who served her time then returned to prison soon after for parole violation. Three years was added to her sentence. Her crime was going to Los Angeles to visit her children. Her mother gave birth at 12; she gave birth in Tijuana at 13. Her reaction when she returned to class was being glad to be back among her friends, where she had food, and did not have to pay rent. By this time, her pregnant kid sister was sharing her cell. Before this, she had shared her cell with her mother-in-law. Some might feel this "criminal family" deserved their punishments. Their collective crime was transporting illegal aliens across the border.

A teacher in prison has to do whatever is helpful for each individual, from the head or from the heart. Although the teacher is cautioned by the prison staff not to reveal personal information or get emotionally involved with inmates, it is difficult not to establish emotional ties. Granted, many people a teacher meets in prison generate fervent prayers that they never be turned loose on society. However, an instructor can be a human being without having it interpreted as a character flaw. Equality and democracy does have a place in a prison classroom.

From Your Students You Shall Learn

Teacher education comes from unexpected sources such as oral history. An assorted group, with one boy just out of high school, met by chance in the library. After the usual "What are you in for?", they came up with the same answer—bank robbery. The sheltered life of a school-teacher was enhanced by a learned discourse on FBI personalities, and judges easiest on bank robbers. In the realm of the born losers, one had held up a bank while an FBI agent was standing behind him. Another had escaped with a satchel of money when a dye bomb exploded, painting his whole body. He rushed home. The FBI caught him in the shower, literally red-handed.

Breakout

A more positive lesson came from a 35 year old man who couldn't read. He had been examined by a psychiatrist, said to have had dyslexia, and had a tutor in jail. After two weeks of refusing to take part in class, he accepted some very simple readers in large print. Part of my regular lesson was to have students read aloud before discussing comprehension questions. One morning after the class reading was finished and the class had begun math, Joe, the non-reader, began reading aloud. By this time, though I was elated, I was fearful that other inmates would slug him for interfering with their math. Nobody said a word. Joe continued for another ten minutes. This was my reward for the capture of a reader.

Vignettes

A scarred, vicious looking criminal glaring over a bookcase saying, "Hey, man! Where can I find an English book?"

Another inmate, not especially liked by other prisoners, leaving class for the last time: "I promise you, Mr. Preece, that I'll go back to school!"

Another image frozen in time: two longtime Mexican women prisoners helping a newly admitted Korean pronounce English words.

A 50 year old Tijuana woman who had attended class regularly for six months was finally sentenced to ten years. She wanted to learn English so she wouldn't have to pluck any more chickens upon her release.

While learning to operate a computer, I was assigned some prisoner experts. Two were jailed for defrauding the U.S. Government. They didn't share their secrets.

A lesser expert commented, "So that's what a computer looks like!" He had stolen fifteen computers from a department store simply by walking out with them. His unpardonable sin was to sell some to an undercover agent. He had never seen a computer out of its box. Before leaving, he informed me he could get me a computer cheap. His rehabilitation needed a booster shot.

Why Do It?

Such is education in one of its basic forms—sometimes satisfying, but always sad. Learning under coercion is academically unsound and maddeningly ineffective. Yet for those who care, it can change a life. For the battle-scarred public school teacher, there are emotional rewards: no parents to hassle you, no grades, and no truancies. Prison teaching may not be something that everyone will get choked up about, but if you make your living as a teacher you go where the customers are.

TEACHING WITH A DIFFERENCE

There are many other alternatives for the offbeat teacher. Although potentially risky in today's world, teaching opportunities abound in foreign countries. Also, teachers wishing to remain home may now branch out into many courses and classrooms never existing until the last several years.

1. U.S. corporations overseas pay very well. Usually, a two year contract is required with round trip travel expenses paid if you fulfill the contract and paid one way if you don't. Companies often specify that you be single, since housing is not available in many countries and the presence of women in countries like Saudi Arabia may pose problems. Life can also be quite restrictive where few American-type activities or entertainment is available. Sunday newspaper classified ads are a good source of information, or magazine ads offering "Teaching Opportunities Overseas" catalogs for a price. Teaching experience, age qualifications, credentials, fluency in a foreign language, interviews are all

variables as conditions of employment. Normally, the position is geared to teaching the corporation employees' children. Although in the context of adventure and travel, the glamor of living out of the United States can wear off fast. This is tempered by the difference in the pay scales of U.S. school systems.

2. Japan and other economically successful countries are avid employers of American teachers. The most direct way to apply is through embassies. If you are employed by a large city school system, notices from foreign countries often appear in the system's newletters or on bulletin boards. In some cases, teachers can request a leave of absence without pay to teach overseas. Housing and meals may be up to you, but paid travel is included if you fulfill the terms of your contract. While the pay will not be so good as that of corporations, it may be better than in the U.S., but not necessarily so. Even with good pay, living in a city like Tokyo can eat up your salary fast. Moreover, foreign countries' schools have much longer hours than U.S. schools, Saturday instruction may be required as well as a longer school year. The intangible compensation emerges from having serious students in a business-like atmosphere and having few disciplinary problems.

3. The federal government is an active employer of overseas teachers. Primarily, the need is for dependents' schools on military bases throughout the world. However, the pay has never been that good for the requirements demanded. Furthermore, the job application paperwork is horrendous. Much of the information requested is virtually impossible to remember, such as dates of when you lived in a certain city and salary received from jobs of ten years past. Unless you are a relatively recent college graduate, obtaining transcripts, letters of recommendation, and evidence of teaching experience early in your career is very difficult to come by. However, if that does not bother you, it is a good way to embark on a career as a federal employee. The best place to start is in a federal building housing a federal employment office. Checking the bound volumes of announcements pertaining to education and scanning the bulletin boards will set you on your way.

4. Another type of government teaching job available is with the Peace Corps. Retired people not needing much additional income or young people wanting to contribute to raising the quality of life for underdeveloped nations may find this a satisfying alternative. Pay is minimal.

Rewards take other forms. Check your phone book, contact Washington, D.C. or wait for recruiters to arrive at your city. This is well-publicized. The Job Corps program is similar to the Peace Corps except that the place of action is in U.S. big cities with big problems, working with the underprivileged.

The possibilities for teaching beyond the public images of classroom teaching are still expanding. While some still remain within the limits of the classroom, students and the subjects are different. Each has its tangible and intangible rewards and drawbacks, but as in any job, the choice is yours to make. The objective should always be to make your teaching an experience in which you can teach without tears.

FOR FURTHER READING

Ames, Louise Bates; Clyde Gillespie; John Streff. *Gisell Institute of Child Development.* New York: Harper and Row, 1972.

Asimov, Isaac. "A Cult of Ignorance." *Newsweek,* (Jan. 21, 1980).

Benjamin, Robert. *Making Schools Work.* New York: Continuum Books, 1981.

Berliner, David C. "Making Changes in Preservice Teacher Education." *Phi Delta Kappan,* 66 (1984), 94–96.

Berliner, David C. and Ursula Casanova Pinero. "Instruction Time: How Can Teachers Manage It Better?" *Instructor* (Oct. 1984):14–15.

Blank, Rolf K. "The Effects of Magnet Schools on the Quality of Education in Urban School Districts." *Phi Delta Kappan,* 66 (1984):270–2.

Block, Robert. "We Already Know the Problems Out Here in the Field." *Phi Delta Kappan,* 65 (1983):183.

Bork, Alfred. "Computers in Education Today—and Some Possible Futures." *Phi Delta Kappan,* 66 (1984):239–43.

Clark, David C. "Better Teachers for the Year 2000: A Proposal for the Structural Reform of Teachers Education." *Phi Delta Kappan,* 66 (1984):116–20.

Clemens, David. "A Teacher Talks Back." *This World,* (Sept. 19, 1982):15.

Connors, Eugene T. "Student Discipline and the Law." *Fastback 122.* Phi Delta Kappa Educational Foundation, Bloomington, Ill., 1982.

Dawe, Harry A. "Teaching: A Performing Art." *Phi Deltan Kappan,* 66 (1984):548–52.

Doyle, Dennis P. and Marsha Levine. "Magnet Schools: Choice and

Quality in Public Education." *Phi Delta Kappan* 66 (1984): 265–9.

Dubois, Nelson F., George F. Alvorson, Richard K. Staley. *Educational Psychology and Instructional Decisions.* Homewood, Ill., The Dorsey Press, 1979.

Evans, H. Dean. "We Must Begin Educational Reform Every Place at Once." *Phi Delta Kappan* 65 (1983):173–7.

Featherstone, Joseph and Helen Featherstone. "Teaching: An Impossible Profession." *American Educator* (1976):39–47. A review of *Schoolteacher: A Sociological Study.* Chicago: Univ. of Chicago Press, 1975, 248 pp.

Finn, Chester E., Jr. "Teacher Unions and School Quality: Potential Allies or Inevitable Foes?" *Phi Delta Kappan* 66 (Jan. 1985):331–2.

Gage, N.L. "What Do We Know About Teaching Effectiveness?" *Phi Delta Kappan* 66 (1984):89–93.

Gibboney, Richard A. "Learning: A Process from Francis Parker". *Phi Delta Kappan* 65 (1983):55–56.

Gilley, Jeanne Mack and B.H. Gilley. *Early Childhood Development and Education.* 2nd ed. Albany, N.Y.: Delmar Publishers, Inc., 1980.

Glasser, William. *Schools Without Failure.* New York: Harper and Row, Publishers, 1969.

Herndon, James. *How to Survive in Your Native Land.* New York: Simon and Shuster, 1971.

Hertzberg, Alvin and Edward F. Stone. *Schools Are for Children.* New York: Schocken Books, 1971.

Holt, John. *Freedom and Beyond.* New York: E.P. Dutton, 1972.

Hyman, Irwin A. and John D'Allessandro. "Good Old Fashioned Discipline: The Politics of Punitiveness." *Phi Delta Kappan* 66 (1984):41–2.

Johnson, Eric W. *How to Live Through Junior High School.* Philadelphia and New York: J.B. Lippincott and Co., 1975.

Jordan, Suzanne. "I Want to Go to the Prose." *Readers Digest* 1977, p. 170. Condensed from *Newsweek* (Nov. 14, 1977).

Kerr, Donna. "Teaching Competency and Teacher Education in the U.S." *Teachers College Record* (Spring 1983):544–6.

Klein, Karen. "The Research on Class Size." *Phi Delta Kappan* (April 1985):578–580.

Komoski, P. Kenneth. "Educational Computing: the Burden of Insuring Quality." *Phi Delta Kappan* 66 (1984):244–8.

Kozoll, Charles E. "Time Management for Educators." *Fastback 175.* Phi Delta Kappa Educational Foundation, Bloomington, Ill., 1982.

Kozol, Jonathan. *Death at an Early Age.* New York: Bantam Books, 1968.

_____. *The Night is Dark and I Am Far From Home.* New York: Continuum Books, 1980.

McDaniel, Thomas R. "A Primer on Motivation: Principles Old and New." *Phi Delta Kappan* 66 (1984):47–9.

McWilliams, Peter. "Attributes of an Ideal Teacher." San Diego *Union,* Dec. 2, 1984.

Merrigan, Charles. "Administrative Solutions." *Phi Delta Kappan* (Sept. 1983):62–3.

Michaels, Marguerite. "The Good News About Our Public Schools." *Parade Magazine* (Jan. 1, 1984).

Mitchell, Richard. *The Graves of Academe.* Boston: Little Brown and Co., 1981.

Morgan, Kirby. "Calm Discipline." *Phi Delta Kappan* 66 (1984): 53.

Murname, Richard J. "Understanding the Sources of Teacher Competence: Choices, Skills, and Limits of Training." *Teachers College Record* (Spring 1983):568.

"NEA Teacher Opinion Poll." *Phi Delta Kappan* 65 (1983):73.

Ohanian, Susan. "Huffing and Puffing and Blowing Schools Excellent." *Phi Delta Kappan* 66 (Jan. 1985):316–317.

Postman, Neil and Charles Weingartner. "How to Recognize a Good School." *Fastback 30.* Phi Delta Kappa Educational Foundation. Bloomington, Ill., 1982.

_____. *The Soft Revolution.* New York: Delacorte Press, 1971.

_____. *Teaching as a Subversive Activity.* New York: Delacorte Press, 1969.

Resnick, Daniel P. and Laura B. Resnick. "Improving Educational Standards in American Schools." *Phi Delta Kappan* 65 (1983):179.

Reynolds, Richard. "The Obsession with 'Good Grades' Can be a Harmful Disease." L.A. *Sunday Times,* 1966.

Riegel, Rodney P., and Ned B. Lovell. "Minimum Competency Testing." *Fastback 137.* Phi Delta Kappa Educational Foundation. Bloomington, Ill. 1980.

Royko, Mike. "Cheating the Children." Chicago *Daily News* (handout to teachers).

Sadker, David and Myra Sadker. "Is the OK Classroom OK?" *Phi Delta Kappan* (Jan. 1985):358.

Satchell, Michael. "Should Children Be Hit in School?" *Parade Magazine.* (March 1985):4–5.

Shanker, Albert. "The Revolution That's Overdue." *Phi Delta Kappan* 66 (Jan. 1985):311–321.

Silberman, Melvin L. and Susan A. Wheelan. "It's Different in the Classroom." *How to Discipline Without Feeling Guilty.* New York: Hawthorn Books, 1980, 172–8.

Smith, Vernon. Book review of *High School Achievement: Public, Catholic, and Private Schools Compared* by James S. Coleman, Thomas Hoffer, and Sally Kilgore. New York: Basic Books, 1982. Reviewed in *Phi Delta Kappan* 65 (1983), p. 69.

Soar, Robert S., Donald M. Medley, and Homer Coker. "Teacher Evaluation: A Critique of Currently Used Methods." *Phi Delta Kappan* 65 (1983):239–43.

Stagliano, Patricia A. and Irwin A. Hyman. "State Department of Education Activities to Reduce School Violence and Vandalism." *Phi Delta Kappan* 65 (1983):67–8.

Stecklow, Steve. "Undercover Schoolboy." Philadelphia *Bulletin,* 9 Nov. 1980 p. 1. Quoted in *Phi Deltan Kappan* 65 (1983):56.

Strother, Deborah Burnett. "Latchkey Children: the Fastest Growing Special Interest Group in the Schools." *Phi Delta Kappan* 66 (1984):290–3.

Weaver, Gilbert G. and Louis Cenci. *Applied Teaching Techniques.* New York: Pittman Publishing Company, 1960.

Wellborn, Stanley. *U.S. News and World Report.* May 17, 1982.

Winn, Ira. "High School Reform: Stuffing the Turkeys." *Phi Delta Kappan* 65 (Nov. 1983):184–185.

• INDEX •

The world seldom notices who the teachers are; but civilization depends on what they do and what they say.

Praise for
The Conspiracy of Ignorance

"Tough, insightful, fearless, and honest, this terrific book drags many a skeleton from the closet of American public schooling and clearly explains how to reverse the decline of that key institution."

> —Chester E. Finn, Jr.,
> Former U.S. Assistant Secretary of
> Education

"Martin Gross leads readers through a compelling, distressing tour of the ever-sinking standards and expectations that have become the hallmark of American public education. His book should be required reading for the legions of politicians and legislators who would have us believe that education reform is an issue that they take seriously."

> —John Silber, Chancellor, Boston
> University, and former chairman,
> Massachusetts Board of Education

"The book lays out a thorough analysis of what is wrong with American public school education today and proposes some far-reaching and much-needed reforms . . . a primer for anyone wishing to take part in the discussions that lie ahead."

> —*Providence Journal* (Rhode Island)

"*The Conspiracy of Ignorance* is a provocative, insightful, and very readable book. It will enlighten anyone who wants to understand why so many modern American public school students are faring poorly academically. I recommend it to parents who must cope with the education establishment and to open-minded educators who want to make needed change."

> —Dr. Leo Klagholz,
> former New Jersey Commissioner of
> Education

THE
CONSPIRACY
OF
IGNORANCE

*The Failure of American
Public Schools*

MARTIN L. GROSS

Perennial

An Imprint of HarperCollinsPublishers

First Perennial edition published 2000.

Designed by Stanley S. Drate/Folio Graphics Co. Inc.

Library of Congress Cataloging-in-Publication Data is available upon
request.

ISBN 0-06-093260-0

00 01 02 03 04 ❖/RRD 10 9 8 7 6 5 4 3 2 1

To my wife, Anita

Education is a companion which no misfortune can depress, no crime can destroy, no enemy can alienate, no despotism can enslave.

At home a friend, abroad an introduction, in solitude a solace, in society an ornament.

It chastens vice, it guides virtue, it gives at once, grace and government to genius.

Without it, what is man? A splendid slave, a reasoning savage.

—JOSEPH ADDISON
"Spectator," 1711

CONTENTS

Contents

THE
CONSPIRACY
OF
IGNORANCE

1

AN INDICTMENT OF
THE EDUCATION
ESTABLISHMENT

*The Decline of Teaching
and Learning*

A large group of eager American 8th graders from two hundred schools coast-to-coast were excited about pitting their math skills against youngsters from several other nations.

The math bee included 24,000 thirteen-year-olds from America, South Korea, the United Kingdom, Spain, Ireland, and four Canadian provinces, all chosen at random and given the same 63-question exam in their native language.

It was a formidable contest, and the American kids felt primed and ready to show off their mathematical stuff. In addition to the math queries, all the students were asked to fill out a yes-no response to the simple statement "I am good at math."

With typical American confidence, even bravado, our kids responded as their teachers would have hoped. Buoyed up by the constant ego building in school, two-thirds of the American kids answered *yes*. The emphasis on "self-esteem"—which permeates American schoolhouses—was apparently ready to pay off.

Meanwhile, one of their adversaries, the South Korean youngsters, were more guarded about their skills, perhaps to the point where their self-esteem was jeopardized. Only one-fourth of these young math students answered *yes* to the same query on competence.

Then the test began in earnest. Many of the questions were quite simple, even for 8th graders. One multiple-choice query asked: "Here are the ages of five children: 13, 8, 6, 4, 4. What is the average age of these children?" Even adults, long out of the classroom, would have no trouble with that one. You merely add up the numbers and divide by 5. The answer, an average age of 7, was one of the printed choices.

How did the confident American kids do on that no-brainer, on which we would expect a near-100 percent correct response? The result was ego-piercing. *Sixty percent of our youngsters got it wrong.*

When the overall test results came in, the Americans were shocked. Their team came in last, while the South Koreans won the contest. The most interesting equation was one of paradox. The math scores were in inverse ratio to the self-esteem responses. The Americans lost in math while they vanquished their opponents in self-confidence. The South Koreans, on the other hand, lost the esteem contest, but won the coveted math prize.

This bears an uncanny relationship to the American Education Establishment, those in charge of teaching our children. They are self-confident, even arrogant, about their modern theories and methods of teaching, which they believe are doing an excellent job. But once again, self-esteem, this time of the teaching vocation, is challenged by the results.

If our children are not doing well—and they are not—are

there other examples to demonstrate a shortfall in student performance? There are many, including contests that show us regularly vanquished by youngsters from around the globe.

In February 1998, the U.S. Department of Education issued the discouraging results of American high school seniors in the Third International Mathematics and Science Study (TIMSS), a worldwide competition among twenty-one nations.

"U.S. twelfth graders performed below the international average and among the lowest of the 21 TIMSS countries on the assessment of mathematical general knowledge," they reported.

This was no exaggeration. The American student scored nineteenth out of the twenty-one nations, doing so poorly in math that they only outperformed teenagers from two underdeveloped countries—Cyprus and South Africa. Dishearteningly, their scores were 20 percent lower than those of students in the Netherlands, a nation that must live on its brainpower—as America might someday be forced to do.

But aside from these defeats in international mental battles, how do our kids do in terms of general knowledge, responses that adults can relate to? After all, we were once in elementary and high school ourselves and took similar courses.

The best estimates of schoolchildren's learning skills come from the "Report Card to the Nation and the States," one of the few successful federal efforts in education. Conducted by the National Assessment of Educational Progress, the "NAEP" tests in reading, math, science, history, and geography provide biennial scores that give us a rude insight into what's *really* happening in American schoolrooms.

What do they show? Very simply, the results are discouraging, confirmation of appalling ignorance across the academic spectrum.

From the American history quizzes, it is apparent that youngsters are not properly taught the story of their nation. Two out of

3

three seventeen-year-olds, most ready to go on to college, did not know the meaning of Abraham Lincoln's Emancipation Proclamation. Less than half the 16,000 high school seniors tested recognized Patrick Henry's defiant challenge, "Give me liberty or give me death."

Even fewer teenagers—punished by a lax, unfocused schoolhouse—knew of the existence of the War of 1812, the Marshall Plan that saved Europe, or Lyndon Johnson's Great Society.

In science, high schoolers displayed frightening ignorance in a nation whose future, in peace and war, depends heavily on technology. The majority could not figure out that a shadow cast by the rising sun would fall to the west. Only 1 in 8 of the 11th graders were judged even "adequate" on a test of Analytic Writing. On a map of the world, most could not find Southeast Asia.

But students are only half the school equation. If they are not smart enough, or nearly as smart as parents believe, at least teachers can hold their own in the world of intelligence and knowledge. Correct?

Hardly. In Massachusetts, in April 1998, the state department of education introduced a new examination for the licensing of would-be teachers, almost all of whom had received a bachelor of education degree shortly before.

The test, as we shall later see, was not designed to challenge the teacher candidates at particularly high levels. But it did expect that they could at least write a lucid sentence. If so, everyone involved was disappointed. *Of the 1,800 test-takers, 59 percent—3 out of every 5—flunked.*

The results were "abysmal" and "painful," said the state education chief, pointing out that not only were many teaching graduates unable to write complete sentences containing nouns and verbs, but their spelling was often atrocious. The test submissions contained such spelling aberrations as "horibal," "compermise," even "universel"—affronts to both educational and literary sensibilities by those supposedly dedicated to upholding them.

So, if both American students and their teachers are below par, what is there to do?

For a while American adults seemed not to care, convinced that since *they* had gotten a good education, perhaps in the 1950s and 1960s, the same must be the order of the day in schools today. Any public awareness of the problem dates back to 1983 when a federal appraisal—"A Nation at Risk"—showed that student performance was falling. That was followed by an enthusiastic call to arms, trumpeted by successive "education presidents" in the White House. They proposed "Goals 2000," pledging that American students would be "number one" in science and mathematics by the turn of the millennium.

Now that we have reached that point in time, how accurate was that grandiose promise?

Actually, it has proven to be ridiculous, depriving Americans of their educational innocence. As we reach the millennium, that hope for superiority has been totally dashed. American schoolchildren, from kindergarten through grade 12, are no more learned today than before, perhaps even less so.

For the past half century, the argument in public education has been between enthusiastic proponents of the "progressive" theories of John Dewey and the "traditionalists," who look back fondly on a vanished rigor. Today the difference still exists, but there is increasing agreement by many on both sides that we are faced with an educational crisis that cuts across all philosophical concerns. Simply stated, American public schools, from kindergarten through the senior year of high school, are miserably failing their students and the society.

The nation is finally aware of the educational crisis. As recently as the 1980s only 2 percent of the population described education as "the most important problem facing the nation."

But by 1996 Americans ranked "the quality of public schooling" as the most pressing concern after crime. Since then the Pew Research Center survey, for three years running, has shown education to be the number one priority issue for Congress, the president, and the people. In 1999, a CNN-*Time* magazine poll reiterated this prime concern.

The power of education in our lives is newly confirmed, and the statistics tear at the fears of many a worried parent. There has always been a gap in prosperity between the schooled and the unschooled, but it has now become a chasm. Bureau of Labor statistics show that a college education adds some $20,000 a year in income, or almost a million dollars, over a lifetime of work.

The cost to American business is just as monumental. Corporations complain that as many as one-third of new hirees need remedial training after high school to become job literate. David Kearns, former CEO of Xerox, estimates that the failure of public school education costs industry at least $50 billion a year.

At a June 1999 symposium on the economic power of high technology, Alan Greenspan, chairman of the Federal Reserve board, reflected that our prosperity was based on the productivity produced by intellect. Though he was proud that our institutions of higher learning were creating people capable of maintaining that prosperity, he warned that the poor state of public school education, from kindergarten through high school, endangered its continuation.

How, then, one might ask, is the demonstrated failure of schooling possible in a nation that is the world leader in technology? If our youngsters are not capable in math and science, as international and domestic studies show, how are we able to maintain our high-tech dominance?

The answer, as sorrowful as it may be, is that American technology runs heavily on the skills of the foreign students who regularly beat us in world competition.

Though American public schools leave the mass of youngsters behind, the nation does have the finest technical institutions—MIT, Cal Tech, Carnegie-Mellon—which attract top students from around the globe. While only a minute segment of our youth make it to those elite schools, foreign students take up the slack, providing the needed talent.

Overall, some 45 percent of all the 13,000 Ph.D.'s in the hard sciences—physics, computer science, mathematics, chemistry, and engineering—are awarded each year to non-Americans, what the government calls "non-resident aliens." In the most vital high-tech fields, computer sciences and engineering, the number of foreign student Ph.D.'s is even higher, some 50 percent. Apparently, failure to properly educate our own has forced us to rely on the outside world for technical expertise. (No one is taking up the slack in the general education of our young, whether it be in reading, literature, the arts, or history.)

The world of education is in chaos for many reasons. One is that the Education Establishment and the public harbor several misconceptions. One distortion, advanced by educators through veiled hints, is that students are underperforming mainly because the public school system is basically made up of inner city students, whether in New York, Los Angeles, Atlanta, or Detroit. Under this false theory, the white middle class has fled to attend private schools from the elite Choates and Grotons to the less expensive Catholic, Protestant, and Jewish parochial schools.

Nothing could be further from the truth. Of the 53 million children in kindergarten through 12th grade (K–12), some 47 million attend public schools. Only 1 in 9 are enrolled in private schools, mainly religiously based. The elite secular schools cater to only 2 percent of the population. The reality is that in almost 9 out of 10 cases white students (88 percent) attend public schools, showing that tales of the "great exodus" are quite false.

In fact, the typical public school student is that same white middle-class child, who makes up the large majority (64 percent) of enrollment and more than two-thirds when overachieving Asian-Americans are added. The reality is that school failure—as we shall see—crosses all racial, religious, ethnic, and socioeconomic lines, affecting every area, from public housing in Chicago to elegant homes in our best suburbs.

The minority school dilemma does, of course, exist. But in a strange anomoly, it is mainly the African-American and Hispanic students, while still performing relatively poorly, who are making any progress at all. In 1971, the reading scores of seventeen-year-old African-Americans were lower than those of white students by 53 points. But by 1998, that spread had closed to only 30 points. *Among young minority children receiving proper traditional education, as we shall see, there is no gap at all.*

The Establishment, flush with self-esteem, has claimed that if only we would listen to its theories and creative demands, our 88,000 elementary and high schools in 14,800 school districts would have new life. We have agreed to cooperate and have spent billions of our hard-earned dollars to put virtually every remedy offered by educators into practice.

To make up for deficient language instruction, we have built thousands of audio language labs. Districts have brought the wonders of personal computers into the schoolhouse, and, more recently, hooked up classrooms to the all-powerful Internet. To integrate the districts, we first tried busing, then reversed mainly to neighborhood schools. To change the structure of the academic beast, we decentralized certain urban school boards. To meet the challenge, we implemented every new theory: "open classrooms," "team teaching," the "new math," even "teacher empowerment."

An Indictment of the Education Establishment

We have constructed "magnet schools" to draw children into specialized art, science, or math studies to escape the punishment of a weak curriculum. We have even launched individualized charter schools to escape the system's oppressive bureaucracy. We have singled out "star teachers" and claimed their success could be replicated everywhere. We have encouraged teachers to take graduate degrees, rewarding them with fatter paychecks.

To attract better talent, pay scales have increased substantially. In New York and New Jersey, classroom teachers earn over $50,000 a year on average. In Connecticut, the average salary has just passed $55,000. Nationwide, according to the National Education Association (NEA), the average teacher now earns over $40,000, including those in small towns and rural areas. With extraordinary benefits and a work year of only 180 days, teaching has become a respectably paid career.

Administrators are often ridiculously overpaid and treated in godly fashion, as in the case of the chancellor of public schools in New York City, who receives $235,000 a year, more than the president of the United States.

The costs of public education are high and rising, with little to show for it. Washington, for all its cackling about its reform program of Goals 2000, picks up only 6 percent of the $350 billion annual charge. The rest is paid by hard-pressed states, and by communities, which support the schools through property taxes, the fastest rising levy in the nation. From 1970 to 1999, the cost of living rose some fourfold, but the cost of education went up eightfold, with the same number of students as three decades ago.

What have all these reforms and trillions of dollars wrought? Have they paid off in better public school performance?

Absolutely not. There has been no significant improvement in the quality of public education, and under present management,

9

there is little hope for the future. Goals 2000 has proved to be an idle dream of naive politicians and educators.

Nothing has worked because the supposed reforms have not attacked the core of the problem: the makeup, theories, and operation of the Education Establishment—the 5 million "professionals," from classroom teachers to state education commissioners, who constitute the near-monolithic force that controls our public schools, from kindergarten through senior high school.

That Establishment has shown itself to be an advocate of low standards, laxity, false educational theory, and poor selection and training of teachers. It suffers from an inability to pass on the accumulated knowledge of civilization from one generation to the next. As time passes, that mental bank decreases, setting up the specter of grave prospects for the future.

Parents are often fooled by a continuous onslaught of Establishment propaganda, but surprisingly, mature students see through the schooling charade. This was clearly demonstrated in a nationwide study of 1,000 teenagers conducted by Public Agenda for the Educational Excellence Partnership—eight organizations, from the Business Roundtable to the American Federation of Teachers. In the survey, "What American Teenagers Really Think About Their Schools," three-fourths of the students complained that they were being short-changed—that they weren't being given demanding enough schoolwork. They would study harder, they said, if only schools would give them more to study and tougher tests to challenge them.

This Establishment is not just a recent thorn in the side of public schooling. In the 1960s, Dr. James Conant, then president of Harvard University, skeptically called the Education Establishment a "closed alliance," whose branches controlled the operation of public schools at every level. He was accurate, but kindly, for the teaching establishment has since shown itself to be more than an "alliance."

An Indictment of the Education Establishment

In reality, it is a self-protective, virtually impenetrable closed circle. It selects our future teachers, trains them in its own academies, issues them its own undergraduate and graduate degrees, certifies them at the state licensing level, hires them for our schools, evaluates and promotes them.

It starts at the classroom level, goes up through the teacher union-guilds, to the principals, the school administrators, to the professors in the schools and departments of education, then up to the superintendents of schools in cities and suburbs. Finally, it reaches the state departments of education, where the Commissioner is usually a leading Establishment figure.

Thus full circle.

Breaking that ring of power has been near-impossible. Its members have much the same background, goals, and values. They attend the same, generally inferior schools and hold the same inferior education degrees at various levels. They also share the same resolve to keep laypeople out of the learning business, which they accomplish by binding together into combined professional cabal and guild-labor unions. They have taken control of our schools away from the citizens, the parents, and their elected officials—who are generally naive about education and overwhelmed by the jargon and obfuscations of the Education Establishment.

In most ways, that Establishment is an unscholarly, anti-intellectual, antiacademic cabal which can best be described as a *conspiracy of ignorance*, one with false theories and low academic standards. Well conceived, internally consistent, it has been powerful enough—thus far—to fight off outside challenges and true change. All this at the expense of our schoolchildren.

We should be aware, however, that it is not a conspiracy of malice. Teachers and educators are, by and large, humane and well-meaning people. Their major sins are that they have discarded traditional scholarship as a major goal and have adopted education.

the psychologist/social work model rather than that of the academic instructor. They will fight compulsively, even unfairly, to maintain their low standards and protect their members from the full examination that could end their monopoly control of public education.

This book is intended as just such an examination of that Establishment and its public schools, in all their facets. It will explore their blemishes, their fallacies, and even their few assets. In this volume, I will set out to prove conclusively that the education of American children, from kindergarten through 12th grade, is a poorly cast and poorly delivered product.

Alexis de Tocqueville, the French seer and author of the two-volume *Democracy of America,* traversed the young country in 1835 and concluded that its public schools were a major bulwark of democracy. America, he said, had a "middling" standard of education. Nowhere in the world were there so few truly learned people. But at the same time, he observed, nowhere in the world were there so few ignorant.

That middling education provided a disciplined environment that prepared children for literacy, life, and work. Over the years that traditional education expanded as the nation grew, providing mass tutoring for virtually everyone. It performed well for most of the baby boomers up through the 1950s and into the 1960s, when it changed in direction and philosophy.

What happened?

Simply put, the goals, ideals, and practices of public education have been quietly, almost secretly, altered over the past three decades, most often without the knowledge of parents, politicians, or the community. As a result, America now has an inferior standard of learning in our public schools. Teachers are selected from an inferior academic pool. Teacher training is thin and faddish. Curriculum has been weakened, especially in our middle and secondary schools. The rigor of prior years is mainly gone.

Meanwhile, Dr. Sigmund Freud has invaded the schoolhouse. The teacher has now assumed more the model of the social worker or even amateur psychologist. Not knowledge, but superior human relations, a sense of self-confidence—"self-esteem" again—and a stronger, warmer rapport among teacher, parent and child have become a new criteria.

It seems hard to fault such objectives. But today, some thirty-five years after the soul of the classroom began to change, we see the result. We have a less apprehensive, perhaps even happier, student body, but one that is academically much weaker and less prepared for the challenges of the twenty-first century.

To turn de Tocqueville's comment on its head, nowhere in the developed world are there now so many ignorant schoolchildren as in America.

I have shaped a Bill of Indictment to outline the specific deficiencies that need essential change. No list can be all-inclusive, but this is designed as an insight into the problems that bedevil us as we attempt, once again, to truly educate young America.

1. The licensing of teachers, what is known as certification, is a ritual without substance, requiring knowledge at the lowest possible level.

2. The curriculum used to teach our children is weak. Most public schools have virtually eliminated formal history and geography and are deficient in teaching composition, grammar, and spelling as well as mathematics and science.

3. Teacher training is lax. The undergraduate degree of most teachers, usually a bachelor of education, is less substantial than an ordinary liberal arts degree. The same hollowness is true of the master's degrees obtained by teachers.

4. Tenure protects the most inadequate of our teachers.
5. Teachers' unions too often operate as political organizations while masquerading as professional groups.
6. The American schoolhouse is heavily psychologized, beginning with educational psychology courses in teacher training up through the psychological testing and counseling of students.
7. Would-be teachers are usually self-selected from the bottom third of high school and university graduates.
8. Evidence indicates that there is no "profession" of education. Laypeople who enter the field with little or no training do as well as graduates of education schools, and often better.
9. More than any other field, education is top-heavy with administrators and bureaucrats.
10. The lack of separation between elementary and high school teachers, in salary and training, makes true scholarship in secondary school difficult, if not impossible.
11. The doctor of education degree, the Ed.D. held by most school superintendents and administrators, is inferior to the traditional Ph.D. degree and requires little academic knowledge.
12. Many schools concentrate on weak students and resist enriching the education of gifted students, claiming that "tracking" is an "elitist" practice.
13. Highly educated college graduates without Education Establishment credentials are usually not permitted to teach in public schools, forcing them into private or college systems, losing superior talent.
14. The Establishment dislikes traditional methods and continually develops new, unproven theories of education, none of which stand the test of time.
15. Parents are regularly fooled about their children's true

abilities through blatant grade inflation, which is rampant in our schools.

16. Too many educators have low expectations for students, resulting in poor performance, especially among minority students.
17. By promoting concepts of "self-esteem," teachers create a false complacency among students, hindering their academic development.
18. Parents, the PTAs, and elected school board officials have abdicated their powers to the hired help, the Education Establishment.
19. State legislators, who have the ultimate power over public education, are generally ignorant about the subject, cowed by educators, and neglect their duty to parents and students.

Some may find this indictment harsh. But as we progress and look into the often-hidden, arcane world of education, I am convinced that the evidence will substantiate the charges. This book is not only designed to provide insight but will offer detailed recommendations on how to correct the ills of public education, point by point as presented in the indictment.

If that is successful, instead of public education—which has had a noble history—threatening to collapse of its own false weight, it can once again become a monument to a knowledgeable democratic people.

2

A TALE OF AMERICAN STUDENT FAILURE

Domestic Ignorance and International Embarrassment

The proud parents of a 6th grade middle school student in an affluent Fairfield County, Connecticut, town surveyed the new bumper sticker on their BMW.

DRIVE CAREFULLY. AN HONOR STUDENT IS RIDING IN THIS CAR.

Their pride was natural, but after a while it became obvious that bumper stickers highlighting the words HONOR STUDENT were proliferating in the town. This could hardly dampen the parents' enthusiasm, but others wondered: "Could there be so many brilliant kids in one place at one time?"

Their curiosity was soon answered by an article in the local paper. It listed the names of the youngsters who had done the town and their parents proud by being named to the Honor Roll. The list looked suspiciously long, however. When it was counted, there were 126 names—a remarkable achievement considering there were only 197 children in that 6th grade.

A Tale of American Student Failure

What the school had accomplished by selecting almost two-thirds of their 6th grade students as "scholars" was to make a caricature, even a mockery, of assessment. It sought to accomplish what was once thought solely in the province of the Creator: the shaping of near geniuses, wholesale.

The reality, of course, is that we are not witnessing the smartening of our young, but the propaganda elevation of student achievement with a stroke of the pen. This fake Establishment touting of academic success is spreading epidemic-like by combining elevated "self-esteem" with blatant grade inflation, all in the hope of masking the failure of American public education.

The theory is quite simple. Since the schools are being attacked by critics armed with strong evidence from the states, Washington, and international competition that they are *not* doing a good job educating the young, why not simply outflank the opposition by producing legions of "honor students"? Nothing increases a school's reputation with parents and taxpaying citizens more than good student performance. If we have so many A students, the schools must be doing a good job, they say. And conversely, proof that the Establishment has been doing a good job is that we have so many A students.

(The bumper stickers have proliferated so rapidly that they have spawned a second, more cynical, version. This one reads: My Honor Student Can Beat Up Your Honor Student.)

The honor student rampage is part of a growing competition among parents and students for better performance, each good mark contributing to the upcoming ferocious battle for a spot in an elite college, the sine qua non of future success.

We see this in the enormous growth of students enrolled in "advanced placement" classes in high school, which offer an opportunity to receive college-level credit. According to the College Board organization, these classes now have an enrollment of 635,000 of the best and the brightest American seventeen- and eighteen year-olds, more than double the number of a decade ago.

This is a welcome development. The more students who can take an advanced curriculum, more rigorous than that usually dispensed in public schools, the better. To educators, it is not only a positive step but like the legions they have named to the Honor Roll, further proof that they are conducting a "world class" operation.

Are they correct? No, the Establishment is quite wrong. Obviously some students are more gifted and more able than others, but by and large, the educational performance of American students is quite low. In fact, even our supposed best are failing in comparison with similar students elsewhere.

This was shown when our highest-achieving students, those in "advanced placement," many of whom were also "honor students," were placed in international competition. As part of the Third International Mathematics and Science Study competition, America entered these gifted students in several special contests, optimistically pitting their skill against the best of the rest of the world.

The results were crushing. Our best are apparently far from good enough.

In the overall math contest, for example, America scored near the basement, fifteenth among sixteen nations. In calculus our smartest teenagers performed almost as poorly—fourteenth out of fifteen countries. In geometry, the academic embarrassment reached its zenith, or nadir, depending on your perspective. The top American youngsters scored at the absolute bottom.

Our leading young science scholars did no better. The American advanced placement high school physics seniors, so thoroughly advertised in the Intel Science Talent Search (formerly the Westinghouse scholarship) and in nationwide science fairs, performed even worse than our best mathematicians. They scored dead last, some 25 percent below the leader, Norway.

This failure of performance is not unique. Rather it is additional evidence of the laxity of American teachers and the entire Education Establishment, whether the students are average or outstanding.

Speaking of the general failure in the teaching of mathematics, the U.S. Department of Education has stated: "Half the 17-year-olds lack math skills commonly taught, not in their 11th grade, but in junior high school." That dismal record would be even worse if it hadn't been buoyed up by studious Asian-American students who tallied 331 in federally supported exams, as against an average score of less than 300 for seventeen-year-olds in general.

The most interesting, and curious, information gained from the Third International tests is that it seems that the longer one stays in American public schools, the less, relatively, one achieves academically.

This was shown by the sharp drop in performance of the older American students, especially as they headed on to college. The young 4th graders scored 545, ranking twelfth out of twenty-six nations, with Singapore winning the prize with a score of 625.

In science, these ten-year-olds did even better, coming out third overall, after Korea and Japan, which was a genuine surprise. However, in the hard-edged physical sciences of chemistry and physics (rather than tests on environment, an American specialty), they ranked considerably lower—in tenth place. Still, it was a victory of sorts.

But the story doesn't end there. As older American students were tested internationally, they performed less well right down the line. By 8th grade, our students were rapidly losing ground. These thirteen-year-olds had to handle more difficult material, and the paucity of good teaching now showed. *The 8th graders scored below average in math (500 score versus 643 for Singapore), ranking a poor twenty-eighth out of forty-one nations.*

Then we come to the seventeen-year-old Americans, who shed little honor on themselves or their teachers. All semblance of good international performance disappeared as high school seniors were faced with considerably more difficult subject matter. By the time they were tested in math, they made that embarrassingly poor performance, coming in, as we've seen, nineteenth out of twenty-one nations. In the next level up, our advanced students occupied the academic basement of the planet.

If this increasing failure by age proves anything it is that as the subject matter becomes even a touch more complex, the American school system sputters, then fizzles out. One simple explanation is that teacher selection and training are geared almost entirely to the needs of small children, who make few academic demands on undertrained, academically deficient teachers. Despite that, even our 4th graders have grave deficiencies, including an inability to read properly.

Barbara Lerner, an analyst who has dealt with mass test results, explains this phenomenon of results fading as American students move up into higher grades, especially as they approach middle school.

Middle school, she states, is "the place where our good news about our kids begins to turn into bad news, the place where American kids who start out so bright and eager and ready, begin turning into the academic laggards we graduate from high school . . . The decline in student achievement scores over the last two decades begins in the fifth grade . . . And we know why: because American schools stopped enforcing standards for academic achievement and discipline for older students in the late Sixties."

Unless there is a radical change in curriculum, teacher selection, and training, America's place in the international standings of 12th graders—the youngsters who are supposed to be the most accomplished as they go on to college—will remain at or near the bottom.

This matters more each day as an increasing number of high schoolers go on for higher education. Only a decade ago some 50 percent of high school graduates went on to college. Today it is an astonishing two-thirds (67 percent), making the inferior high school experience that much more damaging.

We see it clearly in the army of eighteen-year-olds who need remedial work as college freshmen, an oxymoronic situation to say the least. Chester Finn, Jr., former U.S. Assistant Secretary of Education and a knowledgeable critic of the Establishment, points out that in upscale Montgomery County, Maryland (a suburb of Washington, D.C.), where 86 percent of high schoolers go on to higher education, the local community college found that 71 percent of incoming students were deficient in math and half failed to meet the English standards. "When I saw the size of the numbers, I was shocked," said the county executive.

Remedial college courses are the direct result of the academic failure of elementary and high school teaching. Beginning in first grade, the elementary school shifts much of the work that should be done to the middle school. In turn, middle school teachers pass the necessary learning on to the next level, the high school. In this progressive negligence, the failure to truly prepare students is finally dumped onto the university campus.

Diane Ravitch, a scholarly critic of public education and former U.S. Assistant Secretary of Education who is now a research professor at New York University, has outlined the extent of the problem. She explains that 78 percent of U.S. colleges offer courses in remedial reading, writing, or math. "It is fairly shocking, or should be, to discover that 29 percent of all freshmen take a remedial course when they enter college," she writes.

The Conspiracy of Ignorance

The situation is getting worse, not better, as high schools fail to properly prepare students for higher learning. Thirty-nine percent of colleges questioned reported an increase in the need for remedial studies. The problem appears to be most severe in the huge California State University system, where half the freshmen need work in either English or math that should have been taught in high school. The community colleges of the state now spend $300 million a year doing academic repair work.

Much of the breakdown can be seen in the results of the nationwide NAEP tests, given to a large sample of 4th, 8th, and 12th graders, generally every two years. The results conflict with the hope of "education presidents" that we will soon approach the Goals 2000 fantasy of being first in the world.

In the crucial 4th grade, the latest scores in reading, from the NAEP 1998 report, show that 38 percent are reading "below basic" levels, the same failure as in 1992. The 12th graders improved by two points in that category over the last four years but were still three points *lower* than in 1992. When private schools are excluded, all these scores drop even further.

"Below basic," Chester Finn explains, "means essentially non-functional as readers, even though the young people taking the test were within a few months of graduating. And that means last year's graduation ceremonies dumped about 750,000 more semiliterate eighteen-year-olds into the work force with high-school diplomas clutched in their fists."

Equally sobering is that of the 2.5 million high school graduates each year, after twelve years of public schooling, only 6 percent were reading at world-class, or "advanced," levels.

The NAEP tests, on which most youngsters do poorly, are not excruciatingly difficult. A closer examination of the exam in history, for one, shows that our students in history have apparently been abandoned by teachers, who may be as ignorant of the subject as the children.

A Tale of American Student Failure

Only one in five of 4th graders knew enough about either the Alamo, Pearl Harbor, Gettysburg, or Roanoke Island to write even a few sentences. *Three in five didn't know that the Pilgrims and Puritans came here to practice religious freedom.* Only two in five were aware that the Missions were the center of religious activity in the Spanish colonies in America. When asked to describe what happened in Philadelphia in 1776, only one in fourteen wrote anything "appropriate."

Seven in ten didn't know that New York was one of the thirteen colonies that fought in the Revolution. Three in five did not know it was Abraham Lincoln—not Washington or Jefferson or Teddy Roosevelt—who said "I believe this government cannot endure half slave and half free."

The upper grades did somewhat better, but there were signs of inexplicable ignorance that would startle those who went to school in a more rigorous age. When thirteen-year-olds were asked the purpose of the Monroe Doctrine—a staple of traditional history instruction—70 percent failed. Growing up in the system didn't seem to help. The same question given to high school seniors stumped almost 60 percent.

Given a description of Charleston, South Carolina, in ruins, 8th grade students were asked in what year it was written—in 1835, 1845, 1855, or 1865. Less than one-third answered correctly. *Worse yet, 60 percent of high school seniors didn't know when the Civil War was fought.*

Geography showed the same pattern of failure. On a blank outline map, high school seniors were asked to mark (1) Pyrenees Mountains (2) Japanese Archipelago (3) Mediterranean Sea (4) Persian Gulf.

The response? *Seventy-seven percent of the seventeen-year-olds could not locate even three out of the four.*

In the 1996 NAEP math test, on which 12th graders scored an average of 304 out of 500, or some 61 percent, there were enormous, unexplained gaps in knowledge. One test example showed a 6-9-12 triangle with a truncated similar section that was 2-3-? in length. The answer for the third leg of the triangle was obviously "4", but 63 percent of the high school seniors got it wrong.

If American students are usually operating subpar, as testing shows, then why are parents apparently so pleased with their children's teachers and schools?

That peculiar dilemma was explored recently in *Public Opinion Quarterly*. Researchers found that public confidence in public education in general has been declining rapidly. Forty percent had "a great deal of confidence" in our schools in the 1970s. But by the 1980s that number had declined. By the mid-1990s, "fewer than one-quarter" expressed true confidence in public education. Only one in five people gave our public schools an A or B, and almost as many gave them a failing D or F, with C being the usual grade. Not a very complimentary appraisal for a crucial activity that costs us some $350 billion a year.

But that negative view changes abruptly when citizens are asked to grade the school their own children attend. Then two-thirds reward the school with an A or B, and almost none believe it is failing the children. Education in America may be poor or mediocre, they tell us, but their school is doing just fine.

How is that possible?

The answer is threefold. Firstly, schools and teachers do a magnificent public relations job in handling parents. They contact them regularly and set up parent-teacher conferences where, face-to-face, one's loved child becomes the focus of all attention.

Teachers write frequent reports that intimately involve the child's assets and problems. Superintendents of schools routinely send enthusiastic missives to the parents. Many parents also volunteer in the school as aides and gain a vested interest in the operation. As far as the typical school system is concerned, the taxpaying parent is more the customer than are the children, innocents who *cannot* know if they are receiving a good education.

The teachers do not have to fake warmth for the children. If there is one asset the Establishment can boast of it is the personal dedication of teachers to their students and their feelings. The overwhelming negative, as we shall see, is that teachers themselves are poorly educated, are ill-equipped to instruct in a solid curriculum, and have little familiarity with or interest in true scholarship. All of this eventually shows up in poor student performance.

Often teachers seem more interested in the children's adjustment and psyche than in their minds. This does not alienate many parents who agree that they would gladly trade *ignorance* for *happiness*, as if there were a contest between the two—which there shouldn't be.

The second part of the answer is that parents find it hard to question or to be skeptical of teachers. In our culture, beginning in Puritan times, through the Western migration, then after the great immigration, when the public schools successfully handled the Americanization of millions of children, teachers have become honored, almost mythic, figures. Only in the schools did immigrants generally find an absence of bias, an evenhandedness from teachers regardless of wealth or origin. If somewhat less thought of today, teachers still represent our attachment to learning, and many people, especially parents, find it difficult to question their performance.

Most everyone has a memory of a favorite teacher, someone who took a special interest or ignited a love of learning. In such an environment, it is difficult to probe, to challenge how our children are being taught, no matter how necessary that investigation into teacher competence may be.

The third portion of the answer is that most parents do not

really know what their children are learning and how well they are doing in school. The report cards sent home are generally positive, even extravagantly full of praise. They show that *most* children score far above average, a ludicrous statistical trick that science has yet to master.

This sleight of hand, or grade inflation, is prevalent throughout the nation. No matter how well or poorly students are actually doing, almost all get As or Bs, or an equivalent. Almost no one flunks. Unlike a generation ago, very few even get a C, which would be an assault on their self-esteem.

Proof that grade inflation is epidemic in public schools is easy to come by. The Scholastic Aptitude Test people at the Educational Testing Service in Princeton, New Jersey, collect, then correlate, student grades against their scores on the SAT test. This is not a small sample. The SAT is taken annually by 1.7 million teenagers—some 70 percent of all 11th graders.

What do the results show? *That as student SAT scores decline, their school grades go up dramatically, proof positive of rampant grade inflation.* A chart plotting these two contradictory axes shows that in 1988, when the average SAT verbal score (on the new recentered scale) for students who had A grades in school was 582, the top students (those with A, A−, and A+) represented 28 percent of all college-bound seniors taking the exam.

But ten years later, by 1998, the SAT verbal score of A students had dropped 13 points to 569—a substantial decrease. However, their school grades surprisingly jumped upward. From 28 percent of SAT takers having A grades, the figure increased to 38 percent. More students were being labeled smart simply through grade inflation and not because they achieved more.

There is a lesson here for parents: Don't believe too much of what teachers say about your child's performance in school, especially when it is laudatory. The Establishment has set up a self-fulfilling prophecy. To repeat their clever mantra: Since the children are getting As, they must be learning. And conversely, they must be learning since they are getting As.

This and the growing numbers named to the Honor Roll are part of the teaching Establishment's determination to make virtually everyone feel *above average*, whether they are or not. Simultaneously, this lines up more parents pleased to pay the rising school taxes that support the Establishment.

A suburban father who happened to be an engineer and quite proficient in math was pleased when his daughter received an A in algebra. One day he went over her homework with her and found, to his surprise, that she couldn't do simple algebraic equations. After much delay, he finally got an appointment to see her math teacher. He explained that his daughter didn't deserve the A since she didn't seem to understand algebra. The annoyed teacher responded by saying that educators now had different criteria for assessing students from when he went to school. The frustrated father, whose daughter was a victim of grade inflation, did the only thing he could under the circumstances. He took his daughter out of public school and sent her to a private one.

While ballooning Honor Rolls and casually given As succeed in making more parents and children happy, they also do grave damage—both to the youngster and society—in masking the poor education most are receiving and how little they actually know.

(Aside from this academic distortion, the Establishment has violated its own rule of not hurting the feelings of its charges. What about the sensitivities of the overlooked students? Their pain is probably greater today than a generation or two ago when only a handful of the brightest were singled out for special mention.)

If you really want to know how your child is doing, you'll have to check the inflated grades and honors against some other, more standardized criteria. One way is to ask for the average grade given in your child's class. Then you can judge accordingly. If the child has an A, remember that traditionally meant scoring in the top 10 percent of the class. Today, it could mean they are barely above average, which makes it a meaningless distinction.

Another way is to check how well your child has done on standardized tests, whether a state exam such as the Connecticut Mastery Test, or if older, the SAT or ACT college admissions tests, whichever is most used in the 11th grade in your area. Those scores might provide parents with an awakening, especially if they are in sharp contrast to the teachers' Pollyannaish grades.

You might also read your child's textbook in any subject, say American history, and quiz him or her yourself. (That is, if the student has a history textbook, which is becoming an obsolete learning instrument.) You'll probably find that if you want the youngster to truly know history, you'll have to become the teacher yourself.

The question of student performance gnaws at parents and teachers because no one seems to know anymore what students are supposed to know. No longer are there strong, clear, explicit standards by which we can measure performance. It is as if the standards of two generations ago have dissipated into the air and have to be reinvented.

That's exactly what a group called the National Education Goals Panel is doing—trying to establish standards so that our youngsters in 4th, 8th, and 12th grades can become educated enough to handle the twenty-first century.

The group studied the question, then outlined a series of standards. Once that was done, they tested a random sample of students to see how they measured up. Again the sorry refrain. They did not.

In 4th grade mathematics, 80 percent failed to meet the performance goals. As a revealing example, almost 40 percent could not divide 108 by 9. (Naturally, 12.)

A Tale of American Student Failure

In 4th grade geography, 78 percent of the students didn't measure up to the tougher standards. One simple question that many students could not answer was "Which landforms were most likely created by the eruption of volcanoes?" The answer, of course, was "mountains."

In history, five in six couldn't meet the suggested standards. One question failed by 36 percent of the children was: "Which state last became part of the United States?" (Hawaii.)

The 8th grade standards in history were just as unmet as 86 percent didn't measure up. It seems improbable that one simple question fooled 40 percent of the thirteen-year-olds—unless you have children or grandchildren and are aware of how little American history they learn.

"Who wrote the following?" the test asked 8th graders.

"We hold these truths to be self-evident: that all men are created equal; that they are endowed by their Creator with certain unalienable rights; that among these are life, liberty and the pursuit of happiness."

One would hope that children would have learned about the Declaration of Independence and Thomas Jefferson by the 8th grade.

History was no better understood among 12th graders ready for college, 89 percent of whom could not meet the standards. Fifty-seven percent of the 17-year-olds didn't know that the Stamp Act of 1765 was a form of "taxation without representation," the rallying cry at the birth of our nation.

(We should no longer wonder why so few young people over eighteen bother to vote on Election Day. Their connection with America's past is tenuous at best.)

The Education Establishment has well-developed lines of spin to explain away its failures of performance in the classroom. One is money. "If only we had more resources," they claim, "then we could do this and that. Just give us more and more . . ."

The Conspiracy of Ignorance

The susceptible public often yields to this pressure, not knowing that the Establishment equation that MONEY EQUALS PERFORMANCE is untrue. Teachers should surely be reasonably well paid, and increasingly they are. But it's just as equitable for the principals and the administrators to do a much better job with the money we give them.

Supposedly the more cash poured into teaching, the greater the expansion of student minds. It is a tempting delusion, but nothing could be more fallacious. We know this from many sources including the higher academic performance of parochial schools, where expenditures per pupil are 40 percent lower than in public schools. (See Chapter 8.)

Meanwhile, money continues to flow into public schools, with apparently no end in sight and with little or no improvement to show for it. In 1960, Americans spent $375 a year to educate each public school student; $816 in 1970; $6,146 in 1996; and over $7,000 per pupil in the 1999–2000 school year.

In inflation-adjusted dollars, we are now spending two to three times more per child than in 1960, when performance was generally higher.

One of the compelling establishment arguments for more money is their continual push for smaller class sizes, one that touches parents emotionally. If only we could have more teachers and specialists, we are constantly told, performance would surely be pushed skyward.

Parents say "amen." Most Americans are convinced, without real facts, that the fewer children in each class the stronger the teaching. After all, what could be better than more individualized instruction?

That shibboleth of smaller classes, the vaunted pupil-teacher ratio, became a national goal. To meet it, the school districts hired and hired until it hurt. And with tenure, which is usually granted after three years, incompetent teachers were immune to strong discipline or firing.

In 1960, there were 35 million students in public schools and 1.35 million teachers. Today, propelled by the "small class" argument, the number of teachers has doubled to 2.7 million.

Along with the increase in teacher ranks, there has also been an explosion of school administrators, from assistant principals to superintendents of schools, the brahmins of the Establishment. This has created a bloated roster of highly paid, generally unneeded, educational bureaucrats. In the same period, the number of these administrators has more than doubled, from 96,000 to 215,000.

The growth of Establishment employees has included a vast array of support personnel. From 700,000 in 1960, these reading specialists, guidance counselors, special ed teachers, clerical help, teacher's aides, and others, have grown to 2.5 million strong, an almost fourfold increase. Guidance counselors, charged with the psychological adjustment of academically understressed children, were once only 17,000 weak. Today that number has risen almost fivefold to over 80,000. Overall, there is now an army of more than five million school personnel, one for every *nine* students.

(Since little more than half the staff are teachers, America has one of the highest costs of education per student, but is not first in teacher salaries.)

The student body has not followed suit in this massive expansion. From 35 million public school pupils, the ranks have grown only to 47 million, proportionately three times less than the rise in teacher personnel. The revered pupil-teacher ratio has naturally dropped accordingly.

From 27 to 1 in 1955, the pupil-teacher ratio dropped to 25 to 1 in 1965, then to 20 to 1 in 1975, then to 17 to 1 today. Class sizes were reduced and students received more specialized attention in reading, counseling, and other school services. Today the average elementary school class size is twenty-three, considerably lower than it was forty years ago when it was approximately thirty—and even larger before then.

The Establishment theory of smaller classes has been implemented over the decades at a cost of hundreds of billions of dollars and is now being pressed again with a vengeance.

From year to year, the Establishment comes up with its annual "salvation" reform to keep the public hopeful, and guessing, much like a Hail Mary football pass in the last seconds of the Super Bowl. Today smaller class size—which means hiring still more teachers—is advanced as the solution to our educational problems. To this end, California has appropriated hundreds of millions of dollars to hire teachers and reduce class size in the 1st, 2nd, and 3rd grades from some twenty-five to twenty.

The subject has assumed national prominence as President Bill Clinton has promoted a campaign for 100,000 new teachers to create a major turnaround in the fortunes of public education. However, the details of how to pay for it are quite shaky. The federal fiscal 2000 appropriation for this is planned at $1.1 billion, with an eventual layout of some $12 billion over the years.

Will that do it?

It will—if you believe in arithmetic that ranks with the failed "new math." Over a full thirty-year career, the average teacher costs some $1.7 million in current dollars, for salary, retirement and benefits. One hundred thousand teachers will then cost $170 billion. But Washington is talking about a current expenditure of $1.1 billion and a total of only $12 billion. *If we are forced to use traditional arithmetic, that amount will pay for only 7,000 teachers, not 100,000.*

Who will pay the remaining $158 billion? Naturally our already hard-pressed, tax-burdened local school districts.

But what if we did achieve still smaller classes, say twenty to a room instead of the current twenty-three, but still had the same Educational Establishment? What would be the result? To look at the future, perhaps we should look at the past, the best evidence we have. Can we believe the promise of a better education?

Apparently not.

As the pupil-teacher ratio has gone down almost 40 percent from 1955 to 1999 and class sizes have shrunk accordingly, student achievement has not only failed to rise, but has dropped, almost in inverse ratio to the size of the educational staff. In science, for instance, where we have NAEP scores going back to 1969, 12th grade achievement has dropped from an average score of 309 to 296 after almost thirty years.

It may sound illogical, even paradoxical, but perhaps we could speculate that the smaller the class and the more attention given the student, the less is taught and learned. One is reminded of C. Northcote Parkinson's famed law in which he demonstrated that as the British Navy was reduced drastically in size after World War I, the Admiralty staff grew dramatically.

If we look worldwide, we find that this well-ingrained American dedication to smaller and smaller classes may well be a fallacy out of step with much of the developed world. In France, Germany, and Japan, whose students generally best us in international competition, the average class size is about thirty, some 25 percent larger than those in America.

Perhaps more startling is the fact that classrooms in South Korea, which invariably walks away with first prize in the math and science contests, have an average of forty-nine youngsters in 8th grade classrooms, more than *double* the size of those in America.

At the same time, of course, private schools in America generally have somewhat smaller classes—averaging 20 pupils.

There is absolutely nothing wrong with hiring still more teachers, if we want to spend the money. But considering the other liabilities of the Establishment, we should not expect any educational rewards.

The unfortunate reality, which sounds like heresy in today's climate, is that class size probably has nothing whatsoever to do with educational success, one way or another.

On the subject of class size, I am reminded of my own experience in Junior High School 52 in the Bronx, the same school attended by General Colin Powell. In the 8th grade, more than 40 boys were crushed into one classroom. For lack of a seat, I spent some time between the radiators on a wooden board that stretched across the room under the windows. I confess to my rear being heated excessively at times, but I'm convinced it did not damage me or my sardine-packed classmates intellectually, or disrupt the rigorous instruction of the day.

The whole question of the Establishment claim that MONEY EQUALS PERFORMANCE is in doubt. Another breaker of that myth comes from state results, which show that better schooling can seldom be bought. New York State is a perfect example, with special emphasis on New York City, where billions have gone down the schoolhouse drain.

New York, along with New Jersey, leads the nation in spending per pupil. The latest New York State figures show that for the school year 1996–97, the state spent $9,321 per pupil. That figure for the 1999–2000 year, which began in September 1999, has reached an estimated $10,250 for K–8 grades, which is some $3,000 more than the national average.

What do we get for all that money? Not very much. On a statewide basis for 4th graders, for instance, New York scores *below* the national average in reading performance, ranking nineteenth out of the thirty-seven states that were surveyed. The failure is profound. Thirty-eight percent of the children are reading below "basic" levels, a failure that spills over to other subjects— whether history, math, or science. In the 1998 statewide exams for 3rd and 6th graders in reading and math, results showed that student scores dropped two points statewide and were four points lower in New York City.

In the hope of raising standards in English, the state administered a new examination for 4th graders in January 1999 that used the essay form instead of the usual multiple-choice questions. But the effort fell on its academic face. When the results were published at the end of May, it showed that more than half the students in the state had failed, a record surpassed by New York City 4th graders, two-thirds of whom had flunked.

In June 1999, the Board of Education of New York City announced more disastrous results on tests in reading and math taken by 290,000 students citywide the prior April. In 1998, 49.6 percent of the students had been reading at least at grade level when compared to youngsters throughout the nation. But by 1999, that performance had dropped a full five points to 44.6 percent. In mathematics, the results showed an even more severe drop, falling a full ten percent compared with students elsewhere.

Hardly a good return for the enormous amount of money spent in a failed search for quality education.

Though there has been some improvement over the past thirty years, there is still a sizable discrepancy in reading scores between white and African-American youths, who are the major student group in New York City. For example, in the 1998 NAEP 4th grade reading tests nationwide, African-Americans scored an average of 30 points lower on a scale of 500, with an average score of 215.

The Establishment does not wash its hands of the problem. Instead, it uselessly wrings them. They try to put the onus elsewhere—especially on *poverty* and its many side effects. If the children can't read up to grade level, claim educators, it is the fault of the environment in which they live.

But more than likely the failure is due to the incompetence of the Establishment. Too often it has relegated poor children to the academic scrapheap, blaming them, their parents, and the community instead of placing the blame where it belongs—on the school system, its principals, and its teachers.

It is not because of racism, or less attention to African-American and Hispanic children, as some might charge. With federal aid, more money and time, not less, is spent on minority children in general. Much of the real reason, we now know, is that the Establishment theories, particularly those on how to teach reading, are ineffective.

Such contemporary instruction can even be *de-educational*, impeding the traditional ways of learning to read that have been validated over hundreds of years of experience. In the modern classroom, Establishment faddism has overtaken common sense as the modus operandi in the teaching of reading.

How do we know this?

Because right in the center of minority poverty, one of New York City's public schools—P.S. 161 in Crown Heights in Brooklyn—has proven the Establishment absolutely wrong. Instead of faddism, the school relies on proven common sense. The result is that poverty or no poverty, minority students or not, students in its grades K–5 read easily and well.

In fact, 82 percent of the youngsters in the 3rd grade read at grade level, 13 points higher than the city average for all schools and 20 points higher than other schools with similar student bodies.

How is it possible? Are the youngsters *special*, having been selected to attend P.S. 161? No, the K–5 school has a normal community student population who automatically attend because they live in the zoned area. Like the neighborhoods surrounding the Crown Heights school, the students at P.S. 161 are 90 percent African-American, with the rest Hispanic. (There is

A Tale of American Student Failure

one white student in the school.) The students are truly poor, with 97 percent of them eligible for free lunches, the usual benchmark of poverty.

What, then, is the school's secret? And why can't all schools do as well?

The secret is simply that unlike most American public schools, circa 2000—in the city and the suburbs—it is run like a traditional institution in every way. If you blinked your eyes, you might think that you had returned to the 1940s, before the current academic damage began.

The students wear uniforms: plaid skirts and yellow blouses for the girls, and yellow shirts and black trousers for the boys. Even more important, the school is run by a principal who does not yield to modern educational beliefs, about which he is an agnostic at best. By refusing to sign on to current fads, some of which borders on educational quackery, he has proven the power of tradition and common sense. And shown the Establishment to be utterly wrong.

Too often the profession falsely believes that teachers have to continually call on new ideas. One of these, as we shall later examine in detail (Chapter 4), is "whole language" instruction, replete with "invented spelling" of words by youngsters. That failed concept, which first proliferated in the 1970s, is still a major method of teaching reading in too many school districts.

"We try to use common sense in teaching at P.S. 161," Irwin Kurz, the principal, said when interviewed. "It's very traditional learning. If it worked in the 1930s, '40s and '50s—and it did—there's no reason why it shouldn't work today. We don't need new ideas and theories. At this school, we combine phonics—sounding out the words—with a heavy dose of literature. The children easily learn to 'decode' the words rather than just recognize them. Our children start reading in kindergarten, and we have several appropriate age books in volume for them to read as they progress. In addition, on Wednesday mornings, we have a book sale—for $1.00 each—and children and many of the parents attend. In fact, students become members of my Principal's Club in kindergarten and 1st grade when they come into my office and read me a book. The children love reading, which shows in their statewide test scores."

Mr. Kurz, who attended rigorous Jewish elementary and secondary parochial schools, then went on to Yeshiva University before taking a master's in education at City University, is frank about some of the problems in teaching. "I don't think educational training is necessarily the proper background for better teaching. There are too many teachers with insufficient academic schooling. I choose my teachers very carefully."

The Establishment has told us that poor children from deprived homes obviously can't learn to read as well as others because of varied socioeconomic differences. But now that P.S. 161's poor minority students have performed amazingly well, it appears obvious that the cause of reading failure is not societal in origin. Nor is economic poverty to blame.

Rather, it appears that the failure of minority student performance is closely related to the poverty of performance by the Education Establishment, its theories, its administrators, and its teachers.

The failings are not just limited to the minority dilemma but negatively affect public school education across the board, in middle-class and richer suburban areas as well.

That problem goes back to the making of our teachers, from their selection through their training. Please follow me as we enter that world, one in which our educators are shaped. Only if we examine and understand the esoteric, even arcane industry of teacher education can we ever hope to properly educate young America.

3

THE MAKING OF A MODERN TEACHER

Weak Selection and a "Mickey Mouse" Education

necdotes are not proof of a thesis, but when they are personal they can create powerful impressions and sometimes provide hints of more substance to come.

My first impression of teacher education, a subject totally unknown to me at the time, came when I was a senior in college. As part of my undergraduate work in the social sciences, I was required to take one course in "education."

I dutifully showed up for the first lecture and sat there dumbfounded as the professor declaimed about the "profession," and its history and philosophy. I could hardly believe the elusive nature of the material. I had already taken chemistry, history, economics, English literature, calculus—all fields with endless substance that left this student in awe of what he didn't know.

The first, the second, then the third education lecture reinforced quite the opposite feeling. It seemed that there was little, if any, special knowledge. The material was mostly the classification of the obvious, and virtually everything being said was arbitrary. One could easily take a totally opposite view about teaching and come up with an equally reasonable conclusion.

It was difficult for me to handle the intellectual punishment of Education 101, or whatever it was called. I made myself obnoxious in the eyes of the other students, mostly undergraduates training to become elementary school teachers, by questioning the professor, hoping, probing for some substantive answers.

When they didn't come, I challenged him. "Sir, could I be excused from attending this class? I think what little there is to learn—if anything—I could better pick up reading the textbook just before the final exam. If that's all right with you."

"Be my guest," he said, probably thankfully.

I read the book the penultimate day of the course. When my grade, an A, was posted on the board in the hallway, a young fellow student pummeled my back with her fists. "But you weren't even in class," she howled.

"Perhaps that's why I got an A," I answered, surely too sarcastically.

Mastering the thin course was hardly an academic feat, but it did leave an impression that something was rotten in the training of teachers. Since then I have studied the research, virtually all of which has reinforced that early negative impression.

What are the truths about teacher selection and training? First, we should ask two simple questions:

- Are today's teachers and those studying to be teachers bright enough for the demanding job?
- Is the training effective and rigorous enough to provide instructors for our youth in the twenty-first century?

The answer to both questions is a resounding no.

Obviously we have all met intelligent teachers who are a

credit to their vocation. I have known some myself: my students, others as friends and acquaintances, and others as teachers of my own children.

But the fact that there are many bright teachers does not change the documented fact that, by and large, the typical American teacher and teacher candidate are not smart enough or sufficiently well trained to handle the education of students. Nor do they possess enough knowledge to teach youngsters the collective mysteries of 5,000 years of civilization.

The fact is that teachers occupy the lowest level of academe, and most of the nonperformance of our schoolchildren comes from two sources: the intellectual deficiency of their teachers and the wrongheadness of their teachers' training and philosophy.

Who are the young people going into teaching, those who choose that as their life's work?

Firstly, to their credit, most teachers are dedicated to their job. More than physicians, lawyers, politicians, or businessmen, they come to teaching with a relatively altruistic sense of duty. In many cases, teaching is the best they could do professionally. But that does not gainsay the fact that studies show most teachers are drawn to their vocation because they like children and want to help them become successful citizens.

Dedication is not the problem. Teachers work hard and are under continuous stress from school boards, principals above them, and children below them. They handle conflicts in the classroom with general equanimity, much as beleaguered mothers do at home. But the teachers have twenty-five or thirty children to handle rather than two or three.

The problem lies elsewhere. It rests in the fact that our society has selected the wrong people to teach in our public schools and has trained them in a wrongheaded manner.

For most of our history, those who instructed the young were of superior intelligence when compared with the general population. At the turn of the century, for example, the typical adult had a 9th grade education, and even by 1940, only one in four people had graduated from high school. Teachers, on the other hand, beginning shortly after the Civil War, had generally been educated in a two-year "normal school," an institution especially designed to train teachers. As the nation expanded westward, the "schoolmarm" was often a superior, well-educated, unmarried woman for whom teaching was one of the few careers then open.

As the decades progressed, beginning after World War I, teachers increasingly were college graduates. During the depression of the 1930s, teaching was a sought-after vocation. Because of its stability and benefits schools often had faculties of considerable academic prowess. But that superior cadre of teachers seldom exists today. It has been replaced by an entirely new group that is typically very weak academically. Hints that the contemporary teacher is deficient in scholarship come from several studies covering both practicing teachers and applicants for schools of education.

One was conducted by the state of Pennsylvania, which is attempting to raise teacher standards. It studied ninety-one teacher training programs and their student populations and came up with highly discouraging findings.

"When we examined our system of teacher preparation," Eugene Hickok, the state secretary of education, reported in *Policy Review*, "we found a system with limited assurances of competence and quality. . . . Few teacher-education programs had meaningful admission standards. Most undergraduate programs, at best, required prospective students to have a 2.5 grade point average prior to majoring in education. In other words, the doors were open for C-plus students (or worse) to become teachers. Moreover, that requirement could be fulfilled with the easiest classes."

The Making of a Modern Teacher

Students with a C+ average in high school can hardly serve as effective teachers. The U.S. Department of Education confirms the Pennsylvania study: "Too many teachers are being drawn from the bottom quarter and third of the graduating high school and college students."

The SAT scores of those planning a teaching career are further confirmation that the profession is drawing from an inferior academic pool. Dr. Leo Klagholz, of the New Jersey Department of Education and until February 1999 its commissioner, did a study in the 1980s of every student studying to be a teacher in the state's public colleges.

"The results were shocking," Dr. Klagholz stated when interviewed. "We found that these education students had combined—verbal and math—SAT scores of less than 800 on the old scales. Sixty percent of the group scored 399 or lower on the verbal portion of the test." Incidentally, SAT test-takers get 200 points just for signing their names.

The SAT tests, which are familiar to almost all high schoolers, provide a continuous insight into the academic failure of the education community.

The best information comes from the Educational Testing Service in Princeton, New Jersey, which administers the tests. In 1990, ETS checked the SAT scores of 930,000 high school seniors, then asked each student what he or she intended to study in college. The next step was to correlate the SAT scores with the intended vocations.

How well did the would-be-teachers do? Sadly, those who intended to become teachers scored near the bottom. They had a combined math and verbal score of only 864, not high enough to gain admission to most middle-rung liberal arts colleges—surely too low for anyone who expected to teach our children.

By contrast, those just seeking a "general" college education scored over 1,000. Most devastating was that the average for *all* students at the time was above 900, higher than that of the teaching hopefuls.

Since then, the SAT scores have been "recentered," automatically raising the typical score by some 100 points. In 1997, another correlation was made between students' SAT scores and their intended vocations. This time some 1.7 million youngsters took the test, and the results again dampened hopes that our teachers are equipped for quality learning or teaching.

The norm increased to a combined verbal and math score of 1,016.

How did the would-be-teachers do this time?

The unfortunate reality is that the teacher hopefuls had only a 964 SAT score, far below average. They ranked fourth from the bottom of some twenty intended vocations, only surpassing such categories as home economics and vocational training. The most startling fact was that the hopeful educators scored some 200 points below those who expected to train in math and science.

This sets up a most unnerving thought for parents and the entire American society: The typical college-bound high school senior may well have some 50 points more on his SATs than did his or her teachers at the same period of life.

The response from wounded educators is that the study involved only high school students who "intended" to become teachers. Surely, they say, those who actually enter the field score higher.

Probably not. We know this from another standardized test, one taken by college seniors applying for graduate school. The test is the Graduate Record Exam (GRE), which is taken by those who intend to do graduate work in one of eight fields: business, engineering, health sciences, humanities, life sciences, social sciences, physical sciences, and *education*.

We are no longer dealing with seventeen-year-old high school students with a C+ average. The GRE exam is for seasoned twenty-one-year-olds, and older, who are soon to graduate from college and ready to take a master's degree in education. They are either certified teachers seeking further study or college seniors hoping to take graduate work to become teachers. In every respect, this appears to be an accurate sampling of the education community.

How well do they do?

The GRE shows the same failure for these more mature educators and would-be educators.

"Quantitative means [average math scores] are lower in Education at both levels of study than in other fields," the GRE reports dispassionately. In other words, test-takers seeking to enter the field of education came in at the absolute bottom of the eight specialties, with an average score of 499, versus 689 for the leader on the quantitative test, the engineers.

Engineers might be expected to do better on such hard skills as handling numbers. But the disheartening result was that the masters of the slide rule beat the teachers and teacher-hopefuls in the verbal exam as well, by a solid 29 points.

How did teachers do in all three areas of the GRE test—verbal, quantitative, and analytical? Overall, the combined average score for the 1.1 million test-takers was 1,577. The teachers came in last with 1,477, while the physical scientists were at the top with 1,779, followed by the engineers with 1,762. (Incidentally, the scientists also topped the educators on the verbal score.)

Elementary school teachers and teacher-candidates seeking a graduate degree score the poorest among those in education, except for administrators, which is a revealing surprise. Elementary teachers score 33 points below the mean on the verbal test, 56 points lower in the quantitative test, and 32 points below the mean on the analytical test.

Within the lagging education group, the high school teachers scored the highest, though lower than the physical scientists, engineers, and those studying the humanities and the arts.

High school teachers generally major in an actual subject—the one they expect to teach—and minor in education. But a recent study showed that 20 percent of high school instructors majored in the slippery discipline of "general education," something still permitted in half the states. The rest took their major in science, math, social science, English, and foreign languages, even though most high school teachers' degrees are in education.

But there is a gap in their education training that stands out like the proverbial wounded thumb. It is a fact that begs for creditability.

Suprisingly, high school teachers are usually less well prepared in the subjects they are going to teach than are ordinary college graduates. High school teachers-in-training typically take fewer credits in their majors than other students majoring in the same subject.

The Pennsylvania study shows that ordinary math majors in that state had to complete courses in differential equations and advanced calculus to earn their bachelor's degrees in mathematics. But would-be high school math teachers, including those who would teach advanced placement classes, could waive taking these difficult courses. The motive was either not to strain their minds, a common theme in American education, or the Establishment didn't believe they could master the more difficult courses. Instead, they could enroll in a "Mickey Mouse" class in the history of mathematics.

That same Pennsylvania study shows similar deficiencies in the training of foreign language teachers. It reveals that "some candidates in foreign languages were unable to engage in basic conversations in the languages they were purportedly trained to teach."

In Connecticut, which prizes its supposed competency in

public school teaching, it is much the same. At the University of Connecticut, to receive a Bachelor of Science in Mathematics requires 40 credits in math plus 12 credits in such related subjects as chemistry and physics, for a total of 52 units.

But to become certified to teach mathematics in Connecticut public high schools, one needs only 30 math credits plus 9 in related subjects. That is considerably less than the credits required of a *real* mathematician, albeit one with only a basic degree.

This formula for teacher training is not only less than scholarly but makes little sense. It is obvious why American students lag so seriously in math and science skills, as witness the domestic NAEP scores and our abject failure in international competition—including the sorry spectacle of our "advanced placement" math students finishing last.

To train as a public school teacher in America, one does not usually attend a liberal arts college and major in science or literature or history, then go on to teach. Instead, most would-be teachers take a four-year training course at an undergraduate level in one of the 1,200 schools and departments of education, which turn out over 100,000 new teachers a year.

Studies indicate that the American degree in education represents training in a narrow, intellectually deficient, and philosophically weak discipline. To avoid that obstacle, several other nations, like Germany, require that teacher candidates first receive an undergraduate degree in a *content subject*. Only then can they take graduate work in education to prepare for the classroom. That policy both attracts better students and guarantees that the teachers will have reasonable command of the material they will teach.

America usually does the reverse. Most teacher training relies on an inferior curriculum in undergraduate colleges, where students right out of high school major in "education" with little emphasis on knowledge.

The Conspiracy of Ignorance

According to a federal survey, "America's Teachers: Profile of a Profession," more than two-thirds (69 percent) of all public elementary school teachers majored in "general education" and not in a specific subject as undergraduates. Among those with "general elementary" assignments—rather than a specific subject—that number rose to 83 percent.

Education training focuses more on "how" to teach than on content—the "what" to teach—one of the grave liabilities of the present system.

The current training offered by schools and departments of education has been patched together over the years by combining two trends. One is the practical method courses of the old normal schools that flourished in the period before and after the Civil War and lasted until the 1930s. That is blended with the second: the fashionable courses in learning theory, almost all of which are either highly debatable scientifically or outright fallacious.

The result? Instead of teachers-in-training absorbing more hard knowledge than ordinary college students, they are taught considerably less. The content level of their curriculum is quite low, and the course time is siphoned away by nonsubject education courses on how to teach and how to help youngsters adjust.

Is much time given over to nebulous education courses?

Yes, a fact which punishes the study of knowledge. In the case of elementary school trainees, studies show that education material takes up 41 percent of their course time, or some 50 credits out of the usual 120 required for graduation. That leaves only 70 credits for content courses, making their degree little different from that granted by two-year community colleges.

How well do these undergraduate education majors, many of whom entered with a C+ high school average, do? If you believe the marks awarded by education schools—and you shouldn't—they do amazingly well. In fact, from marginal students in high school, overnight they seem to become A scholars. Naturally, that is courtesy of the Establishment and its aggressive grade inflation.

The Pennsylvania survey reveals a widespread academic scheme. In one teacher education program, the majority of teacher trainees who took the course "Curriculum and Foundations" received A grades. In comparison, on the same campus, only 18 percent of those studying either English or physics received an A grade.

This grade inflation is part of the Establishment's promotion of false "self-esteem" for its teacher candidates. Instead of simply calling them "education students," the jargon refers to them as "preservice teachers." James M. Koerner, former head of the Council for Basic Education, has labeled the lingua franca of the Establishment as "Educanto."

The Establishment expends great effort to make its trainees seem smarter and more accomplished than they actually are. A study of fourteen other Pennsylvania universities showed that the average grade in education was a full letter grade higher than in math. The National Center for Education Statistics confirms this grade inflation for teacher trainees throughout the country. The *average grade* in education courses was 3.41 (A−), while it was only 2.67 (B−) in science, even though science students tend to be considerably brighter.

A candid and rather shocking view of the academic caliber of education students comes from a recently retired faculty member from SUNY (State University of New York)–New Paltz who taught English education to teacher trainees for thirty-five years.

"Over time, I saw a steady decline in the quality of these future teachers," writes Sheila Schwartz in the *New York Times.* "Many had writing skills that ranged from depressing to horrifying, especially when we remember that these same people eventually went on to teach writing to high school students. A disturbing number could not write a lucid sentence or paragraph."

When she criticized their grammar, several education students complained that "nobody ever made such a fuss over these things before." If they misspelled a word, some blamed it on their computer Spellcheck. Other students complained that *Moby Dick* was "too long and boring" to read and that *Slaughterhouse Five* was "too hard to understand."

Concludes professor-teacher-retiree Schwartz: "The poor quality of teachers is a prime reason that our public schools are in such poor shape."

In a letter to that same newspaper, Robert Primack, also a former teacher of education trainees, agrees. "I retired last year after 35 years of teaching in an education program, in part because of the poor quality of the students," he writes. "I found that the majority of the current crop of teacher candidates themselves dislike being educated and educating others. Many come from the bottom of the academic pool. . . ."

The teaching community may not be scholarly, but they are wise in the ways of public relations. They know that the community admires advanced training, an understanding that has sent teachers back to school en masse to obtain master's degrees. The effort is noble, but unfortunately the degrees are in education, a suspect discipline that produces an inferior sheepskin.

So fervent is the desire for that credential, both for prestige and an automatic pay raise, that the graduate schools are crowded with ambitious teachers. In one recent year, some 106,000 master's degrees were awarded to teachers. In all, a majority of classroom teachers—actually 54 percent—have that treasured piece of paper.

But lest we be impressed, it should be remembered that these are mainly not advanced degrees in knowledge, such as English or biology, but only in the supposed "art and science" of teaching, adding little that is scholarly to the teacher's armamentarium. One study of 481 master's degrees in education, including several at Harvard and Columbia, showed that the graduate students took 26 credits in still more education courses and only 9 in the liberal arts. Only 1 in 5 were required to write a thesis, and 1 in 25 to show proficiency in a foreign language.

Hardly masters of anything.

But does it make much difference how smart our teachers are, as long as they are dedicated to the children?

Apparently it makes a great deal of difference.

First, there is the intuitive philosophical conclusion that people can only replicate themselves. Aside from some determined or truly gifted students who find their own way despite a weak academic environment, most youngsters will accomplish only what is demanded of them. Because teachers generally create curriculum and standards with which they are comfortable, academic expectations are low, resulting in school failure.

Can they inspire scholarship rather than bare mediocrity, or worse, if they themselves are weak intellectually? Hardly.

Aside from that intuitive conclusion, studies show that smart teachers in elementary and high school produce smarter students. A study by Ronald Ferguson in Texas showed that the performance of teachers on a statewide standardized test correlated positively with student achievement in their classrooms. Another study of high school math teachers, published in the *Journal of Human Resources*, showed a strong connection between the teacher's academic background in math and students' test scores.

Our graduate schools (other than those in education) are convinced of that theorem, that only the outstanding can produce outstanding students. To that end, they hire great scholars in history, math, and science as models to guide and inspire graduate students seeking master's degrees and Ph.D.'s.

The Conspiracy of Ignorance

It should be axiomatic that if we want students to be more scholarly, or at least appreciate scholarship as a goal, then we must have more scholarly teachers in public school. That would mean teachers who score at least 1100 on the SATs instead of 964, and who do not reside academically in the basement of results, as they now do.

The present system of training teachers in undergraduate schools of education turns away the best and the brightest, most of whom wouldn't deign to study such a debatable discipline as education to begin with. They would feel demeaned and never entertain the idea.

The current model of schools of education began near the turn of the twentieth century when the Establishment decided that the methods courses taught in normal schools were not sufficient. They were direct and effective, but they had little mystique.

If the Establishment wanted to achieve professional status for teachers, they would need a new "core discipline." It would have to be different from the simple instruction of children, something that had been going on effectively for thousands of years. They would have to make teaching seem more complex than it actually was, less like the normal school and more like law or medicine, for example.

The most valued word in the lexicon of educators is *profession,* the key to much of the problem. Dictionary definitions vary, but a consensus defines *profession* as *"a calling requiring special knowledge."* Not just specialized in the sense of a full-time activity with reasonable ethical standards (as in the "insurance profession"), but a practice with a command of complex, esoteric material unknown to laypeople.

When educators searched for such a professional core discipline, they decided that *psychology* offered the best possibility. Since teachers dealt with children, why not focus on child development and behavior? Surely this would add to the skill and mystique of teaching.

That decision opened education to new opportunities—and failures. It changed the way teachers taught and looked at their students and led to the new era of frustratingly poor student performance.

That claim of professionalism is central to the Establishment. If they weren't professionals, why would school boards grant them a monopoly in the teaching of our children? One cannot practice medicine or law without special training and state licensing. The Establishment claims that it is equally true of teaching, and courtesy of state politicians nationwide, they have the degrees and licenses to prove it.

Most parents and citizens believe the claim of professionalism. Otherwise why would they countenance, and in many cases support with tax money, the 1,200 schools of education and their graduates, who then become "certified" as teachers by the states?

The Establishment insists that the present structure is a sound one, and has organized itself so that superior laypeople cannot intrude into its monopoly. It protects all 2.7 million public school teachers from charges that they are inadequate and from claims that untrained but well-motivated "nonprofessionals" can teach as well, or perhaps even better.

After all, accomplished mathematicians and historians without backgrounds in "education" teach college freshmen who are only a year older than high school seniors. Is the 12th grade the cutoff point for the profession's jurisdiction and monopoly? Or should it more logically be cut off at the 10th grade? Or the 8th, or the 6th?

The claim of professionalism is directed heavily at parents. "Would you want your child to be taught by an *unqualified* teacher?" they ask, seeking to frighten. They even imply that an untrained teacher could be damaging to the child's mind and psyche. Of course the word *qualified* is defined by the Establishment and is a term critic Thomas Sowell calls Orwellian "Newspeak" since it bears little resemblance to the truth.

The word *qualified*, as used by the Establishment, contains the seeds of paradox, even insincerity. To be qualified ostensibly means that the teacher has graduated from an accredited school of teacher training and has been licensed to teach. But in a startling, rather ludicrous revelation, it appears that of the 1,200 schools and departments of education in America, only 40 percent are accredited by the National Council for Accreditation of Teacher Education, a prominent Establishment vehicle.

And what if all the modern theories of education are false? Do you really have to be a trained "professional" educator to teach well?

Apparently not, which turns the Establishment claims of professionalism into a charade.

How do we know this? Because the evidence has been staring at us for hundreds of years in the success of private and religious schools, most of which turn up their pedagogic noses at public school theorists. By and large, they have eschewed the dubious theories of learning taught in schools of education to concentrate on the accumulated knowledge of the centuries.

Many laypeople are not aware that in most states private schools are exempt from the law requiring the hiring of state-certified teachers. These schools can usually hire any college graduate they want, and they do. On average, private secular and religious schools pay teachers some 10 to 40 percent less than do the public schools, yet by any standard of measurement they do a superior job with students. (See Chapter 8.)

Are most teachers in private schools *qualified*, despite the fact that they may never have taken "education" training?

The answer is that they are not only qualified, but they are often superior. The underlying reason is that the brightest of our college graduates, who usually have disdain for "education" training, are willing to teach in private schools despite the lower pay. A summa cum laude in history from Yale or Harvard, for instance, who is not permitted to teach in public high schools because of lack of training and certification, is welcome in the better private schools, as he or she should be.

At Choate-Rosemary Hall in Wallingford, Connecticut, one of the leading private schools in the nation, there is an unspoken skepticism about state-certified teachers. That is shown by the fact that the school almost exclusively hires *nonprofessional* teachers without education training, who tend to be brighter products of our university system.

"Our teachers do not have to be certified by the state, and we hire few who are," said the assistant headmaster at Choate. He points out that of the 172 faculty members, *none* have the Establishment's talisman—an undergraduate degree in education. Of the 104 faculty members who have a master's degree, only 4 have the degree in education. Nine teachers have their doctorates, but *none* are in education.

It seems that the state-certified teacher has few true credentials as one rises in the world of educational quality.

One important difference between uncertified teachers in private schools and certified teachers in public schools is that the brighter college graduates who go directly into teaching have been spared the *psychological* studies of undergraduate teacher training. That discipline is not only debatable in its accuracy but diverts teachers from the true goal of bringing the world of unalloyed knowledge to students.

Once the Establishment adopted psychology as its core, it evolved a kaleidoscope of new courses in "educational psychology" that soon overran the curriculum of teacher training. Using mainly neo-Freudian concepts, the teacher-model changed from one of academic instruction in knowledge—the university model—to the social work/psychology framework, in which "learning theory" was more important than the study of actual knowledge, whether history or mathematics.

But naive parents, the media, the public, and politicians were impressed, and the Establishment grew in prestige and power.

Most normal schools were transformed into teachers' colleges after World War I. Later the teachers' colleges became the education departments of broader colleges or universities. Their two-year curriculums were expanded into a four-year course for teachers, ending in a B.A. or B.S. in Education.

The names were being changed, but the overwhelming majority of would-be teachers were still "ed majors," and the learning atmosphere was still elementary, no pun intended.

The Teachers College at Columbia University became the fountainhead of the newly professionalized vocation. Beginning in the 1930s, that school championed the research that was responsible for changing the model of schools of education from *instructional* to *psychological*. At the same time, teaching became a cousin to social work, which through the new M.S.W. (Master of Social Work) degree was becoming an appendage to psychology, psychotherapy, even psychoanalysis.

Teaching could do no less. Entranced by the new Freudian revolution, educators delved heavily into the field, from child behavior to clinical psychology.

Its graduates, with master's and doctoral degrees in education, spread out across the country delivering the word: Teaching children was no longer to be a simple case of disseminating information that children had to commit to memory while they learned reading and writing skills. Instead, teaching was now a "developmental" challenge. The teacher was to use the new theories to help children in every way—in personal and group adjustment, in handling sibling and family conflicts, in social harmony, tolerance, and other broad aspects of life.

The Making of a Modern Teacher

A theory was developed that knowledge itself was valueless without the psychological insight that had to accompany it. Otherwise it was mere "rote" learning and did not enhance "critical thinking," which was more psychological in dimension.

(I have to interrupt myself to relate an anecdote. One of my students in a college class was a 6th grade New York City teacher. She explained that the school system wanted to stress critical thinking instead of memorized facts. The problem, she told the class, was that under the present curriculum, "the children are not learning anything they can think about.")

The Establishment decided that its obligation was to influence not only children's minds but their very beings.

Sincere, if poorly educated and anti-intellectual leaders of the teaching vocation believed that this new psychological emphasis was more vital to society than passing on the knowledge and skills of civilization, once the focus of teaching. The concept grew until it captured the public school system, which then became entranced with the new philosophies and theories of learning.

So began the profile of the schoolteacher as not just someone who would ensure that children learned the three Rs—reading, 'riting, and 'rithmatic—but a pseudo–social worker and pseudo-counselor. That emphasis is paramount today, though not openly discussed with parents or the community. Little wonder that knowledge has been left unnurtured in our public schools.

Then opinion began to shift somewhat, at least in academic circles outside the Establishment. Word seeped out of the teachers' colleges in the 1960s and 1970s that much of the activity was hollow, even meaningless pop psychology. Brighter students were labeling education training as "Mickey Mouse" instruction. Noneducation faculty laughed at the curriculum, the professors, and their "made-up" degrees. A counterrevolution was beginning, but unfortunately it never progressed beyond its infancy, where it remains today.

The catalogs of schools of education show the same weak curriculum, especially in their emphasis on debatable psychological theories. Sigmund Freud may be dead in clinical psychiatry, but he lives on happily in teacher training.

Among the common psychology-based courses in ed school today are:

- History and Philosophy of Education
- Personality and Adjustment
- Human Development and Behavior
- Educational Psychology

One course, "Child and Adolescent Development and Exceptionalities," is listed in the catalog of an education college in Connecticut. The description offers a clear clue to the psychological orientation of the Establishment. The course, says the catalog, *"Presents major theories of human development and the social, emotional, and cognitive characteristics of typical and exceptional children, birth through adolescence."*

(This expansive theory comes from a vocation that has trouble teaching nine-year-olds to read English.)

That type of education training, whose scientific base is shaky at best, may make teachers feel good about themselves, but it is far from intellectually sound. It may inspire young teachers to "counsel" their students, even to falsely believe they can evaluate psyches, but it has little proven value in teaching and diverts all involved from the true task at hand. *Supposed* knowledge of "human development," the catchword in modern teacher training, can hardly replace the traditional task of passing on society's accumulated knowledge from one generation to the next—lest it be lost.

This is especially true in the uncertain hands of nineteen-year-old teacher trainees, barely out of high school and having graduated without distinction or even average grades.

The debate over what is central to teaching—information or a particular slant on learning—became the subject of an extended conversation I had with a professor of education in Connecticut, an intelligent Ph.D. with considerable power in the state system.

He was candid and forthright in his opinion. "Passing on the accumulated knowledge of society from one generation to the next is *not* the goal of education," he insisted. "It may have been at one time, but society is changing and education with it."

Detailed information, once the mainstay of our schools, need no longer be taught, according to this education professor. Today, he says, it can easily be garnered from the computer and the Internet, at whose use children are expert. What is now more central to teaching and learning, he theorized, is the understanding that we are no longer a manufacturing society but a service one. People need to learn how to work in groups, not singly. This, he is sure, is what students should gain from school today.

It was refreshing to hear an educator come right out and say what many, myself included, have suspected. *It is not that ignorance is an unfortunate by-product of a poor education system. Rather, it appears that in contemporary teaching circles it may actually be a goal.*

Current educational theory comes down hard against *facts,* which many educators consider "trivia," as this professor labeled them. Instead, the new Establishment paradigm is "learning to learn," as the jargon states but which is unclear in meaning. The Establishment is equally hard on rote memorization.

These theories are interesting but false. No one has ever been able to replace memorization, the retention of information, as the basic method of learning. Nor has anyone been able to replace facts (that is, knowledge) as the core of the educated individual. And despite the professor's skepticism about traditional learning, no one has been able to replace the mind's need to make connections based on information stored in the brain, much like a computer memory board.

From memorized fact A to fact B to fact C, supposed "trivia" can lead to a logical conclusion about situation D. But if fact B is not stored in one's cortex, and is only available on the Internet (if one knows what to look for), the thinking process will obviously be short-circuited. Since conclusions are formed in the brain in nanoseconds, without the raw material there will be insufficient background to complete the process with any validity.

It sometimes seems that people like our professor, and others in the Establishment, fear that too much information clutters up the mind, thereby reducing the skills of "socialization." But if high school seniors, for example, are not taught about the Marshall Plan (70 percent have never heard of it), how can they as adults evaluate intervention in Haiti, or Iraq, or Kosovo? Or understand complex world economic or political crises? Without the *facts*—excuse the expression—what are citizens but pliable fools subject to the whims of demagogues and the media?

This paranoia about facts was also demonstrated by author Charles J. Sykes, who described an interview with an educator in Colorado. His conversation, which was amazingly similar to mine with the Connecticut education professor, confirms the Establishment's strong negative attitude toward knowledge.

The high school principal in Colorado insisted to Sykes that students did not have to learn any specific facts of history or be able to define either World War II, the Holocaust, or the Great Depression. It was, the principal was convinced, "arbitrary" to single out one event in history as being more important than any other. Likewise, students didn't have to know the location of Florida as long as they mastered "geographical thinking," whatever that means.

The Making of a Modern Teacher

When an editorial writer for the *Rocky Mountain News* interviewed a local assistant superintendent of schools, the educator insisted that schools had focused too much on "knowledge" rather than the "application of knowledge." Why, she wondered, should students have to know when the North and the South fought the Civil War?

The answer, of course, is that the chronology of history makes it possible for the mind to create a coherent sequential story that establishes what came before and after and sets up equations of cause and effect. It enables students—and adults—to avoid the warning of the Spanish philosopher George Santayana that those who do not know history may well have to relive its ugliest consequences.

The Establishment's dangerous thrust against facts, or knowledge, is endemic in our public schools. E. D. Hirsch, Jr., renowned author and Professor of Education and Humanities at the University of Virginia, finds its existence rather startling.

"The deep aversion to and contempt for factual knowledge that pervades the thinking of American educators was at first so paradoxical and difficult for an outsider like me to understand or believe that it took me many years to appreciate it," he writes in *The Schools We Need*. "Only gradually have I come to realize that this deep-dyed sentiment has been a powerful cause of our educational failings. . . ."

Hirsch describes a meeting with school principals and administrators at which he spoke. When asked what type of facts a first grader should learn, he suggested, among other things, being able to identify the Atlantic and Pacific Oceans as well as the seven continents. However, one participant wondered of what value it was for children to learn that information. "No one at the meeting was willing to defend the idea of teaching such facts to young children," he reveals.

Soon after, he spoke about the value of students, knowing the relation of the earth and the sun during our planet's year orbit, and why at the equator, spring and fall, not summer, are the hottest seasons. To that an educator responded by asking if that information would make anyone "a better person."

It is hard for laypeople to understand the level of intellectual blindness that dominates the education profession. It has its pitiful aspects, in that these mainly poorly educated people are desperate to appear original, to match the academic successes of science. In making that move, they veer toward the ludicrous, the wild theory, the paradoxical. It may offer them temporary satisfaction that they are probing the limits of philosophy, but their amateurish fantasies are gravely injuring first our children and secondly our entire civilization.

Fortunately, there is a growing minority within the education community who are outspoken about the downgrading of content and knowledge in favor of unsubstantiated theories about "how to teach."

Paul Regnier, an administrator with the Fairfax County, Virginia, public schools, calls this the "illusion of technique." Writing in the education journal *Phi Delta Kappan*, he says that the "current educationist mantra" insists that the most important thing for a teacher is "to know how children learn." They believe, he says, that the techniques "will make teachers more effective without regard to what they are supposed to teach or to what students are supposed to learn."

The constant quest for "new and scientific" approaches to teaching, Regnier says, lures educators "into making claims that appear ludicrous to real scientists and even to educated people in other fields." The result, he concludes, creates "great mischief" in the schools through the "denigration of intellectual life among those involved in K–12 education."

Though many teachers may feel the same, they remain silent for fear of Establishment retaliation against their careers. One survey of 600 experienced teachers revealed some unexpected criticism of concepts they had learned in schools of education. Many called those years "mind-numbing" and "an abject waste of time" during which they were taught "the shabbiest psychobabble."

Commenting on the study, *Time* magazine reported that the teachers "complained that the fragmented, superficial course work had little relevance to classroom realities" and that the preparation work was "woefully inadequate."

The argument over "how" versus "what" to teach still dominates the field, but it has reached a new level of definition. We now also have to consider *why* education trainees are taught to place such strong emphasis on psychology instead of more work in content subjects such as history or math.

One obvious conclusion is that the *how* focuses on the children and their feelings, making schools more "student centered" than concentrated on the needs of society, which would call for "school-centered" learning. In the long run, the latter favors the students as well, but like any vehicle of immediate gratification, the student-centered framework pleases teachers, who are often more interested in the sensibilities of youngsters than in rigorous curriculum, testing, and grading.

Many teachers reject the tougher route because they never enjoyed it as children. Since most were relatively poor students, they prefer an environment that fits their personal goals—a happy, stressless childhood in a lax school regimen, replete with poor performance. There, the student's needs, not those of the school or the community, are honored.

To their credit, they seem to have accomplished their permissive, destructive goal.

They are also convinced that their psychological standards—as our education professor indicated—will create a society more attuned to working in groups rather than as individuals. All their training in "ed psych" tells them that the happy, unstressed child will learn better.

Is that true?

No, learning can be work, even painful. But it can also be joyful and emotionally rewarding once you have passed the threshold, a point most contemporary students never get a chance to reach.

The learning theories of the Establishment are apparently incorrect. If they were not, our *happy* children would be better educated and, in a sense, *smarter*. But has that happened? A quick check of the NAEP test results, as we have seen, shows student ignorance that is often outlandish.

I studied in a "school-centered" secondary institution, Stuyvesant High School in Manhattan, a scholarship school specializing in science. I remember the faculty's indifference to student personal and psychological needs. We studied a rigorous curriculum under the unrelenting demand that we perform *as our teachers wanted*. All the emphasis was placed on the subject matter and, as I remember, very little on the student.

As a boy I was a very good student in mathematics, but my teacher, Dr. Baker, who was also a consultant to IBM, cared little for my sensibilities. As I did a trigonometry example on the board correctly, he would yell out that I must be lazy because I was taking too much time.

Did this traditional theory of education—rigor and relative indifference to student psyches—work well? Stuyvesant has produced legions of scholars in every field and a lion's share of scholarships. Were young psyches injured in the process? I think the reverse, that it produced *true self-esteem* based on hard work.

Those who are learned, from whatever source, value their education as the core of their successful adjustment to life. Joseph Addison summed it up in 1711 when he wrote that education "is a companion which no misfortune can depress, no crime can destroy, no enemy can alienate, no despotism can enslave."

Not every student should be expected to handle an education equal to that provided by New York City's special schools, whether Stuyvesant, or Bronx High School of Science, or Brooklyn Tech, or Hunter High, or Townsend Harris. But the educational route and philosophy that makes scholarship a goal—in contrast to ephemeral theories of "ed psych" and "group socialization"—can serve all students, if at a modified level.

Are students and society better off with the weaker student-centered education of today? Only if we want to accept the trade-off of being among the most ignorant nations in the world, relying on foreign and immigrant talent plus the brilliance or entrepreneurship of a handful of gifted Americans to maintain our civilization.

Today's Establishment is not compulsive about education. That simple truth also came up in my conversation with the professor of education. When I pointed out that in our present system, a high school biology teacher needs fewer credits in biology than an ordinary baccalaureate in the field, he countered, "He doesn't need to be a Ph.D. in biology, as long as he knows enough to teach high school students."

That theory of *enough is enough* dominates the teaching field in every way. It is frightening because it not only permits mediocrity, and worse, but actually encourages it. This compromise with knowledge is expressed by some teachers who in the latest jargon like to refer to themselves as "facilitators" rather than as teachers or instructors. It is their way of saying that students should find their own way through the maze of world knowledge, with the facilitator's help. That is the latest touch of irresponsibility.

The nation will have to pay the price if knowledge—or *trivia*, as our professor prefers to call the accumulated wisdom of 5,000 years—continues to be denigrated by social work–oriented educators. Will the mind of each succeeding generation become more atrophied by the "professionals" appointed to teach the young?

The optimistic hope is that reform is in the air. Several states are trying to raise the grade-bar for admission into schools of education. Pennsylvania, after the recent disheartening study of its teacher training programs, is trying to implement several reforms. Texas is tightening its teacher training programs. It has eliminated the bachelor of education degree, but much of that is window dressing since the state still maintains teacher training in undergraduate schools.

Connecticut now requires that elementary and middle school teachers-in-training major in some solid subject in addition to their concentration of 36 credits in education. That reform also reveals that until a few years ago, would-be teachers in Connecticut studied little else but vacuous education.

These reforms have *some* value, but they are really just surface balm. If we look to history, we will see that teachers are not the first undereducated, if necessary, workers in our society to make false claims of professionalism. A revealing parallel to the present failure of teacher training can be seen in a similar debacle involving medical training in America almost a hundred years ago.

At the turn of the century, medicine was more shaman-directed than scientific. But physicians were well liked, even lauded for their dedication, much as teachers are today. They made house calls at all hours, sitting at the bedside until the "crisis" passed or the patient died.

Science, or better still the lack of it, was the problem. Medical students were chosen willy-nilly, many just out of high school, as the overwhelming majority of teacher trainees are today. Except for a handful of medical colleges like Johns Hopkins, most medical schools had low entrance requirements and much of the learning was not scholarly. The young doctor picked up his skills mainly from an older doctor, adopting his unscientific superstitions in the process.

Medicine, however, was considered a profession, even of the highest order.

In 1910, the Carnegie Foundation gave a grant to Abraham Flexner, a former high school teacher (at a time when they were often scholars) and son of German-Jewish immigrants in Louisville, Kentucky, to investigate the training of physicians. He found that most medical schools were "diploma mills" with little emphasis on science, producing doctors of insufficient skill and learning.

As a result of his report, the states closed down the majority of medical schools, and the rest were forced to affiliate with universities. Within a matter of years, medicine became a *postgraduate* university calling, selecting the better college graduates to become physicians, as it does today.

The parallel is obvious. It prompts the question of why society has put up with an obviously inferior teaching vocation with its weak method of selection and training.

Critic and author Rita Kramer attempts an answer. "The answer lies in the vested interests of the accredited schools, colleges, and departments of education," she writes, "graduation from which is tantamount to certification in most states. It lies in the tendency of legislative bodies, unions, state, district, and local school boards to prefer the status quo. . . . The status quo is a system that does *not* produce the teachers we need, the best teachers our children could have."

Breaking the status quo will require thought and determination. Later I will outline an ideal plan for American public education, K–12, one that will ensure the services of the best and the brightest as our teachers, principals, and administrators, as well as a new, superior curriculum.

Until then, there is one obvious reform—to imitate the present training of physicians and attorneys, something that can be accomplished overnight by our state governments, as they did after the Flexner report.

To do this, we must completely eliminate undergraduate teacher training, which now makes it possible for highly impressionable and not highly competent high school students to enter immediately into schools of education. Eighteen-year-olds with poor academic records are not mature or learned enough to understand that they are being seduced into an anti-intellectual curriculum in which unproven theory is replacing sound, time-tested knowledge.

If, on the other hand, no one could train to become a teacher until they were mature college graduates, much of the damage now being caused to students by ill-chosen and ill-prepared teachers would be eliminated.

The remedy is quite simple.

All fifty states need to pass legislation to close down all undergraduate schools of education. Nor should any schooling or training in education take place at the undergraduate level. Preparation for teaching would consist of a one-year postgraduate program, mainly in methodology and student teaching, plus additional work in a subject-matter specialty. The psychosocial aspects of present teaching dogma would be eliminated as unsound and diverting.

By implementing this plan, college graduates who have majored in a wide variety of subjects would be selected for graduate teacher education—if they have at least a 3.0 average in college. By making education a postgraduate activity for bright, mature students, it would immediately increase the concentration on knowledge in our public schools. Because teaching would finally become at least a near-profession, its elevated prestige would attract better students, as the good private schools now do.

Of course, there needs to be a financial incentive for college graduates who have other options. We should follow the example of Connecticut, which in the 1999–2000 school year is paying well over $55,000 as an average salary, a reasonable prospect for many college graduates.

The starting salary for teachers with a graduate degree in a true academic subject (which everyone would then automatically have) should be appreciably increased nationwide, up from its present $25,000 average. Most of that can be accomplished by a more resourceful use of the $350 billion now spent annually on public education. The goal under this plan should be a starting salary of $40,000 and an average salary of $60,000 nationwide, perhaps more in high-cost areas and less in certain states.

Where would these billions of extra dollars come from?

Though America now spends some $7,500 on each public school student, much of the money is dissipated in excess education "support personnel"—anyone who is not a teacher. Their ranks are now almost as large as those of teachers, a ridiculous situation that exists nowhere else in the world.

By cutting back by one-third on the 2.5 million nonteachers in the system, we can increase salaries for teachers by some 15 or 20 percent without any additional taxes. There is also an additional $11 billion a year in failed federal aid to education programs, which should be diverted to the states as block grants to raise teacher salaries, especially in inner city schools, which badly need better teachers.

But—and this is most important—extra money put into the present system will be to no avail.

It is mandatory to revolutionize the selection and training of America's schoolteachers. They are in the front line of the continuing battle to enrich children's minds and thus their lives. The present pool of teacher candidates is weak academically, and their schooling is distorted by false concepts. No partial and slowly incremental improvement will do the job. Only the forceful intervention of citizens—and their politicians—can rework the rules and create a whole new cadre of teachers and better public schools.

If we fail to eliminate the conspiracy of ignorance that is fervently supported by the Education Establishment, we will never be confident that the nation will be able to prosper in the complex twenty-first century.

4

THE DEBASED READING CURRICULUM

Whatever Happened to Phonics?

One day not many years ago, a grandmother in the San Francisco Bay Area visited her grandson's school and came away shocked.

"This young first grade teacher was reading from an excellent book of stories for young children," she recounted. "But when it came to their turn to read from the book, the students didn't know what to do, and she didn't tell them. I had never seen anything like it in my life. It was absolutely bizarre."

The story of these dumbfounded children has been played out over and over again throughout the nation, all part of a failure that was not accidental, but actually planned. The theory behind that failure was expressed by an Ohio high school teacher, who, writing in an education journal, summed up for naive parents and grandparents much of the Establishment's philosophy.

"We have abandoned rote learning in favor of hands-on learn-

ing and teaching problem solving skills. We now try to teach the child rather than the subject," he boasted.

The rhetoric has a nice ring, but the absence of logic in the statement should be obvious to even the casual observer—just as it explains the "bizarre" incident in California. "Teaching the child" is a typically nebulous Establishment idea. How one can accomplish that without teaching the "subject"—in this case, reading—has never been demonstrated.

What the student learns depends on the *curriculum*, the range and concentration of subject matter, an area which has been declining mightily over the past three decades. If public school education is failing—and it is—part of the blame lies in the fact that less and less attention is being paid to reading, spelling, and grammar. There has been a diminution and distortion of the math curriculum. We have replaced history and geography with soft-core "social studies." In the sciences, the extent and depth of material have been weakened over the years as teachers have been doing just what our high school teacher boasted of—concentrating on the *child* instead of the *subject*.

One of the most grievous failures in curriculum has been in reading, the basic discipline on which all learning hinges, and the sole subject of this chapter. (See Chapter 6 for an examination of other curriculums.)

Reading is in trouble today throughout the nation.

NAEP reading scores for 1994 showed that not only had reading fallen on hard times, but it was failing children of all social classes. In "central city" schools, a government euphemism for those with large minority populations, 47 percent of the 4th graders scored *"below basic"* reading levels, a form of semiliteracy.

But that reading deficiency was not restricted to urban areas. Instead it was widespread across the nation. In that broad band,

The Debased Reading Curriculum

40 percent—or two in five—of all 4th graders were reading poorly.

Has it changed since?

The recently released 1998 reading scores were heralded by the government as a "significant improvement" over previous years. But in reality they were another stark confirmation of the fact that Johnny (and Janie) Still Can't Read.

In the 4th grade, the 40 percent who couldn't read at basic levels has dropped a meaningless two points to 38 percent, back to where it was in 1992, still crippling virtually two out of every five children. Meanwhile the number of advanced readers in the 4th grade stayed at a rather pitiful 7 percent, or one in sixteen children. The only true advance was in grade 8, where public school students reading at the semiliterate level dropped from 30 to 26 percent. But at the same time, the number of poor readers in the 12th grade rose 3 percent over 1992.

Overall, the state of reading in America is status quo ante: our children are reading poorly across the board, one of the main reasons they are performing poorly in most subjects.

The National Center for Education Statistics reveals that there are 42 million functionally illiterate adults in America, and that 1 in 7 *college graduates* have marginal literacy skills. The National Adult Literacy Survey shows that the functionally illiterate cannot even read phone books or voting ballots.

This problem traces back to elementary school, where the damage begins in the first three grades, during which children are expected to learn to read independently. It is not that teacher-power is missing. There are 625,000 teachers from kindergarten through 3rd grade, many of whom have master's degrees. In addition, there are tens of thousands of reading specialists.

Was it always this way? Personal memory of an earlier era could be faulty, but I have a relatively clear recollection of my elementary school, where my fellow students in the Bronx (P.S.

77) seemed to have little trouble reading the basic texts after our extensive phonics training in sounding out words.

During the great immigration of the 1800s, millions used Noah Webster's *Blue-Backed Speller*, a phonics-based book whose first edition was published in 1783 and which became the bible on how to teach children to read, in school and at home. More than 24 million copies were sold, making it second only to the actual Bible. Early reading statistics are not readily available, but in 1910, the U.S. Bureau of Education reported that only 2.2 percent of youngsters aged ten to fourteen were illiterate, and many of those were unschooled.

Then why do we have such monumental reading problems today?

In medicine, illnesses caused by doctors are called iatrogenic disease, *iatro* being Greek for "physician." We may now be facing a parallel in reading, where much of the harm has been caused by teachers and contemporary learning theory. Should we consider the possibility that the epidemic of poor reading is an *edugenic* ailment?

Much of it appears to be the result of changes in the reading curriculum over the past decades, changes that have brought several fashionable and unrewarding trends into the classroom.

For centuries, the teaching of reading has been based on five legs of the curriculum stool.

- First was teaching the twenty-six letters of the Roman alphabet, one of the great advancements in the history of civilization.
- Second was learning the approximately forty-four sounds that those letters create, a system generally called *phonics*. Each of those sounds are called *phonemes*, and a person's ability to hear them correctly is called *phonemic awareness*.
- Third was putting those into practice to "decode," or sound

out, the word, something that was easily done even if the young student had never seen the word, could not recognize it, and had no idea what it meant. (The phonics method is used successfully to teach twelve-year-olds to read Hebrew in preparation for their Bar Mitzvahs.)

- Fourth was doing *some* sight recognition outside of phonics, as per the traditional flash cards that showed DOG and a picture of the cuddly animal.
- Fifth was reading age-appropriate books, either silently or aloud, in school and at home—to self, parents, or the teacher.

This method, which the great majority of children mastered by the 2nd or 3rd grade (the quicker ones in kindergarten and 1st grade), has had a good record of achievement, surely much better than early student mastery of numbers, spelling, or grammar.

But beginning in the 1970s, educational theorists debated the traditional system, claiming that they had a newer, better alternative to systematic drilling in phonics. Reading, they said, was a *natural* talent. With a little help, children could learn to master reading as easily as learning to speak. It merely required making reading "fun" and immersing children immediately into interesting books, where they would surprisingly find their own way.

This peculiar theory was called "whole language," or "whole word." The theory sounds great, except that it's not true.

Reading is not a natural talent. It's more like learning to ride a bike than walking. Speaking is natural. Children pick up language through the ear, easily mimicking what they hear from adults, an endeavor that begins as early as the first year of life. Long before children learn to read, they have a sufficient vocabulary to survive nicely in their young world.

But unlike speaking, reading must be formally taught and

learned. It depends on an eye-brain function that eventually translates the printed scribblings into tangible things and abstract ideas. It requires work, but it can most easily be learned through the mechanisms of the alphabet and sounds. Most words in English can be sounded out, and by the end of the 1st or 2nd grade, children taught first with phonics can use the "code" to unlock 85 percent of English words. The rest have irregular spellings, like *sugar*, and must be learned by rote.

The brain has no inherent knowledge of the alphabet, says Dr. Frank Vellutino, director of child research at SUNY-Albany. It has to be taught.

In the past, that technique made it relatively easy for almost all children—except for those with emotional or neurological problems or poor "phonemic awareness"—to read early and well. It is estimated that about 17 percent of children have such problems and need special help, while 83 percent can easily learn to read the phonics way.

The phonics system is ideal for children whose language is alphabet-based, like English. As intellectual elder statesman Jacques Barzun has pointed out, "the discovery of the alphabet equals that of the wheel" in importance to civilization.

In those nations without alphabets, however, such as China and Japan, learning to read is quite an ardous task. Young children must memorize thousands of *picture characters* and combinations in order to read, an endeavor that would linguistically cripple our own schoolchildren.

But along with other traditional truisms in education, the fanciful, faddish Establishment decided to ignore tried-and-true phonics. They would instead go with a method something like the Chinese-Japanese system, based on word-by-word "recognition," a peculiar reading system for American kids, to say the least.

By the 1970s, the phonics system was increasingly under

attack in fashionable education circles. Critics claimed that it was a boring, mechanical method that blocked children from reading naturally and enjoying literature. The new technique of "whole language," imported from, of all places, New Zealand, was promoted heavily by the Establishment.

Over the last three decades, whole language was highly popularized and adopted by many school systems, which then taught phonics less and less. Instead of decoding words, students were asked to *recognize* them as if they were pictures. That's quite a difficult task considering that by the 4th grade, children have a spoken vocabulary of some 15,000 words. They would have to recognize that number of words just to keep up with their own speech, let alone expand it.

Whole language enthusiasts didn't claim that children should memorize every word. But they did believe that if students were surrounded by books, were read to, and tried to read as best they could, they would "guess" their way through to recognition of words and end up reading.

Literature, they said, was the key: Enough trial-and-error movement through books, with some help on the sound of only the first letter, along with pictures, would reveal the material and make readers of the children. "Students will construct the meaning of the word from the text," they claimed.

In the whole language technique, the writing that children did would also be freewheeling. They would write as they felt and heard, without the restraints of structure, grammar, or spelling. That plus the natural enthusiasm of the children, their desire to find *fun* in books, and their curiosity would liberate them from the supposed drudgery of phonetics, advocates said. Reading would come intuitively and naturally, just like speaking.

Fun, as in many false curriculum changes over the past thirty years, is a main criterion of the whole language system. If children learn to *love* to read, they will learn to read, whole language advocates said. This is a charming, Pollyannaish view of learning, but it sold, not only to the Establishment, but to parents, who bought the false thesis that a happy child would become a smart one. But though it fits contemporary biases in education, *fun* can just as easily become a prime stimulus for the promotion of ignorance.

When it came to spelling words in the whole language system, children were encouraged to be "inventive," to spell whatever they thought was appropriate. According to proponents of this unusual system, reading is a "psycholinguistic guessing game." Students are encouraged to "create" and are not marked wrong for guessing wrong.

The results of the "game" can be quite idiosyncratic. One six-year-old in California named Pablo wrote a story and then read it to his class. As the *San Francisco Chronicle* reported, it ran as follows:

"If I would have magic beans, I would save the beans. And when I save the beans, then I will give them away. The End."

Not too bad for a six-year-old, but the spelling of his written story was more than creative. It was chaotic:

"If I wd hf mg ics I wd save the bses and one I sav the bes then I wd g thm way the end."

Just as they took a dislike to traditional phonics, indoctrinated whole language school superintendents and teachers started to view spelling as anathema. Not only were the weekly spelling lists children used to memorize chucked into the pedagogic wastebin, but in some cases spelling lists were actually taken away from teachers lest they fall back on the ancient mechanism.

In the *Whole Language Catalogue*, Ken Goodman, an Arizona education professor and a prime guru of the system, wrote:

"Whole language classrooms liberate pupils to try new things, to invent spellings, to experiment with a new genre, to guess at meanings in their spellings, or to read and write imperfectly. In whole language classrooms risk-taking is not simply tolerated, it is celebrated."

The very faddishness of the idea struck a responsive chord in the education community, especially in the teacher training schools, with their cadre of impressionable professors and students. Here was another opportunity to show the crusty academic world that they were true "professionals," replete with a battery of esoteric knowledge of their own that was on the cutting edge of modern education theory and unknown to laymen.

"Whole language swept the nation," said William Honig, former superintendent of schools for California, when interviewed. "It pushed out phonics and substituted the new system in many places. It became the gospel in education colleges, where it is very popular, and in many school districts throughout the country. I must admit that as superintendent of education of California during the high point of the whole language era of popularity, I and my department neglected to promote phonics. The results, as shown by the NAEP reading results in California in 1992 and 1994, were catastrophic. The whole language experiment was interesting, but as we found out, the theory is dead wrong."

Since that disastrous experiment, Honig has become a strong proponent of phonics. As an official of the Consortium of Reading Excellence, he supervises the training in phonics of some 15,000 teachers in seventy school districts on the West Coast, especially in California.

But just a decade ago, that state was involved in one of the great battles of whole language versus phonics, a war that is still raging elsewhere.

It began in 1987, when whole language proponents in the California Department of Education convinced Honig and his staff to favor their approach, a decision that he now says was "a mistake." California adopted an English Language Arts framework that virtually ignored phonics and step-by-step skills instruction and promoted whole language, or WL, as it is sometimes called.

By the late 1980s and early 1990s, WL had been implemented in K–3 classes in California. In 1992, the federal government's assessment program, the NAEP, checked out the performance of California children with a sample large enough to compare it with other states. The results, revealed in "NAEP 1992 READ-ING—Report Card for the Nation and the States," were disastrous for California, sending a shock wave through the state, in government, education circles, and among the general public.

The reading scores for nine-year-olds (4th graders) in California public schools were painfully low. California youngsters scored *second from the bottom* of the thirty-nine sampled states, beating out only Mississippi. Worse yet, among their 4th graders, *the majority* (52 percent) were reading below basic levels.

Could it have been a one-year statistical fluke?

Apparently not. In 1994, there was another assessment of reading by NAEP, which confirmed the earlier poor results. This time California scored even worse, if that is possible. California tied for the *bottom slot* with Louisiana, actually beaten out by Mississippi, historically the poorest performer in American education. The two lowest states were the only ones with a raw score below 200, having to settle for 197 out of 350, 5 points lower than in 1992. Worse yet, the number of semiliterate children in California rose from 52 to 56 percent.

Not only were the scores depressing, but parents—in California and elsewhere—began to notice that children were spelling poorly, writing ungrammatically, and were ignorant of punctuation. A survey taken by the National Association of School Boards of Education found that 80 percent of parents blamed their children's reading problems on the lack of phonics training.

One parent in Riverside, California, noticed that her twin boys were coming home from 1st grade not knowing how to spell and unable to read properly. When she learned that 1st grade reading scores had dropped 7 percent, she became a convert to phonics.

In San Diego, which adopted whole language in its 1st grade classes in 1990, reading scores dropped by almost half. A school board member complained to the *San Diego Union,* "From parents I get lines like this, 'You're experimenting with my kid.' I hope we didn't make a mistake—but I feel in my gut that we did."

Even some educators were getting skeptical. In Houston, in the Douglass Elementary School, children were taught reading mainly with the whole language program. "Last year's reading scores were the lowest in twenty years," explained the school's principal at the time. "If the kids can't decipher words, they can't enjoy a whole language program."

When the school switched to an intensive phonics system, the children's reading scores rose enormously on a state reading test, with 98 percent of the children reading at or above grade level.

One teacher in the Crenshaw area of Los Angeles described the frustration of 1st graders asked to read texts even though they didn't know the letters or the sounds. "The children were in tears," she explained. "They look at you with three paragraphs on a page and they say, 'What do we do with this?'"

In the journal of the American Federation of Teachers, a critique pointed out that in whole language, millions of youngsters nationwide were surrounded by "beautiful pieces of literature that (they) can't read." As a result, they would be blocked from entering the economic mainstream, a privilege generally open only to good readers.

By espousing whole language, the Establishment has led teachers, and thus our children, into an abyss of further ignorance, something we can hardly use. Like most of their teaching fads, whole language was accepted by the Establishment with little examination. A five-year survey of the journal *Reading*

Teacher showed just how gullible educators have been. Of 119 journal articles, only one debated the effectiveness of whole language.

Though the California Education Establishment and the state politicians were stung by the NAEP results, some tried to place the blame on the influx of immigrants. It sounded logical. We might even sympathize with the state, especially about the problems created by illegal immigrants who had to be educated in public schools.

But within the figures was an indictment that couldn't be dismissed. It appears that the disaster affected *all* groups, immigrant and otherwise.

In fact, white students in California—overwhelmingly native born—scored the lowest in the nation among other white students. Equally dismaying was that in 4th grade reading, California was also last among Hispanics; third from last among Asians; and fourth from last among African-Americans. A veritable rainbow of academic disaster.

Another state with a similar immigrant and minority population—Texas—avoided the California debacle, concentrating instead on some teaching training reform and standardized testing to regularly measure reading skills. Using the statewide Texas Assessment of Academic Skills (TAAS) exam, they measured all three major student groups—white, Hispanic, and African-American. Although they perform in that order, all three are rising regularly, anywhere from 20 to 40 percent since 1994. That increased performance is shown in the NAEP national tests, where Texas white 4th graders now score 2nd in reading in the nation as against 36th for Californians, while Texas Hispanic youngsters now score 9th compared to 29th in New York and 39th in California.

In California the hero of the whole language fiasco, and the one who directed the shift away from the damaging technique back to phonics, was Marion Joseph, a smart Jewish grandmother who had spent years as the executive assistant to California's superintendent of schools until she retired in 1982.

Mrs. Joseph was the one who was shocked when she visited her grandson's classroom in the Bay Area and found the teacher reading to a dumbfounded group of youngsters who had no idea how to read from the same book when it was their turn.

What Mrs. Joseph had seen was whole language in action. She investigated and found that the state was implementing this strange new method that wasn't teaching her grandson to read. Angered, she went to see Bill Honig, then superintendent of education for California, and explained what was going on. He confessed that he hadn't kept that close an eye on the implementation of the whole language curriculum and had trusted his staff. After he investigated, Honig concluded that she was right and offered to help her crusade for a return to traditional methods.

As a result of Mrs. Joseph's pressure on the state government and the public to get rid of this "bizarre" teaching phenomenon, the governor appointed a blue-ribbon task force to investigate and report back.

Whole language was rejected and phonics came out on top, prompting a new program for state teachers, who were told to stress sounding out over memorizing and guessing at words—something the teachers' grandmothers could have told them. The task force concluded that the state's 1987 policy had failed to "present a comprehensive and balanced reading program [and] gave insufficient attention to systematic skills and instruction."

They warned that unless reading was taught differently, "we will lose a generation of children," who would be doomed to academic and social failure. They recommended that phonics be taught as early as *preschool*, and that language and reading instruction take up as much as a third of the day in kindergarten and half the day in 1st, 2nd, and 3rd grades. The state appropriated $200 million for the phonics program.

On October 11, 1995, Governor Pete Wilson of California signed into law a series of bills that *could* change the face of reading education in the academically beleaguered state. After almost a decade, the bills, designated as the ABC legislation, were designed to restore the primacy of phonics in reading instruction as well as to put new emphasis on spelling skills. To add power to the recommendations, the state set up financial incentives for school districts that stressed the phonics method.

Mrs. Joseph, who had won the day, was appointed a member of the state board of education. "I'm a liberal Democrat," she said when interviewed, "but one thing I learned from all this is that if we want to achieve liberal goals for everyone in society, we have to take a conservative approach toward education."

The power of this one person, who became determined to block the "bizarre" behavior of the Education Establishment when she saw what was happening in her grandson's classroom, should be a moral message and a rallying cry for all parents and citizens, including those outside of California. Whole language still thrives in many places, and to stop it requires that parents and other citizens become active in school affairs and work to reform the present quagmire of de-educational policies.

Now that phonics is slowly coming out of the shadows, studies show both its effectiveness and the damage done by WL. A two-year study in Inglewood, California, revealed that students taught by the phonics method—and phonics *first*—read much better. By the end of the 2nd grade, phonics students scored more than a year above grade level in reading and almost four years ahead in the ability to pronounce new words.

The evidence for the superiority of phonics—still a secondary method in too many schools—is accumulating. The federal National Institute of Child Health and Human Development has funded research into the question of phonics versus whole language at eight major universities, including Yale, and the results have been published in journal articles.

Professor Benita Blachman has summarized those results, pointing out the ignorance of the Establishment in its failure to use the research. "The tragedy is that we are not exploiting what we know about reducing the incidence of reading failure," she says. "Specifically, the instruction currently being provided to our children does not reflect what we know from research. . . . Direct, systematic instruction about the alphabetic code is not routinely provided in kindergarten and first grade in spite of the fact that at this moment this might be our most powerful weapon in the fight against illiteracy."

Amen.

At the 1997 meeting of the American Association for the Advancement of Science, Barbara Foorman of the University of Houston confirmed Professor Blachman's conclusion. She described a study that compared two groups of 1st and 2nd graders who had been classified as "reading disabled" and whose proficiency was at the 25th percentile. Students taught with whole language for a year stayed at that level. But those given systematic phonics instruction jumped up to the 43rd percentile.

In Arizona, in the Peoria Unified School District, one group of K–3 children continued with their whole-word system, while another group used the Spalding Program, a popular phonics-based system. At the end of the year, the control group stayed at the 50th percentile, while the phonics students' scores ranged from the high 80s to the high 90s. The district adopted Spalding for all its eighteen schools, which have scored as much as 30 points higher in reading than neighboring school districts with similar populations.

The switchover from whole language to phonics, although it has only been implemented in California for two years, is beginning to show results. In March 1999, the 1998 NAEP reading scores were published, showing that California had moved up from the bottom to fourth from the bottom, at least beating out Louisiana, Mississippi, and Hawaii. And although still a catastrophic record, the number of chldren with "below basic" scores fell from 56 to 52 percent. Perhaps there's hope for the future.

Research shows that not only is phonics necessary, but it should be taught *first*. If children attempt to read before knowing the sounds, frustration can turn them away.

Author and reading expert Diane McGuinness is even convinced that the school diagnoses of "dyslexia" and "learning disabled" are just ways of saying that the child is having difficulty learning to read. In the absence of emotional problems that could cause it, she believes the remedy is teaching reading by using phonics—the correct way.

Considering the evidence, has phonics won the war for our children?

Not yet. States and schools are rethinking the whole language disaster, but unfortuntely, WL is still alive and doing its pernicious worst in too many classrooms.

"Large cities like New York and Boston are increasingly talking a brave game of phonics," says Dr. Honig, "but much of it is lip service. When I visit public schools in New York, for instance, I see a few posters displaying sounds, but many teachers are still actively resisting the truth."

Every profession has its reactionaries who resist progress, whether it be in law or medicine. We hear stories about certain medical advances that are not incorporated into the daily practice of doctors. However, with such major advances as antibiotics or heart bypass surgery, proof of success prompts the medical profession to accept the reality.

Education is quite different. For a vocation that goes out of its way to profess its "progressive" viewpoint, it is too often stubbornly reactionary. Administrators, professors of education, gullible education students, even many teachers, easily adopt faddist, often false trends with enthusiasm. But simultaneously they obstinately resist scientific evidence.

Their resistance in this area, as illustrated by their failure to adopt phonics and discard most of the whole language concept, is unfortunately a matter of *pride*. That, of course, is the most deadly of all sins, and the one which the highly defensive Establishment often relies on instead of simple, clear intelligence.

The phonics versus whole language war is far from over. In fact, it is just as contentious as ever. At a recent annual convention of the International Reading Association, the animosity came out in the open. Kenneth Goodman of whole language fame not only lashed out at phonics people, but said they were members of the "far right" secretly out to abolish public education. Edward Fry, who publishes a line of phonetic charts, denied the charge, pointing out that he was a Democrat and no "right-winger."

What came out at the convention was what lies behind many of the debates in education: an ideological political battle that plays itself out in the form of teaching and learning concepts. It is not only irrational but a disservice to our children, who are not political, but innocent vessels who will mainly learn what we teach them.

The politicizing of education is far-reaching. When California adopted whole language in 1987, it was promoted by the liberal-left and attacked by conservatives. How can a technique of reading become an ideological battlefield? Either phonics or whole language is superior. What could politics have to do with it?

Whole language is an anti-intellectual distortion forced on us by the Establishment. In its desire to appear to be more humane in the classroom, it has promoted an idea that ostensibly adds fun but that punishes all students, including the weaker ones it was hoping to help.

The charge of right-wing fanaticism troubles some liberals, who are just as interested in good education as anyone else. Michele Zuckerman, a cofounder of PERT, a group that favors phonics, was accused of being a right-winger because of her stand on reading. Ms. Zuckerman, who is a Democrat, was offended. She says she knows that phonics has become a "radical right-wing buzzword" but says it shouldn't be.

The politicization of reading has also offended another woman, Jennifer Welliver, who considers herself a pro-environment, abortion-rights Democrat. When she took up the battle for phonics, she was accused of being a "religious psycho-spiritualist." She adds, "As soon as you start to question the system, you immediately get labeled a conservative. I would like to see this whole thing be nonpolitical."

The attempt to connect those who support phonics with the political right wing, as Dr. Goodman has done, seems uncalled for. It is also the result of a backlash against the Establishment's compulsive need to contest tradition in order to make itself seem progressive, even if that means hurting our schoolchildren.

The advent of conservatives as defenders of rigorous education and high standards has another root as well. It stems from the vacuum created by the average parent and citizen. Their apathy and supine acceptance of whatever school districts and state politicians decide requires that others become the champions of better education.

If conservatives are the main ones—perhaps the only ones—to fight for reading proficiency after its destruction by the Establishment, then more credit to them. Perhaps it will be an incentive for the liberals to match their success by promoting curriculum and standards improvements in the classroom as

The Debased Reading Curriculum

well. As Mrs. Joseph has commented, perhaps the way to achieve liberal social goals is to become conservative about education.

California, finally, has depoliticized reading, which was a counterproductive idea to begin with. That belated event took place when the whole language people admitted they were wrong. Several of the original proponents of WL, mainly liberals, are now behind the phonics initiative. But the same is not true elsewhere in the nation, where the left and the right still line up to do battle over how our children should learn to read—perhaps the most ludicrous ideological contest of our time.

Phonics has won the academic war, and Americans of all political persuasions and social classes should help implement it, just as we did with Noah Webster's *Blue-Backed Speller* in 1783 and for almost two centuries after. We have only to look at the extraordinary success of P.S. 161 in Brooklyn, where minority children read far above the city average because of phonics *first*—plus a rich library of books that are available to all students.

This fight is not over yet. But if American parents can block the politicization of education and ensure that the brilliant discovery of the alphabet is exploited in their own child's classroom, then the struggle will have been worth not only the energy expended, but even the discord.

5

LICENSING AND CERTIFICATION OF TEACHERS

A Nationwide Sham

I n Massachusetts, the appointment of John R. Silber, the feisty chancellor of Boston University, as board chairman of the state department of education, put the Establishment into a state of shock and fear. And they were right to worry.

A scholar of renown, Dr. Silber took a look at the low academic level of new teachers and decided something had to be done. The most likely route, he decided, was to send large groups of graduate education majors packing.

Silber's method was simple. Take the traditional teacher licensing test—which in most states is set at about a 10th grade level—and elevate it a notch or two. After all, the candidates were college graduates (grade 16), even if most had come out of diploma mill teacher training schools where they had majored in education.

Surprisingly, Massachusetts had been among the most lax of

states. *There had been no licensing test of any kind.* Those who completed approved teacher training programs were almost automatically certified for the classroom. Silber was determined to create a true screen that would eliminate the unqualified, which in essence meant that they were not bright enough or skilled enough to teach.

The new exam was custom-developed for the state by National Evaluation Services in Amherst, which tests for eight states, including California and New York. It was first given to 1,800 aspiring teachers in Massachusetts in the spring of 1998. The results were catastrophic. In fact, they sparked a national alert about education and the quality of American teachers almost as potent as the one that greeted the federal government's 1983 "Nation at Risk" critique of American students' achievement.

The exam came in three parts: reading, writing, and a content exam in the subject the candidate intended to teach.

How well did the aspiring teachers do?

The failure rate was so high that it startled those both within and outside the Establishment. Almost three out of five candidates (59 percent) flunked, meaning that they had not passed all three portions of the test and were therefore not eligible to be licensed to teach in Massachusetts public schools.

The rejected teachers and their union, the National Education Association (NEA), were in an uproar at Silber and the state. "What should we do?" several of the failed candidates asked. Find another line of work Silber, who resigned his post in March 1999, responded.

The Establishment was equally frustrated. Veteran teachers were retiring, and schools nationwide had to hire 2 million more over the next decade. How could they accomplish that when Massachusetts was eliminating half the candidates—all of whom had successfully finished a four- or five-year training course in education?

In July 1998, a new group of some 2,100 teacher candidates took the test. The result was almost as startling. Forty-seven percent failed this time. Since the state permitted applicants to take the test an *unlimited* number of times, surely by the second or third time they'd get the hang of it.

That July, some 1,000 of those who had failed the first time tried again. But fate, and the exam, were against them. Only 6 percent passed the second time. The third time around, the failees did a bit better. Eight percent passed that screen. Using some rough calculations, it appears that in the finally analysis, almost 40 percent of the state's aspiring teachers never made it to the classroom.

"We have no objection to a licensing exam," said a spokesperson for the Massachusetts Teachers Association, a branch of the NEA. "But we were dismayed and shocked by this test. We don't think it was fair, valid, or reliable. In fact, we have had a study done by outside experts and they agree with us. The state hasn't yet released the contents of the test, but judging from anecdotal evidence the report concludes that it is statistically unreliable. There are huge differences in scores on retake, and several bright people have failed, including one Fulbright scholar."

She went on to state that the MTA was fooled. Initially they were told the test was going to be a trial run to develop questions. But just a few weeks prior to the testing they were informed that it was "the real thing."

Despite objections prompted by the high failure rate, the Massachusetts test was surely no complex bar exam. In fact, the reading and writing portions were quite simple, much of it composed of essay questions that challenged the test-takers' ability to write lucid and correct English. In the world of education, where so much is *subjective* and knowledge can be called "trivia," such *objective* criteria as correct spelling, grammar, and punctuation had passed many of the teacher candidates by.

The results were "painful," said interim State Education Commissioner Frank Haydu III, who resigned in the political bruhaha that accompanied the testing fiasco.

Many of the test-takers couldn't write complete sentences. The spelling—in a dire reminder of the whole language fiasco—was often atrocious, with such inventive variants as "horibal."

In a way it was poetic justice. Since many veteran teachers had neglected to use spelling lists in their classrooms, they had passed that liability on to their students, some of whom were now failed teacher certification candidates. We are reminded of the vernacular comment "What goes around, comes around."

The Massachusetts test failure became fodder for a Jay Leno opening monologue about the smarts, or lack thereof, of school-teachers. It also prompted a dose of angry sarcasm from a Democratic leader in Massachusetts, who intoned, "I'll tell you who won't be a teacher: the idiots who took the test and so miserably failed and the idiots who passed them." The latter was a reference to the fact that all the test-takers had passed their four-year teacher training regimen, many with flying colors.

In Washington, a disillusioned Democratic senator, Jeff Bingaman of New Mexico, suggested cutting off all federal funds to schools of education if more than 25 percent of their graduates flunked their state licensing exams—a move that would surely shut down most Massachusetts teacher training institutions.

We have seen how a focus on knowledge can set up fears in education circles. In the arena of licensing, the same seems to be true of tests. Teachers increasingly hate to give them, much preferring other methods of assessment, including "portfolios" and inflated grades. That fear seems to extend to tests of their own proficiency, a reflection that many were poor students in high school. Perhaps they still harbor a weak self-esteem, something that may secretly dominate Establishment thinking.

Teacher competency tests are increasingly being pushed by states desperate to raise the bar for licensing. In North Carolina, the state became concerned about the quality of teaching in its fifteen lowest-performing schools. The idea was to test the personnel in these schools—teachers, guidance counselors, and principals—to see if they measured up.

The test was one of general knowledge designed for college juniors in Florida, which should have been easy enough for the North Carolina teachers, who were all college graduates. But the proposal was greeted with an outcry by the Establishment, one far more vociferous than any schoolchild balk at an examination.

The test is "abritrary, irrational, punitive, and counterproductive to our efforts to improve the learning environment at low-performing schools," said the superintendent of schools in Gaston County.

Translation? They feared the teachers could not pass the simple exam.

The North Carolina Association of Educators, the local NEA organization, pledged to support any educator who refused to take the test. The union fought in court for a preliminary injunction against the exam, and pressured state politicians.

The teachers won. State legislators agreed to changes in their Excellent Schools Act of 1997, which was designed to raise both teacher salaries and standards. As the NEA says, "no North Carolina teacher will be required to take this meaningless competency test."

Tests of teacher intelligence, knowledge, and skills are a sensitive subject in the field. Teachers were not superior test-takers as elementary and high schools students, as we've seen, nor do they score well on such standardized tests as the SAT or the GRE. Many still hate any objective assessment of their ability.

Licensing and Certification of Teachers

Obviously they fear they will fail, which will harm their careers, as happened to so many of their colleagues in Massachusetts.

But unlike the new exam in Massachusetts, the typical teacher certification test has traditionally had very low standards. And there is great resistance in the Establishment to raising them.

One imagines a screening process much like the bar examination for lawyers, which one-third fail on first try, and which blocks incompetents from practicing law. Even though the typical teacher competency test is much less rigorous, the Establishment insists on protecting its own.

Rather than safeguard the public by screening *out* untutored teachers, the tests are more often used to screen them *in*. In most states, well over 95 percent of teacher graduates who apply for teaching licenses are eventually certified and move into the classroom unimpeded.

The most common test that teachers have had to take was the National Teachers Examination, which was given by the Educational Testing Service until 1992. That test, which was a one-day affair, has now been converted to a two-part licensing examination called Praxis, also administered by ETS in thirty-six states. The most common teacher screen in the country, it is taken each year by some 620,000 men and women who hope to become educators.

Praxis I, a general test, is taken in the second or third year of teacher training. Praxis II, which includes several tests of knowledge (or "content," as the Establishment calls it) for teaching specialties, is taken at or near graduation from college. If passed, in most states it leads to near-automatic certification and licensing as a teacher.

I received a large sample of questions from Praxis I from the ETS. The test seemed disturbingly easy, which is surely why the overwhelming majority of education students that take it pass.

The Conspiracy of Ignorance

My guess is that it is geared to a 10th grade—high school—level and probably lower.

Some of the questions are an insult to even a marginally educated person. One describes a conversation between a customer and what she believes is TransGlobal Airlines about a flight from New York to Tokyo. But in fact she gets a wrong number. The question is not a difficult one about the distance between the two cities or the time zones, *but a multiple-choice question that asks whether she's trying to reach the airline by letter, radio, telegram, or telephone!*

Shades of extreme ignorance.

Another shows simple bar graphs of world production of crude oil in 1974 and 1975 in nine countries, from the United States to the United Arab Emirates. One of the two years is shown in solid black and the other is shaded. The question is not a complex one about the countries or petroleum reserves. Instead it simply asks how many of the nine nations had produced more oil in 1975 than in 1974. All that is required is to look at the graph and count first one, then two taller bars in 1975.

The question is more suited to a 4th grade student than to a college graduate, let alone a would-be teacher.

In mathematics, Praxis asked what was the probability of each of three tossed coins coming down either heads or tails. The answer, which is known to almost all 8th graders, is 50 percent no matter what the situation.

A geography question shows a blank map of Africa and asks which country with a black majority was controlled by minority whites in the 1970s. The letter E is marked at the bottom of the continent, and the answer, of course, is South Africa, something virtually every high school student knows, or should know.

There is something pathetic about the simplistic nature of the test. But the test-makers are aware of the academic deficiencies of new teachers, as are the state departments of education, though they are loathe to admit it. Otherwise they would not approve such meager screens. If pressed, I would say that almost all the questions could be answered by a twelve- or thirteen-year-old, let alone someone about to teach our children.

The Massachusetts test appears to be a *bit* more difficult than most, which is why some 40 percent of teaching candidates will never enter a public school classroom in that state.

The test asks candidates to define *abolish*. It also asks "What is a preposition?" One question involves correcting the grammar of the sentence *"A distinguished scholar and a great teacher, Professor Smith's famous lecture on the pyramids are not to be missed.*

There are two obvious errors: his "lecture" does not modify Smith, and *is* should be used instead of *are*. To rewrite it, they suggest: *"Because Professor Smith is a distinguished scholar and a great teacher, his famous lecture on the pyramids is not to be missed."*

The test samples also include a lengthy passage on James Madison and the Constitution. Test-takers are asked to write a summary of what they have just read. The Massachusetts Department of Education published sample responses, some of which were unnerving.

One teacher candidate wrote: *"Interperting the Constitution rases many questions."* Another wrote: *"The major problem with this passage is that, there was no documentery of the debat, so the delegates kept them secret."*

Still another response was picturesque: *"James Madison was the Father of the Constitution. But he was no good at notes. He wrote a lot of notes on the debats. But also left some stuff out. What we will never know. In the convention, delegats had to debat and compermise. 42 people did not sign and thanks to James Madison we will never know, why?"*

The failure of so many Massachusetts candidates only reinforces the fact that many teachers come from the lower ranks of academe, a situation the Establishment helps to maintain through its general laxity in licensing and certification.

But a skeptic might ask, hasn't it always been this way? Haven't schoolteachers always been academically deficient in relation to the rest of the population?

As we have seen, the reality was quite the opposite. Before World War II, teachers were among the best educated of the population. Though the normal school, the typical teacher training center, was not a complete university, it attracted bright, generally female, candidates, and as time progressed, more teachers took a full bachelor's degree. The typical undereducated parent was awed by the schoolteacher, who appeared to be the fountainhead of knowledge.

Today the situation is almost reversed. The average college-bound senior (67 percent of high school graduates go on to college) may well have an SAT score that's 50 points higher than the one his teacher earned—1,016 versus 964. In the higher socioeconomic suburban areas, where students routinely score 1,100 or more on their SATs, the difference may even be greater. And on the Graduate Record Exam, education school graduates score at the bottom of eight professions.

Today most suburban parents have gone to college, as have teachers. But the typical college-educated parent has taken a more sophisticated college curriculum, with greater emphasis and more credits in liberal arts and sciences. Though there is no available measure of parents' SAT scores, most probably did as well as their children, who on average score higher than their teachers. And as students go on to college in ever increasing numbers, the educational spread—in favor of the community over the teachers—continues to grow.

Changing that is the challenge. I have already suggested closing all undergraduate schools of education, which would create a much better universe of teacher candidates from which to draw.

Another step is a more demanding certification test, which would weed out perhaps the entire lower half of the teaching and administration Establishment. If one were to administer a rigorous, if not excessively stringent test of academic skill, what percentage of teachers would pass? I would hazard a guess that only one-third would ever make it to the classroom.

The threat of more rigorous teacher tests has alarmed the education community, especially in Massachusetts, whose newly found rigor seems to have no limits. Dr. Silber and the department of education have even sponsored legislation to test all of the state's *current teachers*, a threat that has driven the Massachusetts Teachers Association into fits of hostility. At the same time, it seems to have invigorated the state's determination to sweep away a generation of laxity.

"Our concern is not for the teachers but for the parents of our state," says a representative of the Massachusetts Department of Education, which appears to be in a to-the-death struggle with public school educators. "Last year, as part of our legislated mandate to recertify all teachers every five years, we proposed adding a written test they would have to take. If teachers couldn't pass it, after a retake, we would be able to fire them. The bill died in Education Committee, but we're trying again this year."

If teachers are not fully capable and have trouble passing simple licensing tests, how about the schools that produce them?

In the last few years there has been an attempt to accredit those teacher colleges that are worthy and ignore the rest. It is a strange demonstration in which the Establishment turns its back on the very institutions whose graduates it strenuously defends even if they are academically backward.

The accrediting organization is known in the trade as NCATE, the National Council for Accreditation of Teacher Education. Of the 1,200 schools of education—undergraduate and graduate—in the nation, only 500 are accredited. Why? Well, it is a voluntary operation, and since 1987, only 700 schools have even bothered to apply.

NCATE, which is supported by thirty-three educational institutions, including the teacher unions, says it turns down some schools because of lack of standards.

"We revised our standards in 1988, and over the next three years, our denial rate went up to 30 percent because schools couldn't meet the criteria," says an NCATE spokesperson. "Then in 1995, we upgraded our standards again—mainly to insist that there be more subject content in teacher education schools. About 15 percent were rejected, and 15 percent more were put on probation."

The group would like the same powers that the Joint Commission on Accreditation enjoys in the hospital arena. But many schools are not interested. This includes not only minor schools, but such giants as Columbia Teachers College, which is not part of NCATE. However, in some states, including Maryland and Alaska, teacher trainees must attend an accredited school if they want to be licensed.

So why are the majority of education schools not involved with NCATE?

Some claim it is for ideological reasons, specifically "political correctness," a reminder of the phonics versus whole language battle. Recently the same kind of warfare erupted in the accrediting of teacher training schools. Four education colleges in Iowa dropped out of the NCATE accreditation system claiming that they did not agree with the diversity and multicultural requirements in terms of faculty and curriculum. They felt that NCATE was politicizing education, which appears to be true.

The battle only reinforces, for some, the suspicion that Establishment leaders often have an agenda that goes beyond public school education. Instead, teaching and learning become vehicles for propagating their own ideological agenda, resulting in a disservice to our children.

In an article in the education journal *Phi Delta Kappan*, Jonathan K. Parker argues that the Iowa schools were right to drop out of the Establishment accrediting system. He says that like himself, the four college presidents are "simply frustrated with an organization that sometimes seems more concerned with promoting a particular political and social agenda than with professionalizing teaching."

We've seen no such improvement in education. But this hasn't deterred the Establishment from continually trying to convince the public that *it is going to do something.* The latest move in that direction, one that imitates the Establishment's favorite medical model, is to create "board certification" for teachers, much as we do for gastroenterologists.

The organization attempting this is a relatively new one, the National Board for Professional Teaching Standards, or NBPTS. (Educators are prone to use tongue-twisting names.) The program has been in operation for only three years, so the roster of "board-certified" teachers is minuscule. Out of 2.7 million teachers, only 1,835, or 1 in 1,500, have been certified to date.

There are twelve different certificates, arranged by topic and age-grouping of students, such as "Middle School English" and "Early Adolescent/Generalist." The candidates who apply or who are recommended by their school districts go through a screening process that includes a full day of testing, then the production of a portfolio, which requires 200 to 300 hours of work, videotapes of themselves in the classroom, lesson plans, and other assessments.

"About 47 percent of the candidates are certified in the first go-round, which takes a year," explains a spokesperson for the NBPTS. "Those who do not pass can continue to seek certification for a period of three years."

The program is backed by the federal government, the Carnegie Corporation, other philanthropies, and industrial firms. The NEA doesn't provide any funding, but union representatives sit on the board of directors of the NBPTS. The goal is to raise standards and simultaneously to impress the public with these "star" teachers. The hope is that the desire to become board-certified will brush off on other teachers and build a core of the truly qualified.

The major teachers' union agrees and shows its dual motivation in an article in its trade paper, *NEA Today*. Says the union:

"We finally have our chance to be accorded the professionalism that doctors, lawyers, and architects have achieved for years. National certification, many believe, will help teachers achieve greater respect from local communities, even self-respect. Maybe we'll reach the day when we never again have to hear a colleague say, 'I'm just a teacher.' "

This is the professional side of the equation. But the NEA never forgets that teaching is a dollar-and-cents business as well. "We should start thinking about draft language that can be bargained into contracts to support teachers who want to apply for board certification," adds the article about a process that costs a good deal of money and takes time away from the classroom.

Of course there is nothing wrong with this attempt to professionalize teaching and raise standards. But it is being built on a shaky foundation. *If* they had a competent academic universe to draw from, the present procedure would take a hundred years to involve most teachers. And with the current population of the Establishment, the standards would have to be lowered considerably to involve the majority, making board certification little different from contemporary low-level licensing and certification.

If education is ever to be considered a profession, the licensing screen must be racheted up enormously, probably far past the level of the Massachusetts exam, which is washing out some 40 percent of the poorly trained applicants. Perhaps that screening exercise should begin *before* students start expensive training in education, much of it at public expense.

Praxis I was intended to do something of that nature, but it is a ridiculously easy exam, which a 10th or even 9th grader could pass.

To safeguard the community and public school students, the states must insist on tougher licensing exams and a test for recertification of all teachers—plus one to screen out incompetents before they begin a long teacher training process that may lead to nowhere.

Just as good liberal arts colleges insist on reasonable performance on the SATs—a score of at least 1,100—and a minimum 3.0 grade point average in high school, so undergraduate schools of education must become as rigorous. (All this until such time as these schools are legally closed and replaced by postgraduate teacher training.)

As the Massachusetts Department of Education says, their responsibility is to the parents and the children, not to the teachers. As citizens of a Republic, we can do no less.

6

THE DEBASED GENERAL CURRICULUM

Whatever Happened to Geography and Trigonometry?

There is a general rule that seems to dominate educational thinking in America. If the curriculum in any subject is not strong enough, and students are failing—as American youngsters are—don't simply raise the requirements. That might well work.

Instead, the Establishment does an intellectual backflip at every sign of failure. It starts to modify, change, weaken, and reinvent the curriculum to provide more show than light and make it appear that it is up to the challenge.

That is what happened in the reading fiasco. Whole language was brought in to replace phonics, which had not failed but had just not been used enough. Now the same misdirection in curriculum is taking place in mathematics, at which American children seem to be particularly unskilled.

At the Third International Mathematics and Science Study, a

competition graded in 1998, Americans scored near the bottom, often 20 to 25 percent lower than students in the Netherlands and Norway, nations that exist mainly on their brainpower. The shortsightedness of American middle and high schools in teaching math became evident as students' performance in these international contests seemed to sink by age, going inexorably downhill from 4th to 8th to 12th grades.

Why?

Luther Williams of the National Science Foundation points out one obvious reason. Other countries are way ahead of us in the complexity of math they require students to study. Middle school youngsters (generally aged eleven to fourteen) in other developed countries quickly graduate out of simple 4th grade arithmetic by that age and move into algebra and geometry. But in America, where middle school teachers are not well trained in math, Williams explains that "basic arithmetic is still the staple of 8th-grade math."

In simpler terms, the American student is mired in a backward math program.

From the 1996 NAEP mathematics report for 4th, 8th, and 12th grade students, we can see our children are *not* learning. That volume of results also offers examples of math questions and answers from the test. We should take a peek—unless we become easily aggravated by the failures of American students and, by extrapolation, their teachers.

Here's the summary of one question from the NAEP test. If Sam is going to buy lunch consisting of a sandwich that costs 90 cents, juice that costs 50 cents, and fruit that costs 35 cents, how many dollar bills does he need in order to buy that same lunch for five days?

Before I give the answer, I have a question for the reader. How many of the 4th graders (nine-year-olds) failed to come up with the answer? Ten, twenty, even thirty percent of the nine-year-olds?

The first answer, of course, is that it requires nine dollar bills—$8.75 for the food with 25 cents in change. *The other answer is embarrassing: 83 percent of the students got it wrong.*

Shall we try again? If we create teams of 8 from among a total of 34 students, how many are left over to play as substitutes? The simple answer of 2 (4 × 8 plus 2 equals 34) was missed by 61 percent of the nine-year-olds. Not many Einsteins here.

In the 8th grade test, here is a simple problem for thirteen-year-olds that was answered correctly by only 26 percent of the children: If a car odometer registered 41,256.9 miles and the car went another 1,200 feet, what would the odometer show? There were four multiple-choice answers. The correct one showed that the car went another .2 of a mile, for a total of 41,257.1. But these middle school children mainly guessed incorrectly, a quarter of students choosing one of the three wrong answers.

Were 12th graders—high school seniors—any smarter?

We've already seen these youngsters in action, with 63 percent failing to recognize that the third side of a truncated triangle of 2 × 3 × ? within a similar larger triangle of 6 × 9 × 12 was 4.

The math performance in American schools is weak, sometimes aggravatingly so. Overall many more students failed than were proficient at math. Only 20 percent of the 4th graders were considered "proficient" or "good," and 38 percent failed, or scored "below basic." In the 8th grade, 23 percent were proficient, and 39 percent failed. In grade 12, only 16 percent were good at math, and 31 percent failed.

One potent reason for this failure is the weak math curriculum in public schools. As we've seen, the middle school is heavily mired down in simple arithmetic. In high school, not enough children take intermediate algebra or even simple algebra. Trigonometry, the basic discipline for building and surveying, has nearly disappeared from the curriculum as being too difficult.

A recently published study by the U.S. Department of Education, based on the high school transcripts of a nationwide sample of 25,575 students in 340 representative schools, shows the curriculum shortfall. Of the fifty states, only *three* required more than two years of math in high school for graduation, a low threshold for knowledge. Most required only two years and others even less.

The transcript report shows a relatively strong record for private schools in math but a weaker one for public schools. More than a third of public high school graduates *never* took a full course in basic algebra. Almost half (45 percent) never took intermediate algebra. Geometry fared somewhat better, being studied by 68 percent of students. But trigonometry is apparently a lost art. Only 1 in 8 students did the minimum work in that vital math subject.

Obviously math preparation needs beefing up in every way. It seems incredible that someone can graduate from high school today without having taken even simple algebra, as is the case with almost a million eighteen-year-olds each June.

Algebra 1 and 2 should be mandatory in all schools, as should geometry. And all states should immediately raise the math requirement to three years of study, reaching eventually to a four-year curriculum. School districts with a little rigor in their bureaucratic bones should make trigonometry a required subject for graduation.

Advanced math, which is the future of our technology, is shortchanged as well. On a national level, only *2 percent* of 12th grade students are studying at an advanced level. Only 1 in 11 students take calculus, and 1 in 50 study statistics and probabilities.

We will have to institute a much more rigorous math curriculum if we hope to compete in the world without having to rely on foreigners for much of our brainpower, as we do today. As in engineering, a near-majority of the Ph.D.'s in mathematics granted by American universities are awarded to foreign students.

Another generally unspoken problem is that our teachers are not well trained. In too many cases they are teaching subjects, especially math and science, with little or no background in the field.

The scandal of secondary school teaching—both middle school and high school—is that many of the people teaching math are not, by the largest stretch of imagination, mathematicians. We have already seen that the requirements for certification as high school math teachers are lower than for those taking a simple bachelor of science degree in math.

Now we learn from the "Schools and Staffing Survey" conducted by the National Center for Education Statistics that almost *half* the secondary school math teachers are not equipped to teach the subject. Among teachers whose major assignment is math, 11 percent had only a minor in math. *But 34 percent had neither a major nor a minor in math.*

(Of those who have math as a second assignment, it's worse: 71 percent have had no training in math at all.)

Are there other bad signs on the math horizon? Unfortunately, yes. And one of them is a very dangerous and irrational piece of pedagogy.

Rather than increase the rigor of math teaching to make up for the general failure, the Establishment—as usual—is moving in the opposite direction. It is setting up still another new methodology, the second since the New Math of the 1970s.

This *New, New Math*, sometimes called *Whole Math*, or *Constructivist Math*, holds that too much effort is spent on math drill and computations. What good is all that multiplying, adding, dividing, even simple algebraic equations, they say, if the students don't understand "concepts"?

This new approach seems to have a deadly cousinlike relationship to whole language, which eschewed phonics, spelling, and grammar and also talked about the glories of "concepts."

In the case of whole math, one of its early moves involved a classic case of Establishment permissiveness. Many schools now permit students to use calculators in class and even on tests! This, of course, obviates all computational discipline, which is probably at the core of the brain's understanding of mathematical principles.

One simple explanation of whole math can be found in a new piece of curriculum, *Mathland*, used in many 6th grade classes. Teachers are instructed on how to guide students through one problem:

"I just checked out a library book that is 1,344 pages long! The book is due in 3 weeks. How many pages will I need to read a day to finish the book on time?"

The obvious answer can be found by dividing 1,344 pages by 21 days, to come up with 64 pages a day. But that does not satisfy *Mathland*, which explains in its guide that they want students to figure out other ways to solve the problem.

The *Mathland* guide explains that "division in Mathland is not a separate operation to master, but rather a combination of successive approximations, multiplication, adding up and subtracting back, all held together with the students' own number sense."

One of the faddish secrets here is "successive approximations," as if it is best for students to come up with continual raw scores that are wrong before zeroing in on an answer they would otherwise get in seconds. It makes no sense. If you understand the real concept—that each day one does a piece of the work until it is all done—the idea is *perfectly* explained by dividing 1,344 by 21.

The Conspiracy of Ignorance

The great beauty of mathematical computations is that they cut to the heart of the problem, without staggering like a punch-drunk fool unable to understand the concept of division. Are our students now supposed to forget technique and throw away the power of 5,000 years of mathematical method in favor of a theory—and a highly unproven one at that—and then use a calculator as a crutch for an idle brain?

The new theory is the product of the National Council of Teachers of Mathematics, an Establishment organization seeking new ways to do old problems that were once easily solved. Thomas Romberg, an education professor of mathematics at the University of Wisconsin and chairman of the commission which set it up, explains the new, new math in an op-ed piece in the *New York Times*.

He claims that math reasoning must be learned through "personal and social experiences" and even in "groups," which is highly unlikely. Some of our finest mathematicians (and I have known one or two) have the worst possible social and personal skills, seldom operating in groups, a fetish of whole math. The minds of good mathematicians are highly individualistic and usually enveloped in equations and thought exercises far removed from social experiences, sometimes even from ordinary reality.

Another professor, this time of business, and a mother as well, writes in the *Wall Street Journal* about her unfortunate contact with whole math. Her daughter, then in the 8th grade, was using a calculator to figure out 10 percent of 470, a computation that should take the human brain—even that of a thirteen-year-old—a second, without a calculator. The mother also had to explain to her daughter about fractions, that one-fourth was the same as 25 percent. She relates that a youngster in a fast-food restaurant asked her if the change he had given her was correct. His computer was down.

The Debased General Curriculum

In the *Times*, Professor Romberg finds it necessary to apologize to the public for excesses and "horror stories" perpetrated by teachers in the name of whole math. This, of course, is a cover-my-fanny approach typical of faddish theorists in education when they see how ridiculous their concepts become in actual operation. This professor explains his theory, but then also offers regrets and apologies.

- The Council does not say students should use a calculator "for all computations."
- Though the Council wants students to be "comfortable" with calculators, "nowhere does it argue that students do not need to memorize multiplication facts."
- Teachers may prematurely teach the Council's problem-solving ideas "without having students learn algebraic procedures."
- Having students work in groups, a whole math tenet, doesn't mean that teachers should give up discussions of "individual assignments."
- Teachers may not have enough training to translate the Council's new theories "into a learning experience for students."
- It's unfair to attack the Council's entire program because of "initial missteps."

One continuing horror story that has accompanied whole math is the ridiculous idea of allowing, even encouraging, the use of calculators in school computations, trying to make a silicon chip replace the atrophying student brain.

Because it has crept up on us, most parents are not aware that in many schools their children are not doing multiplication and division but are using little $10 calculators to do their schoolwork—not at home surreptitiously, but right in the classroom, and in some places, even on tests.

I checked the school in my hometown, and yes, it permits calculators both in math class and when taking the statewide Connecticut Mastery Test, thereby giving schools and individual parents and students a false idea of the students' ability to do *real* computations. This will serve them poorly as they advance and attend schools of higher education that may not permit calculators, or when they take some standardized tests, like the Stanford Achievement Test, where they can't use calculators, and suffer from a brain unconditioned to do arithmetic.

(The College Board's SATs do permit the use of calculators, which is itself an affront to standardized testing, our only way to properly assess students.)

It would be wise for all parents to query their schools about the use of calculators. If the school permits it, parents and others should complain vociferously because they're destroying your child's mathematical mind.

Since most teachers were themselves poor at math as children, they tend to favor systems that favor weak students, often at the expense of the talented, or even the average ones.

One of their most permissive tools is the *"math portfolio."* In *Childhood Education,* an assistant professor of education at the University of South Florida writes that math tests are often unfair because they emphasize computational skills, a contemporary no-no. "Not all students perform well on tests," he says, adding that "anxiety, fatigue or learning disabilities" can adversely affect children's performance.

(He fails to mention that many students do poorly on tests because they have never been taught the material.)

Instead, he believes that more emphasis should be put on the *portfolio,* a collection of student- and teacher-selected work that reflects the child's supposed success in math—a kind of carefully prepared scrapbook that invites good assessments even when the student is mathematically tone-deaf. But a portfolio, he assures us, "gives a more accurate picture of a student's performance than a conventional letter grade that is compiled from traditional tests and assignments."

Nonsense. It is a rather pathetic excuse for bad teaching and learning, all part of contemporary educational paranoia, which detests facts, tests, knowledge, and information. It ignores true assessment of children's skills, preferring stage-managed methods developed to promote self-esteem and the perpetuation of ignorance.

Opposition to whole math is now being organized, just as was the opposition to the fiasco of whole language. One group is led by Marianne Jennings, the mother who wrote the *Wall Street Journal* piece. She is a founder of "Mathematically Correct," a group of parents and others intent on combating the whole math formula.

"We are supposedly a conservative group, but we are being joined by a number of liberal Democrats who are beginning to realize that they have been taken in by the education people," she says.

In the noneducation academic world, there are several professors of mathematics horrified at the thought of whole math. One of them is Dr. Richard Askey, professor of mathematics at the University of Wisconsin, where ironically, whole math was born in the Math Education Department.

Professor Askey believes that the concept is all wrong. If students do not learn the techniques of computation, he says, they will not have a foundation on which to build concepts and theory. He calls *Mathland* an absolute disaster and is equally opposed to the use of calculators.

"I became involved in math education when I realized that many of my calculus students hadn't been well prepared in public school," the mathematician recounted when interviewed. "Several of them told me that they did almost no serious math work in high school. Since then, I've done a good deal of research on the subject, and I've learned that math instruction and the curriculum in elementary and secondary schools are at a very low level. As one of my colleagues has said, it's 'a mile wide and an inch deep.'"

Dr. Askey reminds us of the poor math performance of Americans in the TIMSS international competition, where Japan—whose nation depends on brainpower—usually excels. In that country, 60 percent of the high school students take advanced work, which includes trigonometry and some calculus. The other 40 percent are in a lower track.

"If our students could do as well as the slower Japanese track, it would be an advance," says Askey. "Secretary of Education Riley talks about our becoming number one in math, but even the new higher standards he advocates are no better than those of the slower Japanese. It's ridiculous. Our middle school is a good place to get students started on more advanced math, but we've made no progress. In 1923, the Mathematics Association of American advocated teaching algebra in the 7th grade instead of the 9th grade. Over seventy-five years have passed and we still usually wait until the 9th grade. In fact, math teaching in the middle schools of America is generally a disaster."

The mathematics curriculum is constantly being roiled, without advancing, and generally regressing. In the sister field of science, there is also an attempt to reduce traditional learning with the same "constructivist" theory. One professor of education at Pembroke State University in North Carolina describes it as "student-activated" instead of "teacher-oriented" instruction. In the former, which she favors, she says that students "interact with each other, they reexamine, reflect, and alter their thinking based on evidence and logical reasoning." Little, however, is said about scientific knowledge, once the foundation of science teaching.

The Debased General Curriculum

"Whole science" has not advanced as rapidly as whole math, but it threatens logic and learning as well in thousands of schools. It is another attempt to play down fundamentals and have children handle "concepts" without having sufficient background. Scientists are alarmed at these shortcuts, and the tendency of schools to make science "fun," which leads to a watering down of the curriculum into what one scientist calls "science appreciation."

Nobel Laureate Glenn T. Seaborg, who passed away in 1999, believed that science education must feature rigorous memorization of fundamentals. Otherwise, he said, students will never learn to think abstractly—an approach which is the reverse of flawed contemporary educational theory.

Seaborg, two other Nobel Laureates, and thirty other scientists offered to write a K–12 science curriculum for the state of California, gratis. They were turned down, and the contract was given to professional educators for $178,000. The educators charged that Seaborg et al. were pushing traditional science, which they feared was "too elitist." Their proof? Science was dominated by white males.

Other scientists are equally disgusted with the state of the science curriculum in our public schools. Leon M. Lederman, Nobel Laureate in Physics, recently addressed the problem.

"The causes of science illiteracy—the superficiality, misinformation, ignorance and downright hostility toward science we encounter at virtually all levels of school . . . are numerous," he writes. He is particularly appalled by the absence of physics in the high school curriculum, which guarantees that students will "have little idea of the fundamental forces that govern atomic and molecular interactions."

Today youngsters generally study biology in the 9th grade, the first year of high school. Some go on to chemistry in the 10th grade, then abruptly halt their science education. Dr. Lederman would reverse the curriculum. Ninth graders would first learn physics, including "concepts of motion, energy, heat, electricity, light and the nature of the atom." In the 10th grade they would study chemistry, "armed with a good grasp of the structure of atoms and the forces that give rise to bonding."

In the third year of a *required* high school science curriculum, they would study biology, gaining, he says, an "understanding of biological molecules that would come naturally as a part of a broad understanding of chemistry."

I am in no position to evaluate the Nobel Prize winner's suggestion of reversing the curriculum to make physics the first course. But I can point out that if his suggestion is to be taken seriously, we will first have to radically upgrade the science curriculum. *At present, physics, his choice to be studied first, is a nearly extinct subject in American high schools.*

While 93 percent of students in public high schools take biology and 54 percent take chemistry before they graduate, only 24 percent—or less than 1 in 4—study physics.

One would assume that a high school education would include all three, as Dr. Lederman suggests. But the federal transcript study shows that only 20 percent of high school graduates—1 in 5—take all three basic science courses.

In many European nations, the study of physics, which is never taken here by most students, begins in middle school. The top-achieving science nations, like the Scandinavians, teach physics *every year* beginning in the 6th grade. In America, only a handful of schools, usually private ones, are beginning to promote physics. St. Mary's Academy, a Catholic college prep school for girls in Portland, Oregon, has taken Dr. Lederman's suggestion and reversed the curriculum in order to push physics. All 9th graders take it, and many elect for a second year of physics as well.

America's pronounced scientific illiteracy starts in our public schools, highlighted by undereducated educators. In whatever order, all three major sciences—biology, chemistry, and physics— should become required subjects for graduation in all fifty states.

(This failure to educate students in science extends all the way up to the Ivy League. At Harvard, a nonscience major can take one course, "The Atmosphere," and fulfill all physical science requirements for graduation!)

The American students' results in world science competition are often poor, as we have seen. Domestically, the 1996 NAEP results for science are just as disappointing, proof of the failures of curriculum and undertrained teachers. The national average score on a scale of 0 to 300 was 150, but states performed quite individually, either better or worse.

For example, in the 8th grade, Maine led the list with a score of 163, followed by North Dakota and Montana, while Louisiana was at the bottom with a score of 132. New York and Texas were a little below average with scores of 145. Catholic schools beat the public schools in the 8th grade by a commanding amount, 162 to 148.

Overall, science achievement in American schools is generally static in the lower grades and moves downward as the curriculum becomes more difficult. In the 4th grade, there has been a small increase in scores since 1970, from 225 to 230, out of a maximum of 500. In the 8th grade, the performance has been level. But in the 12th grade, where the critique of the Nobel Laureates should be taken to heart, scores have dropped from 305 to 296.

As in mathematics, many public schools science teachers are not well equipped for the job. A federal staffing survey shows that of science teachers in our secondary schools, 40 percent never majored in science. Another 12 percent only minored in the subject, meaning that the *majority* are not well trained enough for even our present weak curriculum, let alone one that requires chemistry and physics. Where a teacher has a second assignment to handle science, the figures are worse. There, 49 percent never majored in science, and another 14 percent only minored in the subject.

Hardly a teaching staff that can solve America's scientific illiteracy.

Like physics, another disappearing segment of our public school curriculum is geography. In one NAEP geography exam, 57 percent of the students failed, many finding it difficult even to find the United States on a map.

For years, geography was heavily taught in elementary school, then as a separate subject in junior high. But geography has long since been replaced by social studies, a grab-bag discipline that can cover *anything* the teacher and the school desire, including ecology, community relations, sex and race relations, history, geography, or whatever.

In earlier periods of American education, the geography of the globe, including maps of every continent, with the identifying and naming of states, nations, capitals, rivers, and mountains, was part of the required curriculum. With that emphasis on geographic facts, children gained a full concept of their own nation and the world and could easily recognize important places, giving them a global view.

Much of that discipline is gone in the teaching of geography, which is now a minor item in the social science curriculum. In most high schools, geography doesn't even exist as a separate course, required or elective.

The subject has trod a difficult road in public schools as the Establishment has played down the study of places and their names as being too reminiscent of rote memorization, the bête noire of modern educators. Of course "rote" is the key factor in learning, but one that many educators have learned to hate.

The result? Students too often react with a blank stare if

asked to pick out Turkey, or Nepal, or Pakistan, or the Caspian Sea—let alone Chicago—on a map. Or even Bosnia, Haiti, Yugoslavia, and Iraq, places where our national interests are now involved. Students could once name most of the U.S. states, along with their capitals. That is not only a lost art, but one denigrated by educators as too mechanical and as "trivia," the new Establishment euphemism for knowledge.

"When social studies came about in the public school, geography fell by the wayside," Ms. Osa Brand, a Ph.D. and president of the Association of American Geographers explained when interviewed. "The results of the NAEP tests in geography show poor student performance. This is unlike Europe, where the high school teaching of geography is taken seriously and students work hard at it. In America, most students never even take a single specific geography course. The problem is the politics of the classroom, the resistance of organizations like the National Council for the Social Studies against geography as a separate subject."

We see the growing geographic ignorance of our students in the NAEP evaluation. The questions, which reflect the current curriculum in social studies, dwell heavily on natural resources, topography, earthquakes, ecology, and other phenomena. But when it comes to locations and names of places, the students are in a perpetual quandary, with only a vague notion of the world they live in.

One simple question on the NAEP test for 12th graders clearly explains what has happened to geographic knowledge in our schools. As we have seen, two-thirds of the students could not correctly mark three out of four blank areas of a map, even though they included such obvious places as Japan and the Mediterranean Sea. In prior years, when geography was honored, most 8th graders would have gotten all four right.

Today, one assumes that responsibility for teaching geography must have been shifted to high school. Wrong. The reality is that geography is virtually ignored at that level as well. A survey of high school curriculum nationwide shows that only 25 percent—1 in 4—of students study geography for even a single semester by the time they graduate.

What then are high school students in history to make of the fact that France established a puppet regime in Mexico in the 1860s if they have no idea where France is? And perhaps Mexico as well.

The situation is dire, but Dr. Brand, who grew up in Europe, sees some light ahead, pointing out that interest in geography is rising. The Southern Governors Association, for one, has made strengthening the geography curriculum a priority. "We have a marvelous window of opportunity," Ms. Brand says optimistically, "for good things to happen to the study of geography."

Hopefully, parents will take advantage of that window and push their schools to provide a renaissance in separate geography courses, especially in the recognition and naming of places, from Toledo (in Ohio or Spain) to Timbuktu (in Mali, where sub-Saharan Africa begins).

American history has suffered almost the same fate as geography in public schools, where it has been relegated to the position of a second-rate discipline, far behind the more fashionable ancient and foreign history. Social studies is once again the culprit. Within that vague rubric, little American history need be taught. And little is.

Recently the *New York Times* ran a front page piece on the restoration of Mount Vernon. The reporter interviewed a ten-year-old who was visiting Mount Vernon with his parents. "Do you know who George Washington was?" the reporter asked the child. He *thought* that Washington was "one of the American presidents," but didn't mention his being the "Father of Our Country" or even the first president.

The Debased General Curriculum

How is that possible? Easily. One should understand that this display of youthful ignorance is not an isolated example. Children untutored in American history are a dime a million. It is a symptom of the *downsizing* and *revision* of American history throughout the curriculum, from 1st grade to senior high school.

Little wonder that in a federally sponsored quiz of 16,000 high school seniors nationwide, few had ever heard of Tom Paine's revolutionary pamphlet, "Common Sense." *Perhaps worse, only half the graduating eighteen-year-olds knew that the Bill of Rights guaranteed freedom of religion.*

Let's look at the history curriculum of an affluent Fairfield County, Connecticut, community where teachers make an average of $65,000 a year and where lack of money is surely no excuse for any lack of performance or inadequate curriculum.

In grades K–5, social studies concentrates on the "community," not the nation or its founding. In the 3rd grade, children learn the history of their town, starting with the Indians and going up to the present era. In the 4th grade, there is no history at all. In the 5th grade, they offer a little history, beginning with the European explorers and going through the expansion westward.

They have still avoided the Founding Fathers, the presidents, the Revolution, and the Civil War—which, if typical nationally, would explain a child's not knowing that Washington was our first president. In middle school, more time is spent on other world cultures than on the American story. In the 6th grade, for example, the students learn about "Ancient Peoples," from the Eskimos to those of the Indus Valleys to the old Egyptian culture. In the 7th grade, the emphasis is on older world cultures as well, ending in 1600. But still no mention of America.

Not until the 8th grade—when students are now thirteen and fourteen—do they get a real introduction to the story of their

121

own country. Then, just one social studies course is devoted to U.S. history, from colonial days onward.

Actually, this district's history curriculum, as deficient as it is, may be better than one in a nearby, almost as affluent Fairfield County community where my grandchildren go to school. The eldest, in the first year of high school, has *just* taken his first dedicated course in American history. An excellent student, he suffers from a weak curriculum. In middle school, he learned a little about the American Revolution in social studies class, but not in any organized way.

Finally, at the age of fifteen, he is studying the Revolutionary period up through the Articles of Confederation and the Constitution in reasonable detail. But after that point in the first semester, American history instruction stopped, with no word on when they will return to it. Naturally, there has been no coverage of the Jacksonian period, or the Mexican War or the Civil War, or Lincoln or Teddy Roosevelt, let alone FDR. My grandson is familiar with Washington, Adams, Jefferson, and Madison, but not with Monroe, John Quincy Adams, Jackson, or the later presidents.

The younger boy, another excellent student, is in 6th grade, where history is a sometime thing. Like most his age in the modern school system, he hasn't been taught the date of the Declaration of Independence or that of the Civil War (dates are anathema to modern educators), but he has learned something of Lewis and Clark and their Indian guide. Surprisingly, his teacher has also spent some time on the Boston Tea Party and Valley Forge—surprising because the social science curriculum seems to vary school by school, teacher by teacher.

Now to return to the history curriculum requirements of our first school district. How much American history will they take— two or three years? Not even close. This high school, which boasts that 87 percent of its graduates go on to college, requires only one course in pre–World War II American history to graduate.

Actually, require is too strong a word. In the 9th grade, they study "World Themes." In the 10th grade, the school requires *either* "American History" or a substitute course called "The American Experience," which although interesting, eschews conventional sequential history in favor of an "interdisciplinary" English and history course concentrating on writing.

"Contemporary America," a history of the United States since 1945, follows in the 11th or 12th grade, which is a good concept. However, if the student missed "American History" in the 10th grade, there is little background for this course.

So what would be a proper curriculum in American history, enough to prepare the student to be an active citizen and voter?

That training should begin early, with areas of study as follows:

- 4th grade—the Plymouth Colony, the Puritans, Boston, other settlers including William Penn and the early western frontier
- 5th grade—the later colonial period, up through the Declaration of Independence
- 6th grade—the Revolutionary War, the Constitution, and the Jeffersonian period, including the Louisiana Purchase and the Lewis and Clark expedition
- 7th grade—the War of 1812, the Jacksonian period, the Mexican War, the slavery debates, up to the Civil War
- 8th grade—Lincoln, the Civil War, the Reconstruction, and the Johnson impeachment trial, up through Teddy Roosevelt

In high school, four full years of U.S. history should be compulsory. In the 9th grade, the course should start in colonial days and go up through the Civil War. In the 10th grade, the course should cover the period up to World War I, reworking all the material from elementary and middle school in a much more sophisticated and detailed manner. In the 11th grade, the seventeen-year-olds should pick up their study after World War I, then proceed through the Great Depression and World War II up to the present.

In the 12th grade, a compulsory course in "American Civilization," combining history, literature, and economics, would help high school graduates understand their nation while learning to appreciate the concept of scholarship. An original, lengthy paper on some aspect of American culture should be required as well.

Too much American history?

Hardly. What could be more vital to a democracy in the twenty-first century than for its youngsters to understand the dynamics of how we got here, with sufficient knowledge to help them divine a proper course for the future?

To make this new curriculum, including the study of geography, succeed, we should eliminate social studies as a discipline beginning in middle school. From then on, history, geography, and economics should be separate courses taught by specialists in the fields. At least two years of geography should be required in high school, which is now seldom the case.

If the teaching of history is insufficient and sometimes nebulous because of the Establishment's fear of facts, is it at least accurate?

I raise that question because there is a strong *revisionist* movement in the teaching of American history raging in the universities, which are in turn trying to foist their biases onto our elementary and secondary schools. That bias, simply put, is that America is not a land of freedom and democracy, as our students once learned. Instead, the world's premier nation has ostensibly been tainted with the stain of Columbus from its beginnings up through a tortured and rather tawdry history.

The Debased General Curriculum

The center of that revisionist activity is National Standards for the Teaching of History, a self-promoted organization that despite its title has no official standing. It is located at UCLA, the University of California at Los Angeles. In 1993, the U.S. Department of Education and the National Endowment for the Humanities, another taxpayer-supported agency, gave the group a $2 million federal grant to develop a history curriculum for grades 5 through 12 in all middle and high schools in the nation. Congress approved, hoping it would beef up the thin history curriculum and teaching.

Instead, the result was nearly catastrophic. The UCLA group issued a curriculum report that was totally unbalanced, casting America in a poor light as a nation whose history was basically one of racism and imperialism.

A careful study of the document makes it clear that it was a blatant attempt to disparage the nation in the eyes of our students and play down the history of the successful world-leading (and saving) democracy. Tales of slavery, the Ku Klux Klan, and McCarthyism were highlighted along with the conquest of Native Americans, with few counterbalancing tales of freedom, open immigration, and a Civil War that freed the slaves at the cost of more lives, proportionately, than World War I and II combined.

George Washington is never mentioned as our first president, and many historical persons from Paul Revere to Thomas Edison to the Wright Brothers, disappear from the scene. The Constitution is mainly seen as an example of how the movement to stop slavery was quashed. The curriculum comes down hard on American industrialists but extolls the ancient emperor of Mali, a contemporary revisionist hero. It covers Harriet Tubman, as it should, but omits Daniel Webster, Miles Standish, and Eli Whitney.

Twenty thousand copies of this distorted history curriculum, courtesy of the American taxpayer, were shipped out to schools throughout the nation before the U.S. Senate finally reviewed and killed the project. But perhaps too late, for much of the damage had already been done.

Upgrading to a more advanced, more accurate, more rigorous curriculum in all subjects has been difficult because of opposition by the Establishment. Overall, they prefer a weak curriculum, possibly for two reasons.

One is their false idea that specific, codified, sequential information, including time and place, weakens "understanding," which is ostensibly their goal. That theory is, of course, exactly the opposite of the truth. Understanding comes from the ability to draw on stored knowledge, either academic or experiential, and apply it to the present problem, or even to the future. Without facts, or *knowledge*, there is no brain road map to understanding.

The second reason is that since most members of the Establishment have not themselves excelled under a rigorous curriculum, they project their own academic inadequacies onto their students—lowering expectations for performance, the sin of a bad teacher.

Many educators feel more comfortable supporting lower curriculum requirements, which they can more easily handle in class and which will reduce their own concerns about their competency and lack of self-esteem.

This was seen, almost in caricature, in California. In 1998, the state finally passed a series of education reforms designed to get the state out of the educational basement where it had sunk. Public hearings were held on new, tougher curriculum standards, at which the public and educators testified. The California Teachers Association, the union, stayed neutral, but a number of teachers rose in opposition to the changes.

Once more the villain was "facts," as they called what is better known to the educated as knowledge. They told the board that they were afraid the contemplated new standards involved too many *facts* and stressed memorization.

"If you start boring kids to death with fact, fact, fact, especially in social studies, you're going to lose them," said a middle school teacher in Huntington Beach. A science and math coordinator for Irvine also objected, stating that the new standards were too tough for youngsters, probably meaning herself. "We can all do better, but we've got to be reasonable," she complained.

Since we cannot rely on the status quo or the falsely innovative Establishment to improve the curriculum, change must come—as in California—from state legislators pressured by a concerned public. Unfortunately, the public at large is not yet sufficiently informed or mobilized to call for overall change. When it becomes increasingly angered at the ignorance and anti-intellectualism in our schools, that will happen.

Meanwhile, there are many curriculum guideposts the public can learn about and use to educate their local school boards, perhaps moving them into action. In this and the previous chapter I have outlined several—from reading to mathematics and history. Another source is the Core Knowledge curriculum from the work of E. D. Hirsch, author of *Cultural Literacy,* and a series of guides for teachers in grades K–5.

Hirsch has established a foundation that now works with 800 schools nationwide to introduce a curriculum that is robust and in which *everyone* involved knows what the children are supposed to learn. The curriculum includes Egyptian history in the 1st grade; American history in the 2nd grade; math in the 3rd grade, including fractions and geometry; science in the 4th grade, concentrating on electricity; American history and geography in the 5th grade; and literature and essay writing in the 6th, from the *Odyssey* to Robert Louis Stevenson's *Dr. Jekyll and Mr. Hyde.*

The Conspiracy of Ignorance

The concept is that knowledge builds on knowledge, which stimulates understanding, then makes it possible to absorb and understand still more knowledge—the exact opposite of flawed contemporary Establishment theory.

In science, for example, which is taught each year from kindergarten through the 6th grade in the Core Knowledge curriculum, the students start with magnetism; go on to matter and atoms; then magnetic fields in 2nd grade; protons, neutrons, and electrons in 4th grade; the periodic table of elements, molecules, and compounds in 5th grade; culminating in heat, temperature, and kinetic energy in 6th grade.

Compare this with the typical elementary school curriculum, and be prepared to laugh at the vacuous nature of public school teaching.

7

THE PSYCHOLOGIZED CLASSROOM

Counseling, Personality Testing, and Dr. Freud

Answer *yes* or *no* to the following questions:

1. Have you ever thought of or attempted suicide?
2. Have you ever thought of or attempted to harm anyone else?
3. Are there any family problems upsetting you?
4. Do you hate coming to school?
5. I believe I have special powers others do not have.
6. Do you like yourself?

These queries are sampled from a forty-three-question personality test in which students are asked to confess private matters about themselves and their families. It was not administered by a psychiatric clinic, as one would expect, but was given to schoolchildren in a Pittsburgh suburb. This questionnaire, and many like it, are representative of a growing educational movement that views American public schools as adjunct mental health clinics.

The 1983 federal report spoke of students as being "at risk" academically. Today the Establishment views the student body as being at risk emotionally as well, and therefore in need of the school's supposed help in dealing with psychological problems and suspect feelings.

As dedication to knowledge has decreased, the probing of youthful psyches has increased, reaching a pinnacle today. With the help of teachers and principals, a legion of psychological specialists in our schools coast-to-coast are questioning children from kindergarten to senior high school, seeking confessions of conflicts, family troubles, fears, even neuroses—with no evidence that it has helped students, and may actually have had a negative effect.

"A lot of this psychological work is being done in the school without the knowledge or permission of parents," says Representative Sam Rohrer of the Pennsylvania legislature, who supplied me with numerous psychological tests given to schoolchildren in his state.

"Not long ago the federal government gave a grant to a local psychiatric institute," he explained when interviewed. "The personality testing they gave to students was exposed in a local newspaper. When I learned that the parents didn't know what was going on, I put in a bill requiring parental permission—or allowing their child to opt out of the psychological testing. But because of the strong education lobby, it was killed in the House Education Committee. I'm trying again this year. I don't think this type of activity belongs in the schoolroom. It violates the privacy of both the children and parents."

The case that triggered Rohrer's bill involved the federal National Institute of Mental Health, which gave a grant to a local psychiatric institute to study the psyches of schoolchildren in three local school districts. The institute's job reportedly was to profile the students psychologically, seeking out emotional problems, including "attention deficit disorder," a fashionable ailment that is often overdiagnosed, resulting in the medication of students.

This is just one of scores of grants made by the NIMH to peer into the minds and behavior of our schoolchildren from a psychological, or even psychiatric, point of view.

"There are a lot of schoolboys in my district who have been diagnosed as having ADD and were given Ritalin to make it easier for teachers to handle them," says Representative Rohrer. "Much of that started with psychological testing in the schools, which gave school personnel leads to follow up, some ending up in a psychiatrist's office. I know of cases where school officials told parents not to bring the child back to school until he was on medication."

The amount of psychological probing of students varies from school district to school district, but it is widespread nationally. It is often treated as a near secret and seldom discussed with parents or the community. In many cases, knowledge of the practice is withheld from the school boards as well, as it was in the Pittsburgh probe.

The variety of psychological and personality tests is endless, all seeking out student vulnerability, which is probably aggravated by supposed professional attention. One test, called the Student Stress Survey, used in a 6th grade class in middle school, consists of twelve true-false questions, including:

- "I fight with my parents often."
- "My parents treat other children in my family better than they treat me."
- "My parents are headed for a divorce."

If the student answers *yes* too often, the school advises the youngster to talk it out with a teacher or guidance counselor.

This type of intervention involves children as early as 3rd grade. One test given by the guidance counselor in a Pennsylvania school district tries to quantify the child's "worries," simultaneously teaching the student the false view that privacy is not an important quality.

This test, called "Worrying About Life," states "I worry about . . ." The nine-year-old is asked to answer "often," "sometimes," or "never" to such items as "I worry about some past things I have done"; "my parents growing old"; "what people think of me."

These are not just ad hoc tests dreamed up by individual schools. The Pennsylvania Department of Education sponsors a test called Strengths and Weaknesses, which asks 7th graders to complete such statements as "If I ran for President, my opponent would say my biggest fault is . . ." and "My parents say I need to. . . ."

On the one hand, the schools try to boost the child's self-esteem academically, generally beyond reasonability. But in their probing of psyches, they do quite the opposite, planting seeds of psychological doubt and vulnerability.

The typical psychologized schoolhouse has what they call a "mental health team." It starts with the classroom teacher, and includes psychological personnel from the guidance counselor (now simply called "school counselor"), to the school social worker, to the school psychologist.

Since it is a public school, this psychological intervention must by law have some educational rationale. The Establishment claims that it is required because emotional problems can hinder learning. But the reality is that many schools operate in much the same way as psychological clinics.

Once a child has been "profiled" and seems in need of help, the team works up an "education plan" that tries to divine how the student's emotional state is hindering learning. After the child is further tested by the school psychologist, the parents might be called in and told that the student needs further help— either from the school psychologist or from an outside therapist. The recommendation might even include the name of a psychiatrist who can order medication for the student.

School psychological teams were rare in the 1950s but have proliferated in the last thirty years. *By now their work as counselors, probers, testers, and even as unauthorized, unlicensed therapists is taken for granted, as if this were a normal function of the American school—which it is not.* (Politicians, please note.)

As instruction in knowledge has diminished, the schools have expanded their jurisdiction to the "whole child," much as they have done with "whole language." If less interested in the context of the Gettysburg Address or the Bill of Rights, they have become compulsively interested in the child's feelings, attitudes, emotions, even his or her beliefs.

Some think this interest parallels the Establishment's desire for increased control of the child, decreased influence of the family, and greater power for the schools with children and thus over society. This suspicion (paranoia?) fits in well with the self-image of teachers as following the social work/psychology model rather than that of the time-tested instructor, which is the university paradigm.

The result is that the ranks of school "mental health" workers have risen alarmingly. In 1958, the federal government passed the National Defense Education Act, an attempt to move us ahead in the space effort after Sputnik. But included in the act was federal support for guidance counselors, most of whom were then called vocational counselors. Originally, they were mainly interested in helping students choose the right college or the appropriate career, which was the true intent of the bill.

With federal help, the number of counselors increased dramatically. Meanwhile the neo-Freudian influence in society at large rose with the glamorization of psychoanalysis, psychotherapy, and psychological testing—in popular literature, television, and films. The emphasis of counselors increasingly shifted from offering students practical advice to the more glamorous, if more subjective, arena of "feelings" and "conflicts."

In 1958, there were only 12,000 school counselors, a number that the Department of Education says reached 88,000 in the 1995–96 school year. According to the American School Counseling Association, it is now over 90,000 and may be approaching 100,000.

School psychologists have risen in number even more dramatically. The U.S. Department of Education states that forty years ago, in the 1959–60 school year, there were only 2,054 school psychologists, a number that has grown to some 25,000, according to the National Association of School Psychologists.

In profiling students with psychological tests, the schools' motives are often well disguised. In some districts students are tricked into believing that the tests involve learning, when in fact they are being led to reveal their feelings—now considered within the Establishment's province.

In Pennsylvania, Representative Rohrer explains that there is a statewide test called the Education Quality Assessment, which sounds like an evaluation of the student's knowledge. But the *majority* of questions involve emotions and attitudes rather than information.

For example:

"You are asked to sit at a table with retarded students. In this situation you would feel (a) Very comfortable (b) Comfortable (c) Slightly uncomfortable (d) Very uncomfortable."

Naturally, there are "correct" answers—those that fit the school's concept of how a child *should* feel.

The probing of student values, once the province of the family, is now done by many schools as well. Sometimes the inquiry is surreptitious, as in the Pennsylvania test. But it may also be open. In one case, an ethical values test was given to students in a high school honors class in biology. The youngsters were told to respond by answering whether they agreed or disagreed with such queries as:

"If you preferred blue eyes to brown eyes, it would be acceptable to employ gene surgery to modify the genes to produce a blue-eyed child" or

"I would choose to abort a fetus shown to be genetically inferior."

In many cases, tests of values can split parents and children by intimating that the belief systems of the two generations are inherently different and that the child's *true needs and values* are better expressed by the school than by the parents.

This type of indoctrination, where it exists, starts early. A questionnaire entitled My Beliefs—My Parents' Beliefs, was given to a 3rd grade class of eight-year-olds. It stated such beliefs as "Religion should be an important part of everyone's life," then had students fill in the blanks for "My Beliefs" followed by "My Parents' Beliefs." Other such items included "Women should stay home to raise their children."

There is a growing suspicion that schools have adopted an antiparent stance demonstrated in many ways—a continuation of the Establishment's view that they know better psychologically than do parents.

Columnist John Leo in *U.S. News & World Report* states that "using students to 'reeducate' their parents is standard fare now in the schools." He describes one "health" program in which a toucan, Miranda, encourages children to confess problems at home by writing secret messages to their teacher. In a "values clarification" class in Oregon, students were asked "How many of you ever wanted to beat up on your parents?"

In California, he reports, 9th graders in one school district were told to judge whether their families operated in an "open" and "democratic" way or were "closed" and "authoritarian." There is no more effective way to break down cohesion between parents and children, and the Establishment's psychological cohorts apparently know that all too well.

When students come in voluntarily to see a counselor (perhaps triggered by such indoctrination), they are assured of "confidentiality." But what is actually meant is that the information is shared in the school, and only the parent may be kept out of the loop.

"We do not repeat to parents what our students tell us," stated an official of the American School Counselors Association when interviewed. "Students come to us as self-referrals with many problems, most of them developmental ones. High schoolers will tell us that they want to stay out late but that their parents won't let them. Or a girl will complain that her best friend stole her boyfriend. Most school districts do not require that we contact the parent when we do short-term counseling, what we call 'behavioral teaching,' which might involve one session a week for six to eight weeks. If the situation is more profound, involving a deep-seated problem, we would usually send the student to the school psychologist for longer-term counseling."

"Shouldn't parents know what's going on?" I asked, perhaps naively.

"The student is our client. We need the youngster's permission to notify the parent. Counseling is a confidential one-on-one relationship," she responded.

In the case of a private counselor or psychologist, the parent is always involved. Yet the public schools have decided that what goes on in their counseling sessions is often none of the parent's business.

"What if a young high school girl is pregnant?" I asked. "Do you then notify the parent?"

"No, not if it's a normal pregnancy. But we would ask the girl if she would agree to attend a conference with the counselor and her parents. We believe confidentiality is important. Otherwise the students wouldn't come to us with their problems. But there are exceptions to our rule. If we think the student is dangerous to herself—contemplating suicide—we will notify the parents and the administration. The same is true if the child has threatened another student."

School counselors will do "short-term" mental health work or "behavioral teaching" with a student, but they scrupulously shy away from the "P" word—psychotherapy. That's because school counselors have never been authorized by law, nor are they sufficiently trained, to do psychological probing, especially not psychotherapy. That has a professional and legal meaning beyond their licensure as guidance counselors. But that apparently doesn't stop them from engaging in psychological intervention with students for a month or two on a regular basis.

To make sure there are enough clients to justify their numbers, some counselors advertise to students with flyers. One—headlined "Do You Need Help With Family Problems?"—was produced with little cartoons and four boxes.

Three of the boxes were provocatively headed as follows: "Do You Feel Your Parents Don't Understand You?"; "Is There Too Much Pressure From Parents? (Do they worry too much about grades?)"; and "Do You Fight With Brothers and Sisters? (Is it lack of caring—or just not enough privacy?)." The fourth box was the psychological pitch: "Talking over these problems with your counselor can give you a better perspective."

The obvious conclusion is that the counselors are seeking to capitalize on differences between parents and adolescents, an age-old trial of the species.

Longer-term intervention in the child's psyche is handled by the school psychologist, often by referral from the counselor or teacher. But neither is that activity legally permitted *if* it is considered psychotherapy. School psychologists are supposed to do testing, mainly to evaluate whether a child is learning impaired and requires "special education," the fastest rising category in American schools.

In the mid-1970s, the federal government initiated the IDEA program, an acronym for Individuals with Disabilities Education Act. One would expect perhaps 5 percent of children to be considered "disabled" or "special," enabling the school district to get aid in educating them. But the high enrollment in the program surprised everyone as an avalanche of youngsters became "special ed" students.

Aside from physical impairments such as blindness, deafness, autism, mental retardation, and physically crippling symptoms, the law listed seven other categories, which were somewhat psychological and vague. They included "specific learning disabilities," "serious emotional disturbance," and "speech or language impairments." These syndromes are so loosely defined that it has resulted in an explosion of special education enrollment.

The result is that the roster of IDEA students has now reached over 6 million children, considerably more than anyone anticipated.

The cost of special education has reached phenomenal proportions, some $100 billion a year, or $17,000 a student. Each special ed student costs taxpayers more than twice as much as a regular student. In New York City, it runs almost triple the cost, $22,000 a schoolchild. Of this monumental cost, Washington contributes only $7 billion a year, but like much that emanates from the capital, they wag the dog.

The federal government has created a mainly unfunded mandate under IDEA legislation that *requires* school districts to provide detailed services for every child labeled "special." In some cases, this even requires districts to send children to expensive *private schools*.

Like most federal mandates, the money comes out of local pockets, placing an enormous burden on school taxpayers. One major cost is for the salaries of 270,000 special education teachers.

The gatekeeper in cases of "emotional problems" and general "learning disabilities"—the person who has the responsibility to test and admit students into this program—is that same school psychologist.

What percent of children are educationally "disabled," according to the formula? Nationwide, it is an amazingly high 12 percent, or 1 in 8—more in inner cities and less in suburban districts. But in a flagrant distortion of common sense, the upscale community of Greenwich, Connecticut, where more than 80 percent of the youngsters go on to four-year colleges, announced in late 1998 that *1 in 5 high school students, or 19.8 percent*, were "disabled" according to the strange IDEA criteria.

Greenwich school authorities stated that the majority of these students had disciplinary problems, poor attendance records, and did not do their homework. In this therapeutic age, where we have 125,000 school counselors and school psychologists, it appeared inevitable that some of the undisciplined, less bright, or uninterested students would now be labeled "disabled."

In prior, more rational times, those students would probably have decided that they were not college material and would have dropped out and gotten a job, retaining their dignity.

Of course some students do have serious emotional problems that keep them from performing well, especially on tests. No one knows how many children are truly qualified for special ed programs, but for those who are, it can be a valuable program, one that can even include one-on-one tutoring from a special ed teacher.

The Conspiracy of Ignorance

In Greenwich, however, almost 22 percent of the entire school budget was being spent on special education children. This in a town where 70 percent of the adults are college graduates, where the mean household income is $120,000, and where the average house sells for $1.1 million.

Only the Establishment could turn sociology upside down and find that 20 percent of high school students were in some way "learning disabled" in such a privileged, educated community. A spokeperson for the Greenwich schools states that much of the blame rests with parents, who want to enroll their children in the special education program because it is reportedly an excellent full-service operation for students who need extra help.

"The parents know the law—that we have to provide it if the child qualifies by federal IDEA standards," she states. "Years ago there was a stigma to being labeled 'disabled,' but no longer. Now parents threaten to sue us if we don't put their child in the program, which is quite expensive. But so are legal fees defending the district against parents. Now, we are trying to cut down the special education enrollment."

Nationwide, many special ed children covered by the IDEA program were diagnosed by one of the 25,000 school psychologists. *But in a strange anomoly, it turns out that the great majority of these supposed psychologists are not psychologists after all.* To be licensed to practice psychology, one must usually have a Ph.D. in the subject. But of the 25,000 school psychologists, only 7,000 have that advanced degree. Although they are not permitted to do psychological work in the public arena, they can practice on schoolchildren, all taxpayer paid.

One would think that a school psychologist's credentials would have to be stronger than those of an ordinary psychologist. But exactly the opposite is the case. Not only are the overwhelming percentage of them not licensed psychologists but they generally have only an Ed.S., an educational specialist degree.

Even less well-trained teachers are drawn into the school mental health watch as well. In one professional journal, guidance counselor Irving Doress tells teachers not to shy away from their psychological role. Instead they should confidently accept themselves as *teacher-therapists*, the first line in mental health prevention work.

"Don't sell yourself short because 'I'm not a therapist' or 'I had only three psych courses' or 'I might destroy the child's psychological balance,'" he writes. "Take a chance, follow your instincts. You'll probably do no more harm and much good."

Many teachers take that chance, often focusing more on Johnny's psychological problems than on his multiplication tables. Of course, those "three psych courses" the guidance counselor speaks of are potential landmines, which can do more harm to students than good. Not only is amateur psychology dangerous in the hands of teachers, but that emphasis detracts enormously from the proper goal of educating children—which is to impart knowledge and not play Dr. Freud at taxpayers' expense.

The view of the classroom as a psychological laboratory was advocated some years ago when Dr. Stonewall B. Stickney, former director of school mental health services in Pittsburgh, wrote in the *American Journal of Psychiatry* that "schools are our community mental health centers." Stating that of the 390,000 students then in the city's school system, 39,000 were "emotionally disturbed," he believed it was the school's responsibility to test and screen them out as a prelude to therapy—perhaps the guiding inspiration for many psychologized school systems today.

As we've seen, a spokesperson for the national counseling organization tried to soft-pedal the psychological aspects of its work, especially its fear of the "P" word. But a professor of educational psychology at the University of Michigan, Lawrence M. Brammer, has advised them not to be faint-hearted.

In his article "The Counselor Is a Psychologist," he tells counselors that "social workers and psychologists look with mild contempt on school counselors who identify only with the guidance model." The answer, he says, is to join with other school mental health people and become part of the "counseling psychological model."

History indicates that most school systems have followed his advice.

A school psychologist in Westchester County, New York, when interviewed by me, explained that much of the counseling and therapy work done in schools is extralegal, a euphemism for illegality. "We school psychologists are here because the law of New York State says that in order to label a youngster as mentally retarded, he must be diagnosed as such by a school psychologist."

The original intent of the law was to have school psychologists test students for their ability to learn, then diagnose those who were unable. That mandate expanded until school psychologists tested larger and larger numbers of students and for different, less significant reasons.

Their regimen generally includes such tests as the Wechsler intelligence measure along with a battery of others to probe the child's personality, fears, and supposed "inner self." The latter include such controversial *projective* instruments as the famed Rorschach inkblots (for which special training is required) along with the Thematic Apperception Test and the Draw-A-Man Test, both of which are Freudian "deep probe" instruments open to many interpretations.

The problem is that these tests are too subjective, while the more simplistic personality questionnaires are generally inaccurate, can be faked, and have grave statistical flaws. I explained that in my book *The Brain Watchers*, then testified before Congress, which subsequently passed legislation making it illegal to use such tests in the hiring of federal government employees. The same strictures should apply to public schools and their usually undertrained non-psychologist "school psychologists."

Another danger is that excess mental probing can do damage by placing negative ideas into a child's impressionable mind. One test, labeled Health Education, deals with suicide as a subject. It begins with a suicide note to her mother and father from a fictional teenager, Jennifer, who is about to kill herself.

Jennifer mentions that she did a report on the poet Sylvia Plath, who killed herself. "Dying is an art, like everything else. I do it exceptionally well," Plath wrote. Jennifer adds, "You see, I'm the same way."

The test asks the student to analyze Jennifer's suicide note and what it reveals about her. They also want to know how the reader reacted. "How did you feel?" it asks. For every counselor who believes this is an adventure into better mental health, there should be a parent who believes that overimpressionable teenagers should not be presented with such overstimulating material in school.

The continuing debate over the use and misuse of counseling in the school setting revolves around whether or not district personnel are capable of practicing even a modified form of psychology and whether or not what they do is psychotherapy, which is not authorized by law.

"The way I see my job is to look after the best interest of the youngster, from the point of view of mental health," the Westchester school psychologist said. "I don't do psychotherapy, I counsel."

"What's the difference between the two?" I asked.

"Counseling is different in that it is more pragmatic and short term. It is the application of psychological skills to help people manage, to deal with stress, to be all right."

Either one is a stretch of the school psychologist's original responsibility as a tester of mental deficiency. It also represents an intrusion into the privacy of the family structure by the schools, especially when no parental permission is required. In fact, by labeling what is essentially psychotherapy as counseling, no matter how long the process, schools may be inventing a semantic subterfuge to circumvent the law.

Some skeptical psychologists outside the school system question both the ethics and the accuracy of the school psychological operation. Dr. Henry Winthrop, formerly on the faculty of the University of South Florida, saw it as operating in "bad faith."

Writing in the journal *Mental Hygiene*, he complained that school psychologists may be treating inaccurate psychological tests with undue reverence, as if they were gospel. "Consider the terrible situation in which a silly and overserious psychologist decides that a student is mentally deranged and bases that decision only upon the results of a few, routine psychological tests," he advised.

Winthrop also attacked schools' *lack of confidentiality*. "What shall we say of the school therapist who, in dealing with a student who comes for counseling in good faith, assigns that student a psychiatric label, which he then inserts in the counselee's folder so that the diagnosis can follow the counselee for years and impair the transfer from one school to another?"

A school psychologist, this one in Connecticut, once described to me how he scouts out psychological customers rather than waiting for them to come in. He makes initial contact with large numbers of students through *class meetings*, a kind of primitive group therapy session that parents are often unaware of. The children are aware that they are being encouraged to talk out their problems in front of other children. "The kids know it involves feelings, behavior, emotions, and getting along," he revealed.

If either the teacher or any member of the "team" believes a student is having difficulty learning, or has problems in personal social adjustment, it can trigger a full psychological evaluation by the school psychologist. Large numbers of children can be involved.

After being observed in the classroom, the student is put through a battery of educational and psychological tests, followed by psychological interviews, which often include the parents as well. A school social worker may also be called in. If further treatment is considered necessary, the child might be referred to a private psychiatrist.

Despite promises of confidentiality, the results, including the scores on psychological tests and reports on counseling sessions, are entered in the child's school record. The record stays there from its inception, perhaps in kindergarten or 1st grade, through the completion of high school. The details may not go on to college, but often the fact that the student has been seen by a school psychologist is noted and becomes known to the university admissions officer.

"The child may be too shy or withdrawn, or exhibit any behavior which the teacher feels is beyond expected behavior: inattentiveness, extreme physical activity, pugnaciousness, or unhappy or depressed behavior," the Connecticut school psychologist explained. "The philosophy behind what we do is that modern education is more than just the three Rs. Getting along with other people is part of the democratic social goal."

This modern educational concept of the primacy of "getting along" has several major flaws. That is especially true in the development of children who may one day become leaders, either because of a strong personality or academic success, or a mixture of the two.

One flaw in the school psychologist's thinking is that the bugaboo of "inattentiveness" may be the defense of a bored bright student forced to put up with the inadequacies of public school teaching and a limited curriculum. "Pugnaciousness" may be a problem for teachers and school psychologists, but it can also be a prime trait for future chief executives of corporations, movie producers, entrepreneurs, radio talk show hosts, investigative journalists, even crusading politicians. "Depressed behavior" now and then can simply mean that the youngster is a member of the human race.

Much of this is an instrinsic part of the *neat* and unexceptional ethos that permeates our schools and, by extrapolation, our society in general. Psychological emphasis in the public schools seems to have several major results. Among them are the denigration of idiosyncratic behavior, the hallmark of many true achievers; the mental corraling of creative youngsters; the too-easy application of psychological labels when uncalled for; and perhaps most important, strengthening of the forces of conformity in an already conformist society.

All are detectable within the Establishment when they speak of the enemy—the critics of public schools—as "elitists," an insult often aimed at those of superior intelligence, especially when contrasted with themselves.

The "elitist" concept is, of course, at the spiritual center of such extraordinary schools as Choate, Stuyvesant High, the Bronx High School of Science, Groton, Andover, and Exeter. Not every child can handle such an education, but the infusion of a touch of the elitist mentality into the Establishment might go far in dispelling the pap pop psychological rationale of the public schools and raise their present antischolarly goals.

Mental health work in the school setting seems more pigeon-holing than it is preventive of anything. Special ed programs can help certain children who are bright but have emotional problems that hold them back, but it is now obvious that by and large, psychology has been oversold in the schools, both in the training of teachers and in the probing of young psyches—which have a devilish way of growing up without intervention, thank you. It may also wreak havoc in the parent-child relationship and cause oversensitive youngsters to exaggerate normal fears and vulnerabilities, especially at puberty, resulting in potential damage.

There is no doubt that the Establishment's psychological emphasis is mainly unwarranted, but parents must shoulder some of the blame. Too often they fail to keep up with what's happening to their children in school, which gives the school tacit permission to invade their and their child's privacy. Too many parents abdicate responsibility, trusting their child's psyche to the school district, which can be an error of judgment.

Most important, there is no scientific evidence that the psychologized schoolhouse is of any advantage to the great majority of students—that it has in any way reduced anxieties or emotional conflicts or calmed the perfectly normal fears and uncertainties of early and later adolescence.

Nor has it been effective in preventing the epidemic of school violence, or predicting which students would be involved. Perhaps what is required in the school setting is not more psychology, but more spiritual guidance. Like most Americans, I insist on the general separation of church and state, lest we adopt the undemocratic concept of an established theology. But *voluntary* spiritual guidance is part of our tradition, as witness the large number of full-time clergy attached to our armed forces. The regular presence of ministers, priests, and rabbis on school sites, available to counsel students, might do as much or more than all the psychological personnel and their Rorschach inkblots.

The overwhelming and apparently ineffective presence of psychology in our schools exists mainly because the Establishment has hung its tottering professionalism on that unsteady base and seeks to expand that province in every way possible. In fact, a strong case can be made that in addition to diverting attention away from sound academic instruction, the psychologized school has been one of the great neurotic stimuli of all time.

To remedy the situation requires a retreat from psychology in the school setting and a strident advance into the more difficult but more rewarding world of scholarship.

8

PRIVATE, PAROCHIAL, AND CHARTER SCHOOLS

Superior Education and a Matter of Choice

Presidents are proud of their concern for education, and the title of "education president" is one they seek almost as fervently as they do their official one. Federal aid to education is their tool, even if it is usually ineffective.

But those presidents with school-age children of their own have to approach the situation more personally. Where in Washington, D.C., should they send their offspring to be educated—to the weak public city school system or under the protective umbrella of an elite private school?

This dilemma challenged two of our youngest presidents, Jimmy Carter and Bill Clinton, both of whom had a school-age daughter. But they faced the challenge in decidedly different ways.

In 1977, Amy Carter, the First Couple's daughter, had to attend elementary school in Washington, D.C. The Carters, long admirers of public education and integration, decided to act on their ideals. They sent Amy to a public school in the District, whose school system scores at the very bottom in federal NAEP test results. Without fanfare, she spent four years in a Washington public school before returning to Georgia.

In 1993, the Clintons faced the same dilemma. Chelsea, then almost thirteen, either had to tread the public school path of Amy Carter, or not. After all, Mr. Clinton, following the lead of George Bush, had named himself an "education president," with a strong, vested political interest in the public school system, the teachers' unions, and an egalitarian ethos.

But the Clintons' concern for their child apparently overwhelmed those ideals. Until she went off to Stanford University in 1998, Chelsea studied at Sidwell Friends School, an exclusive, expensive private academy in the fashionable northwest section of the District that charges $15,620 a year tuition for its upper school.

Many parents face that same dilemma, as I did when my children were young. In New York City, there are occasional islands of excellence. I was fortunate enough to live in the relatively good P.S. 6 school district on the Upper East Side, saving me the cost of private schools in the elementary grades.

Why fortunate? Are private schools so overwhelmingly better than public schools, And if so, why?

In terms of decorum, discipline, and behavior of the students, the answer is assuredly *yes*. There are many reasons for that, but the major factor is that most private schools simply will not countenance poor behavior or, generally, excessively lazy students. They simply ask students to leave, a solution not available to public schools. That one advantage makes private schools, if one can afford them, a reasonable alternative to public schools.

But advocates of private schools point to another, perhaps more important attraction. They perform better academically.

There is no doubt of that. Take the SAT scores. In 1998, public school students had a mean score of 1,011. Religiously affiliated schools—Catholic, Protestant, and Jewish—had a mean of 1,042. Independent secular private schools scored considerably higher than either, with a mean of 1,111—100 points above that of public schools. In the years 1997 and 1996, the relationships were almost identical to those in 1998.

The NAEP scores show much the same gap, with the private schools solidly ahead. In the 1996 science test results, 8th graders in public schools scored an average of 148, compared with Catholic school students, at 163, and other private schools, at 161. In history studies, the spread between public and private was just as large. Students in Catholic and other private schools beat out the public ones by 20 points.

Which brings up the age-old question: Do children in private schools perform better because of the teaching and curriculum or because the student body is better academically to begin with?

When we speak of private schools, most think of the elite secondary institutions with high intellectual standards—the famed prep schools. Those include Choate, JFK's alma mater, which he attended before going on to Harvard; Groton, FDR's school before Harvard; and Philips-Andover, where George Bush prepped before Yale. These schools are not only academically strong, but quite expensive. In 1999, for instance, tuition at Groton was $19,420 *without board.*

When hiring teachers, the elite secondary schools turn up their noses at education graduates, cognizant that most are not qualified to teach their bright students. Just as Connecticut doesn't require Choate to hire state-certified teachers—with their inadequate academic background and peculiar theories—so Massachusetts gives similar leeway to private schools such as Groton, where students average an outstanding 1,380 on their SATs, some 400 points more than education majors. Like

Choate, Groton hires "untrained" scholars as faculty members, often a prime determinant of school quality.

But the elite prep schools are not typical of the 6,357 independent private schools that are not affiliated with religious organizations. Most of these schools have no national reputation and do not necessarily have scholar-teachers. But they still perform considerably better than public schools.

Many private schools only teach children from preschool through the 9th grade—schools such as the Country Day School in Greenwich ($15,000 tuition) and the Rippowan-Cisqua School in the Town of Bedford (tuition $17,000), where many of the wealthy in Westchester County, New York, send their children.

"We do not discriminate against anyone, except intellectually," says a spokesperson for the National Association of Independent Schools, which represents 1,100 academies. "Our schools are all 501-C3 nonprofit organizations and cover the spectrum from preschool through the 13th grade. They are mainly secular schools, though some have a religious tradition. But they must not be attached to a church and must have an independent board of directors. Our minority enrollment is 17 percent, which, though lower than in public schools, is considerable. Our schools are of every type. Some are very competitive, and others are nurturing."

The total enrollment of this group is only a half-million, or some 1 percent of the total student population. Members of the NAIS represent almost three-fourths of all 769,000 students in independent private schools.

The second group of private schools is religiously based, with a sizeable enrollment of more than five million children, or some 10 percent of the U.S. student body. The largest among the religious schools are the Catholic, or parochial, schools, which educate children through grade 12, with a student population of 2.6 million. Of the nation's 28,000 private schools, 21,000 are church-affiliated, with Catholic schools making up 8,248 of that number.

The Catholic education network is massive, paralleling the public school system in most larger cities. In structure, they are not very different. In many Catholic dioceses, the teachers—as in public schools—are required to be state certified. Nuns and brothers also teach, but some 85 percent of the faculty are lay-people.

What makes them different from public school teachers? There are four factors:

1. Catholic school teachers get paid considerably less, closer to $25,000 a year than $40,000, which is partially explained by their being "called" to the work.
2. Their religious faith is part of their teaching commitment.
3. Many are graduates of Catholic colleges, which place less emphasis on the *nonsense* aspect of contemporary teacher training, including the faddish antifact, antiphonics, self-esteem theories. Instead, many stress traditional teaching, including effective, if unfashionable, "rote" learning.
4. They have a stronger regard for discipline, order, and homework, all ingredients of a better education.

The results are rather extraordinary. According to the National Catholic Education Association, they graduate 97 percent of their high school students and send 94 percent of them to either two- or four-year colleges, a record that dwarfs that of the public schools. On the SATs and NAEP tests, as we've seen, Catholic school students outperform their public school cousins.

But, shouts the Establishment, the comparison is not fair.

Why? Because, say public school advocates, Catholic schools don't have to educate masses of minority children. That charge is simply not true. In reality, Catholic schools have a sizable minority enrollment of 25 percent, almost equal to that of public schools. Most important, a minority graduate of a Catholic high school is three times more likely to earn a college degree than is a minority graduate of a public school. Their chances are some 25 percent (1 in 4) versus less than 9 percent (1 in 11) for public schoolers.

But, the Establishment complains once more, minority children in public schools are poorer than those in Catholic schools.

There are no exact figures by which to weigh this, but it's evident that the superiority of Catholic education often extends into the depths of the poorest inner-city neighborhoods. The Hales Franciscan parochial school in Chicago, whose student body is mostly African-American, programmed its answering machine a few years ago to say, "One hundred percent of our students were admitted to college."

Most children in that school—which concentrates on math and English—are poor and on some form of financial assistance.

In 1980, the late James S. Coleman, a prominent University of Chicago sociologist, studied performance in high schools and found that students in Catholic institutions learned more than those in public school. Controversy surrounded the report, but in 1987, he produced follow-up material that confirmed his original study.

He rejected the public school claim that Catholic school students performed better simply because they were more talented or because they came from "better" (richer) families. The difference, he said, was in the schools: Students learned more in Catholic schools than did those of similar background and ability in public schools. He also concluded that Catholic schooling lowers high school dropout rates.

More recently, in 1997, Derek Neal, an associate professor of economics at the University of Chicago, conducted another study. Using the data from the National Longitudinal Survey of Youth, he concluded that Catholic schooling increased the chances of graduating from high school by 26 percent, basically confirming Coleman's findings.

Neal found that African-American and Hispanic students in Catholic schools in urban counties actually had a higher (91 percent) graduation rate than urban whites in public schools (87 percent). Meanwhile, only 62 percent of urban African-Americans and Hispanics graduated from public high schools.

To disprove the poverty theory, Neal compared urban minority Catholic school children with similar students in public school in terms of parents' education, occupation, family structure, and reading materials at home. The poorer Catholic students had a graduation rate of 88 percent, somewhat less than their peers but still much higher than the graduation rate of minority public school students.

Increasingly, the success of Catholic parochial schools is being gossiped about in many communities, granting them star power. Their attraction is not just to minorities but to higher-income professional and executive parents of all backgrounds who are angered by the poor education and decorum in many public schools.

In the *New York Observer*, a paper published in Manhattan with a large upper-income secular readership, Anne Roiphe writes, "There are paths through the blackboard jungle. The Catholic schools do better. They offer discipline, hope and order, and they beat the streets . . . through the fierceness of the will of the teachers, through the imposed order of the church and its representatives."

In *America*, a prominent Catholic magazine, Gail Lumet Buckley adds that in parochial schools, the children "are also taught respectful behavior and self-control, two secrets of future success."

Despite their good academic record, Catholic schools are, of course, not for everyone. Most Protestant and Jewish parents who want to leave the public school system would prefer to send their children elsewhere.

For those who cannot afford the elite independent private schools, there is a large network of Protestant academies, from kindergarten through high school. These Christian religious schools are collectively almost as large as the Catholic network, with 13,000 schools and 1.8 million students, an enrollment that is growing.

One of the largest groups is the Association of Christian Schools International, which represents more than half the students in Protestant day schools.

Tuition is much lower in these Christian schools than in the elite private ones, yet achievement is almost as high. On the Stanford Achievement Test, for example, the almost one million children in ACSI schools scored considerably above the national norm at every grade level. In the 4th grade, where the national norm is 4.5, these Christian school students scored 6.5, some two grades higher than their age group.

What is the secret?

"Our schools cover almost all the Protestant denominations including Baptist, Lutheran, Episcopal, Presbyterian, and numerous interdenominational faiths," says Tom Scott of the ACSI. "We try to keep the tuition as low as possible, and I would say it runs about $3,000 a year for elementary schools and $4,000 for high school, although our actual costs are higher. Our curriculum is also stronger than in public schools."

In Protestant high schools, he explained, that typically includes at least three years each of math, a foreign language, science, and history and at least a year of geography. The students generally take prealgebra in the 8th grade, algebra 1 in 9th, and algebra 2 in 10th.

"Most students in the college preparatory programs also take advanced math," he adds. "In some schools we are beginning classical studies in Latin and Greek. About 94 percent of our students go on to higher education, with between 80 and 85 percent to four-year colleges."

Aside from a strong curriculum, Scott says that there are other, more spiritual, advantages for students and parents in Protestant schools.

"We don't seek to fulfill the immediate needs of the child as the public schools do. Instead we are concerned about the needs of the whole family within the community. The Bible sets a moral tone for the school in establishing what is right and what is wrong," Scott emphasizes. "I once taught in public school in Ohio, where I was told that we had no right to correct the child on matters of morals. We were just 'facilitators' and were not to become involved in teaching moral values. Here in our Christian schools it's exactly the opposite. Our children learn moral lessons along with knowledge. We also have the advantage of teachers for whom it is not just a job but a life's endeavor based on faith."

One of the surprises in the religious private school area is the growth of Jewish schools, yeshivas, and day schools sponsored by various groups, including the Orthodox, the Conservative, and the Reform adherents of that faith. In a nation of some 6 million Jews, 170,000 children attend Jewish day schools, which proportionately represents a larger percentage of students than that of Protestants who attend religious schools.

One Jewish parent, a professor of education at the University of North Carolina, writing in the liberal publication *Tikkun*, debated his decision to send his daughter Sarah to a religious day school instead of to public school. "While I find the pedagogy too conventional," he writes, "my daughter has found the place to be nurturant and loving. She has, for the most part, found delight in being there—a place where schooling has sustained her, not opposed her life."

The Conspiracy of Ignorance

He argues with himself as he must make a decision on where to send her for the 6th grade. While he admires her Jewish schooling, on the other hand he appreciates the value of public education. "In its ideal rendering," he says, "public schooling represents a space where all of our children may be educated."

What did he decide? He ended his piece still struggling. "The ultimate value of Jewish education is not found in my daughter's capacity to read or speak Hebrew . . . but whether she will become a human being deeply concerned for the worth and dignity of all the lives that share our world."

"Yet," he concludes, "I worry that my desire for this education will also boost the arguments of those who favor 'school choice.' "

Dr. Svi Shapiro, the author, had put his finger on the strongest debate in education of the upcoming millennium—how to create a rich, rewarding private educational experience not just for members of the educated upper middle class, like himself, but to grant that same privilege to other children, minority and otherwise.

The debate on vouchers rages hot and fast. The Establishment fears vouchers more than any other challenge to its supremacy. Vouchers represent free tuition money for parents, thus far anywhere from $2,250 to $4,900. With that in hand, they can exercise "choice" and enroll their children in any private school that will accept them, secular or religious.

The attraction of vouchers is especially strong for poor families, who feel trapped not only economically but educationally. They are required to attend the local schools even though the majority of children there might be reading below grade level. One recent poll showed that 68 percent of African-Americans favor vouchers, while most liberal whites oppose them as being potentially destructive to the future of public schools.

This debate—whether public funds should be used to pay

tuition for private schools, religious as well as secular—now roils the educational waters with little prospect that a definitive resolution will come anytime soon. Meanwhile, both sides, the public school Establishment and those who favor choice, are testing each other, the law, the Constitution, and public and political opinion.

The teaching unions fiercely oppose vouchers, seeing them draining money from public schools to private institutions. They also fear choice as a competitor for students, a competition in which they would probably be long-term losers, greatly reducing public school enrollments.

But in an anomaly within the dispute, public school teachers prefer to exercise choice for their own children. In Milwaukee, Wisconsin, it appears that public school teachers in two of the city's Central City districts prefer to send their own children to private school rather than to the schools where they teach. This is not a minor revolt: Some 43 percent of teachers have enrolled their youngsters in local private secular and religious institutions.

The fierce battle over vouchers is presently set as a tale of two cities: Milwaukee and Cleveland.

"School choice in our town was pioneered by Polly Williams, an African-American state legislator who represents the inner-city community of Milwaukee," explains Jeff Fleming, a spokesperson for the mayor's office in that city. "She took the idea of vouchers to pay for private schools to Mayor Norquist, a Democrat, and to Governor Thompson, a Republican, and they got on board. In 1991, the legislature passed the Milwaukee Parental Choice Program, and we now have 6,200 children going to private school, all paid for by the state."

The Milwaukee program is making educational history in America. Not only does it cover secular private schools, but in 1996 it was expanded to include religious schools as well. The idea was quite explosive, and many groups, including the Milwaukee branch of the National Education Association and the American Civil Liberties Union, attacked it as violating the Constitutional guarantee of separation of church and state, and sued.

"Initially, the lower state court ruled their way—that it was unconstitutional," explains Fleming. "Then it went to the state appeals court, which backed the lower court's ruling. The idea of the state paying for the education of students in religious schools would have been dead, but in June of 1998, the Wisconsin Supreme Court ruled that it was constitutional, which surprised a lot of people. The opponents of the program appealed the decision to the U.S. Supreme Court. But in December of 1998, the high court refused to hear the case. So, as of now, the Wisconsin court ruling holds and the program goes on."

The voucher plan is income-based, with a family ceiling set to accommodate poor youngsters in Milwaukee. Four out of five of those chosen were either African-American or Hispanic. The income cutoff point is 175 percent of the federal poverty level, which for a family of four comes to a reasonably high $29,000 a year. The voucher check is made out to parents, but it is sent to the private secular or religious school of their choice. Parents then come in to sign it. The maximum voucher is some $4,900 or the cost of tuition, whichever is lower. The only restriction is that the schools cannot require voucher students to participate in religious activities.

The present state legislation calls for a maximum of 15,000 vouchers in Milwaukee, the only city in the state that is eligible, and observers feel the program is on its way to reach that target.

The peculiar aspect of this voucher system is that the entire official education community of Milwaukee and the state of Wisconsin, including the state superintendent of education, is heavily opposed to it. Yet it operates. The majority of the elected Milwaukee public school board is also against the program. The Common Council, the city's legislative body, has not taken a stand. Its advocates are the mayor, the governor, and the state legislature, whose combined power overwhelms the opponents.

"We object to the Milwaukee voucher situation for two reasons," complains Terry Craney, head of the Wisconsin Education Association Council, which has 86,000 members and is the state branch of the National Education Association. "We were disappointed by the state supreme court decision in June 1998, which saw no problem with it. But despite what they say, we believe the constitutional issue is quite clear—taxpayer money is being used to support religious schools. We feel that is a violation of the church-state separation in the United States. The second reason is the cost, which runs about $25 million a year—every penny of which comes out of the state aid to schools, cutting into our public school budgets."

Mr. Craney admits that the public schools in Milwaukee could use improving.

"Don't the religious schools do a better job with minority children than the public schools?" I asked the local NEA president.

"I don't know, but if they do it's because they are cherry-picking the best students. We in the public schools can't choose. We have to educate everyone."

The improvement Mr. Craney admits is needed may be starting, observes Mr. Fleming of the mayor's office. But if it is taking place, he gives the credit to the voucher program acting as a competitive goad to the Establishment. Fleming sees a "glimmer" of hope in Milwaukee in a few recent moves.

"We are expanding the number of public schools that use the Montessori method in the early grades. The city government has sponsored three independent charter schools supported by tax money, and we're increasing that to seven. The University of Wisconsin in Milwaukee is thinking of starting one, and most interesting, the Medical College of Wisconsin may be setting up a special science school in the city. Right now my son is going to a

Catholic school in Milwaukee, where he's receiving an excellent education—studying the post–Civil War Reconstruction period in the 4th grade, for example, But if they start that special public science school, I'll probably transfer him back to the city system."

The arguments are clear in Milwaukee. The city is torn between two sides. The debate is between better education—which the regular public schools don't seem able to provide—and the cost of vouchers and the concept of separation of church and state. There are strong adherents on both sides of the question in Milwaukee and increasingly throughout the country.

Perhaps the person in the most strained position in Milwaukee is Charles Toulman, who runs the voucher program, which is now operating in eighty-six schools, fifty-six of which are religiously based. The strain comes from the fact that Mr. Toulman works for the state superintendent of public instruction, who is against vouchers.

"Even though we don't support the program, I run it to the best of my ability," Toulman said when interviewed. "Our objection is that there is not sufficient accountability. The students in every public school have to take a statewide achievement exam, and the teachers must be licensed and go through a background check. But the private schools are exempt. We ordered an evaluation of how the 'choice' students are doing in private schools, conducted by John Witte, a professor at the University of Wisconsin at Madison."

"What were the results?" I asked.

"Inconclusive. The students are not doing dramatically better," he answered. But he then added that "if the public schools in Milwaukee were doing great, we wouldn't have a voucher program in the first place."

That, of course, is the crux of the argument. Good schools don't need replacing or abandoning. The competition of private schools has always helped elevate public schools. But with vouchers, the comparison is now more immediate and pressing. And most important, there are few complaints from parents who received enough money to transfer their children to better, more ordered school environments.

Milwaukee's voucher plan has successfully met the legal challenge of constitutionality. But the choice program in our second city, Cleveland, is still laboriously making its way through the courts.

"I believe the landmark case on vouchers before the Supreme Court will come out of our program in Cleveland," says Bert Holt, who runs the Cleveland Scholarship and Tutoring Program. "We have had two court decisions in our favor, including the Ohio Appellate Court in 1997. Now the ACLU and the teacher's union, the American Federation of Teachers, is appealing it to the Supreme Court."

The majority of the 3,744 children in the Cleveland choice program go to religious schools, including Catholic, Protestant, and even three Muslim schools. The students are chosen by lottery—with a chance of about 1 in 2—and the parents receive up to $2,500, less 10 percent, which they must pay personally.

"The program is mainly for poor African-Americans, who make up 68 percent of the public school population in Cleveland and 68 percent of those in the voucher program," explains Ms. Holt. "As far as I'm concerned, choice is the only solution to the problem of poor education in our public schools, especially for minority children. Personally, I believe that *every* school in urban America should be a school of choice. Then either the public schools will have to come around and become outstanding or they'll have to close."

The teaching Establishment in Cleveland is up in arms about this substantial threat to their future. In fact, Ms. Holt believes that there has been an attempt to sabotage the program through lack of cooperation. She states that money for tutoring in the public schools, some 36 hours per child, has been appropriated by the state legislature as part of the plan. But most teachers refuse to participate.

"Not only that," she says, "but they're trying to stop non-teacher tutors from coming in to help the children."

The battle of vouchers versus full public education has engulfed Milwaukee and Cleveland in bitter battles between the Establishment and many in the minority community who see choice as the way out of the inner city. That war has now spread to a third city, the Big Apple, New York, the largest and most powerful in America.

In 1995, Mayor Rudolph Giuliani brought in Rudy Crew from Oakland to be the chancellor of a public system of over one million children. Hopes were high that this experienced educator would turn the city around and raise its rather pitiful reading scores, for one. There has been some small improvement and a few miraculous case histories, such as Irwin Kurz's P.S. 161. But overall, public education in New York City, where some 75 percent of the students are minorities, is still a classic case history in failure.

In March 1999, the new NAEP scores on reading were announced. As we've seen, New York State showed no gains on 4th grade reading, and scores for African-American and Hispanic students were lower than before.

In January of that year, Mayor Giuliani publicly announced that he would try to put in a voucher system for poor minority children as a last resort. That promoted an uproar of outrage from the Establishment, including the chancellor himself, who once had a strong fraternal relationship with the mayor. When delivering a speech in Miami, Mr. Giuliani said that vouchers and school choice were "the most important thing that has to be done with education in America."

"If the mayor brings vouchers to New York," Chancellor Crew announced, "I will resign."

That unsettled the air, after which Dr. Crew declared he would *not* resign as long as the voucher program was run by City Hall, a compromise of sorts.

"If the mayor wants to run his own voucher program, that's between him and the taxpayers," Dr. Crew stated. "It would not put me in the position of having to implement something I find onerous."

Mayor Giuliani hoped to mirror the Milwaukee experience by putting $12 million in vouchers in just one of the city's thirty-two school districts. The mayor has temporarily backed away from seeking approval from the seven-member school board, and the chancellor backed away from resignation for a while after which he was replaced. New York may, or may not, be the next large city to adopt vouchers.

The future of school choice depends on the resolution of what may be the crucial case from the educationally beleaguered city of Cleveland. In May 1999, the Ohio Supreme Court put a temporary roadblock in the way of that city's voucher system, ruling on a technical issue—that the state had improperly paid for the program through the state budget rather than a separate appropriation. That was corrected in time for the 1999–2000 school year with a $5.25 million authorization. In the city's favor, the court ruled that the voucher program *did not* violate the church-state separation of either Ohio or federal law.

That fall of 1999, the case went to the federal district court in Cleveland, where the presiding judge ruled the opposite of the Ohio court. He stated that the voucher program *did* violate the Establishment clause because much of the money went to parochial schools.

Judge Oliver did, however, issue a stay that those children who had *already been* in the program could continue until appeals were concluded. But the U.S. Supreme Court intervened and issued an expanded "stay," meaning that new children receiving vouchers could also be educated in private schools until the federal court of appeals rendered its verdict.

As of now, the legal situation is mixed. The Wisconsin courts have upheld the voucher program, including the use of the money for tuition in religious schools. However, Maine has ruled against vouchers on the church-state issue.

So far, the U.S. Supreme Court has refused to hear the voucher cases, but sooner or later, that august if capricious body of jurists will have to face one of the great dilemmas in education.

What do I personally think of vouchers?

Since I am usually decisive, this question presents an unusual challenge. The Education Establishment is a wreck, a pitiful institution that has failed to raise the scholarly level of our schools and equip our children for a complex life in the next century. Its failure is masked in middle-class suburbia by giving youngsters a bare skeleton of knowledge that limits their minds, a carefully orchestrated charade in which just enough is taught to keep unknowing parents from rebelling.

But when it comes to teaching minority children—who are the majority in many cities—and raising them out of poverty through knowledge, then American public education is surely an unmitigated disaster. That is why there is strong pressure for private school vouchers, a movement that will only increase in political power. *As of now, the choice movement is accelerating as a strange political marriage is being made—one between mainly white Republicans and African-American and Latino Democrats.*

This is seen most dramatically in Florida, where in April 1999, Republican governor Jeb Bush announced a statewide voucher program. Cleverly, it is not openly based on race, ethnicity, or poverty. Instead it rests on the simple thesis that if any school in the state is not performing adequately, based on student test scores, then *every* child in that school will be eligible for a $4,000 voucher.

Initially, only a handful of failing schools were identified. But state officials predicted that as performance requirements were raised, the program could eventually affect several hundred schools, involving a quarter of a million vouchers worth *$1 billion.*

However, as in the Cleveland case, the courts have put a road-block in the way of the Florida voucher program. A state court in the 2nd Judicial Circuit has ruled the program unconstitutional on the same grounds of separation of church and state. (The current program involves four Catholic schools.) The court also granted a stay until appeals are completed. While the first year's program only involved two schools with "F" grades for achievement, that number is now up to 80 Florida schools with enrollment of 60,000 students.

Middle-class groups may eventually protest this type of voucher program as representing racial and ethnic favoritism, but there is little doubt that whether or not it is seen as hurting public schools over the short range, the mechanism of vouchers has a life of its own—only finally stoppable through being ruled unconstitutional by the U.S. Supreme Court.

Public opinion in favor of vouchers is growing, even from the most unexpected sources. The latest advocate is none other than Arthur Levine, president of Columbia Teachers College, the fountainhead of liberal public school support.

In a *Wall Street Journal* op-ed piece entitled "Why I'm Reluctantly Backing Vouchers," Levine explains that although throughout his career, he has been an opponent of school voucher programs, he is now changing his mind. "However, after much soul-searching," he writes, "I have reluctantly concluded that a limited school voucher program is now essential for the poorest Americans attending the worst public schools."

Of course, Dr. Levine does not explain why those public schools are the "worst," since so many teachers are either graduates of his college or have been heavily influenced by its teachings.

So, am I for or against vouchers?

I am torn. I am a product of an older, excellent public education experience—good elementary schools in New York City, then an extraordinary education at Stuyvesant High School. If everyone today could be educated in the same manner, there would be no discussion of vouchers. But time has eroded our public schools and changed the dimensions of the argument.

Since excellence no longer seems possible under present conditions, except in isolated cases, I am, like Dr. Levine, reluctantly—and regretfully—in favor of vouchers as long as they are needed. But unlike the Columbia educator, my cutoff point is not when enough vouchers have been handed out to assuage educators' guilt over failing our children, poor and middle class alike.

What is my cutoff point?

When we have flooded the market with millions of vouchers, enough to painfully squeeze the Establishment and force it to either abdicate its teaching monopoly or permanently drop its false pedagogy and return to rigorous traditional education. Once that is done, vouchers will no longer be necessary, as they were not a generation or two ago.

One of the fastest growing school choice movements is home schooling, which has accelerated since the outbreak of school shootings. At the core of the movement are Christian parents who want to protect their children from what they consider the lack of moral values in the public schools. They prefer to keep the youngsters at home and teach them themselves.

The number of students enrolled in home schools is growing, says a spokesman of the Home School Legal Defense Association (HSLDA), which has 55,000 members who pay $100 a year to have the organization defend the right to instruct their children in private without interference from the state. He estimates that 1.5 million children are now home schooled and that the number

is growing by some 15 percent per year. "The shootings in Little-
ton, Colorado, and elsewhere have increased that number," he
points out.

Up until the recent legal victories in court, home school parents were considered breakers of the truancy law and hounded
by authorities, even arrested. "But now," says the spokesman,
"home schooling is legal in all 50 states."

That doesn't mean that the parents are always permitted free
reign in educating their children. But in a series of court victories, the home is increasingly becoming an authorized site for
education rather than for official persecution. One of the greatest
obstacles to home schooling were laws that required that all
teachers be "certified" by the state—a criterion that fits only one-
fourth of present home school parents.

The DeJonge family of Grand Rapids, Michigan, were
arrested on April 23, 1985 for home schooling their children
without the presence of a certified teacher. The case was handled
by attorneys of the HSLDA, all of whom are home schoolers
themselves, at a cost of almost $100,000. Finally on May 25,
1993, the Michigan Supreme Court struck the teacher certification requirement for religious home schoolers.

More recent legal victories for home schoolers include a 1997
bill signed by Governor Jim Edgar of Illinois which abolished
the State Board of Education's control over private schools,
including children schooled at home. In California, a federal district judge ruled in favor of home school parents whose home
had been forcibly entered by local police, and awarded them a
cash settlement. In several areas, daytime curfew laws—aimed
at labeling home schooled children as truants—were declared
illegal.

But what of the quality of their education? How could
"untrained" parents possibly compete with "certified" school
teachers? According to several studies of standarized tests, home

schooled children not only do as well, but on average, far better than students in public schools.

One of the most telling studies involved the ACT college admission test, given to some 1.7 million high school students each year. As we have seen, the norm score on that test is 21. Home schoolers scored higher than the norm in 47 of the 50 states, with a substantial 22.8 average grade. In some states, home schoolers received ACT scores that would grant them admission to the nation's finest colleges, as witness a 30.5 score in Vermont; a 25 in Massachusetts; a 25.7 in North Dakota; a 25.8 in Wyoming; and a 24.9 in Oregon. Home schoolers did particularly well in the reading (24.6) and English (23.4) sections of the ACT test, far surpassing the performance of public school students.

So parents do have some choice, in private, religious and parochial schools, in the possibility of the expansion of the voucher programs, in home schooling, and in a vibrant new system that is offering competition to the Establishment—charter schools.

They are not private schools, but despite the fact that they are supported by taxpayer money, they are not the usual public schools either. Charter schools are a new hybrid of the two and have been taking children and funds away from public schools as parents exercise their choice.

The first charter school was opened in Minnesota in 1991, and they have since become the fastest-growing element in the educational mix. There are approximately 1,000 charter schools operating in twenty-nine states and the District of Columbia, with some 150,000 students, small by public school standards but expanding rapidly.

A charter school can be started by virtually anyone—an individual, a teacher, a principal, a museum, a foundation, a college or university, even a profit-making organization. States pass legislation authorizing them, then a school district or the state, or a combination of the two, can issue specific charters. Most of the charters are contracts granted for a five-year period with a proviso that they will raise the academic achievement of their students or risk losing their charter.

The charter schools are supported by the school district and the state, which usually pay the school on a per student basis. The typical stipend is 90 percent of what the district normally spends on the child. However, the charter schools do not receive capital costs, which means they must scrounge for real estate, desks, and supplies. In the initial stage, money is the gravest problem, and in some cases they receive help from outside corporations, foundations, and individual donations.

Typically the school sites are catch-as-catch-can, in renovated buildings, apartments, former stores, museums, even—in some cases—in regular public or private schools that have converted to charter status. According to a study conducted for the U.S. Department of Education, 56 percent of the charter schools are start-ups, 33 percent were once regular public schools, and 11 percent were formerly private schools.

Chester Finn, then at the Hudson Institute and now president of the Thomas B. Fordham Foundation, was one of the leaders of a team of researchers who conducted a two-year study of this new school phenomenon supported by the Pew Charitable Trusts. The report, "Charter Schools in Action," was summarized by the team in the education journal *Phi Delta Kappan*. They surveyed 4,954 students (5th grade and up), 2,978 parents, and 521 teachers in a variety of charter schools.

Calling the schools "genuine centers of innovation," Finn and the team said we should "welcome charter schools as a giant step toward the reinvention of public education in America. Charter schools are creating a new kind of American public school and much can be learned from them."

Some charter schools have already proven their worth. In Los Angeles, Yvonne Chan, principal of the Vaughan Next Century Learning Center, has won a McGraw Award for her work. The school's 1,200 Hispanic students opted out of the local school district to attend her charter school and have already improved their attendance and test scores.

But other charter schools have done poorly, and several have been closed in California, Arizona, and Michigan.

We do not yet have evidence that most are achieving academic excellence. But they should be looked at, as the Finn report says, as educational R & D—research into what can be accomplished once the Establishment's inferior standards and bureaucratic micromanagement are eliminated. One California principal who now runs his own charter school says, "The charter school approach offered us a way to get the monkeys of the state and the district, with all their rules and regulations and the bureaucracy, off our back."

Charter schools come in all varieties, flavors, and styles. In some states, only certified teachers may teach; in others, they are free, like private schools, to hire whom they want as teachers. In one strong innovation, the superintendent of schools in Kingsburg, California, led a movement that resulted in the entire school district becoming a charter district.

In Boston, the City on a Hill charter school was started by two public school teachers, who then enrolled a small group of students, mainly with minority backgrounds, and housed them in a YMCA. The school soon set up partnerships with the Boston Ballet and the Boston Symphony.

Parents have also started charter schools. In Oakland, California, those who wanted a drug-free school for their children in a heavily drug-ridden area, worked with the Pacific Research Institute. Despite, as the report says, "intense union and board interference," the school was created, headed by the former principal of the local public school. As one parent stated, "We began to think we could do better for our kids than the district was doing. Sure as hell we couldn't do any worse."

Charter schools vary in educational philosophy, and one started by two fathers in Mesa, Arizona, accommodates divergent theories. The Sequoia School has two programs coexisting within its walls: a traditional "back-to-basics" program operating alongside a team-taught "progressive" one.

Several schools are run by for-profit organizations. The Edison Project, started by Chris Whittle, a media entrepreneur, operates the Boston Renaissance School, which spans grades K–8 and has over 1,000 students, mostly minority children. The Edison people stress standards, curriculum, tests, and performance.

A number of charter schools in Colorado have adopted the Core Knowledge program of E. D. Hirsch. In Arizona, a charter school is using the Montessori method for young children. At Excel Academy in Michigan, by state law all the teachers have to be certified. But none of them are members of the union, and there is no tenure. They can be dismissed for not meeting the school's standards.

The attraction of charter schools is that choice is involved at various levels. If they do not achieve their objectives, the schools can be closed after the five-year contract period. If students or parents are not pleased, they can vote with their legs by leaving and returning to the regular public school system. It is quite early in the experiment to assess results, but the opportunity for choice is already putting pressure on nearby public schools.

In Arizona, a leading state in the charter school movement, the public schools are losing students, and with them funding of some $10 million a year. To fight off the competition, the Mesa Unified School District ran a full-page ad in the local paper.

"There's no better place to learn than in the 68 Mesa public schools! . . . Don't miss out!"

In one of the poorest areas of Phoenix, the school superintendent says that 300 of his students have left for charter schools. These losses, he says, are a "wake-up call." He even phoned the parents to find out why. "The main theme that's coming across is that we have not been sensitive to the needs of the parents," he concludes.

Support for charter schools as one method of breaking the Establishment monopoly makes strange bedfellows—conservative think tanks such as the Heritage Foundation, liberals such as President Clinton, traditional Republicans like former president Bush, and media giants such as Mortimer B. Zuckerman.

In *U.S. News & World Report,* Zuckerman writes:

"A generation ago, public schools were usually the solution to students from poor or immigrant families trying to work their way up. Now the same schools are usually the problem. . . . An answer may lie with the charter school. . . . They can hire teachers who share their unique educational vision, so they can build a staff united in its emphasis and thus attract parents who want the same approach."

Charter schools are surely no panacea, no antidote to the miasma of ignorance that now permeates the public school system. But they offer one more choice, one more opportunity to try to provide better education.

What public education requires is radical reform prodded from the outside, a multilevel attack from every direction, whether it be the training and certification of teachers or the competition provided by private schools, religious schools—and now, charter schools.

The Establishment monopoly has mainly benefited the Establishment and its cadres, not our students. This is hardly the formula for a nation in desperate need of learning and scholarship, for *all* its children.

9

ALTERNATE CERTIFICATION OF TEACHERS

Competition from a Brighter "Untrained" Cadre

When former president George Bush was just out of Yale in the late 1940s, after he had served in the U.S. Navy and had settled in Texas, he had a thought:

Why not teach high school? That sounded like a socially useful activity, and he was apparently well prepared academically. He was a member of the Phi Beta Kappa honor society, and in his junior year had won the class award as the "outstanding" Yalie.

He approached the school board of his Texas town and applied for the job, convinced that he'd be accepted by acclamation.

"Sorry, Mr. Bush," he was told, "you don't have a degree in education so we can't hire you."

It seems incredible that a Yale "Phi Bet" should be turned down by a community that routinely hired academically marginal people as its teachers. But that is still the crushing anomaly of American education. When staffing our schools, we go out of our way to create legal barriers against the best and the brightest who want to teach.

This story about President Bush was told to me by an educator who shared a podium with him when he related the anecdote as an argument for bringing talented outsiders into teaching as part of the Goals 2000 program. Perhaps more than any other example, it describes how the Establishment protects its public school monopoly by rejecting superior people who haven't attended its inferior schools of education.

But don't teachers have to go to schools of education to learn how to teach our children?

Apparently not, as proven by our best private schools, which often hire brilliant young "untrained" scholars to teach. In most states, private institutions and religiously based schools are exempt from the education laws that protect the Establishment public school monopoly. Educators constantly lobby state legislators to have them require that only state-certified teachers may be hired by *all* schools. They usually fail to extend their monopoly to private schools, but the Establishment just shrugs as it fiercely guards its own turf. *In the $350 billion public school system, it insists that its teachers and no one else, regardless of academic qualifications, hold sway in the classroom.*

The Establishment has the unknowing public and beholden politicians as allies in a cabal that the Federal Trade Commission would call restraint of trade in any other situation.

But increasingly today, often because of a teacher shortage in the era of the baby boomlet—the children born to baby boomer parents—there is an interloper in the equation that might one day destroy the *conspiracy of ignorance*. That new player is "alternate certification," a system being established in several states to permit often superior untrained personnel to come into the field.

Alternate Certification of Teachers

Under this system, which has expanded in the last few years, college-educated laypeople are invited in to teach school on a permanent basis. They have never attended a school of education and have no training in teaching whatsoever. They generally know nothing of the trade babble and invented learning theories and wouldn't know "ed psych" or grade inflation from a Dow-Jones ticker.

Alternate-certification teachers generally come to the classroom as a second career. They all have at least a bachelor's degree, whether in English, history, math, science, or business. Many are older and are switching careers because they want to teach, or in some states, especially in the Northeast, partially because teaching is becoming a relatively well-paid occupation.

The phenomenon is just fifteen years from its infancy and growing rapidly, with an estimated 75,000 of the nation's teacher roster having come into the classroom through this alternate route.

How well do they do? Since they teach in the same classrooms in the same public schools and are *eventually* licensed and certified like all other public school teachers, their performance is comparable to that of teachers Establishment-trained in schools of education.

Are they as competent in subject matter (what the trade calls "content") as those with education degrees? Are they as able in the more elusive art of *how to teach* that the Establishment speaks of so fervently?

New Jersey was the innovator in this field, under the guidance of Dr. Leo Klagholz, who until mid-1999 was the state's commissioner of education. His program began as a pioneer movement in 1985 and has grown immeasurably in stature and size and is now being imitated to some degree in forty-one states, and aggressively in a handful of states, including New Jersey.

I asked Dr. Klagholz how well his "alternate" teachers are doing.

"Superior in most respects," he responded. "They have at least a bachelor's degree in one subject, and 1 in 5 have advanced degrees, including doctorates. But not one of them has a degree in education. Most of the men and women are between twenty-five and thirty years old, with more life experience than regularly certified teachers. And some of them are as old as fifty. Overall, I'd say that they come from more selective, better universities than do our regular teachers."

Since 1985, when the program started, New Jersey has increased the number of alternate-certified teachers from the outside each year. *In 1999, they represented one-fourth of all New Jersey teacher-hirees.*

They start teaching in their own classrooms immediately after being hired and are assigned a teacher mentor from another classroom who helps them during the first year. Meanwhile, they take method courses in their spare time at one of the fourteen regional state centers, their major contact with so-called professional training.

After a number of years, Dr. Klagholz did a peer review study of the alternate-certified teachers. It showed that their "trained" colleagues thought them as good, or better, than they were.

What does this prove about the supposed validity of the "profession"?

"It's become obvious," said Klagholz, "that in teaching there is no clear link between training and practice. Competence in teaching is equally distributed between the trained and untrained."

Perhaps without realizing it, Dr. Klagholz has framed the argument and posed a massively important question. It's hardly possible that an untrained person could perform brain surgery, build a skyscraper, or draft a complicated will for a large estate that would stand up in court. But if untrained teachers do as well or better than trained teachers, why do we need the Establishment, its schools, its licensing, its theories, and its massive, expensive superstructure?

That plus Klagholz's tantalizing statement that his "outside" teachers come from better schools and have better academic credentials makes the Establishment look weaker, more inefficient, and less necessary than ever before.

"The alternate certification movement started in 1983," says Dr. Emily Feistritzer, president of the National Center for Education Information in Washington. "The people from New Jersey—Saul Cooperman, the commissioner at the time, and Leo Klagholz, who was then in charge of certification, met with several of us at Princeton to move alternate certification forward. When it began, the opposition from the American Association for Colleges of Teacher Education was fierce. But when they saw that these nontraditional teachers were doing well in the classroom, they backed off. The teacher unions have always stayed on the fence."

Dr. Feistritzer is optimistic about the future of alternative certification even though it is still only a small fraction of the whole.

"We find that the alternate teachers are older and more mature, and have a better retention average—that is, they stay longer on the job," she stated when interviewed. "Troops to Teachers, which brings former service people in as teachers, is an example of that. Meanwhile, statistics show that between one-third and 40 percent of graduates of teacher training schools do not even go into teaching."

The once-vocal opposition of the AACTE may now be muted, but much of the Establishment is still in mortal fear that alternate-route teachers will raise the bar on competence and eventually push "regular" teachers out. Dr. Feistritzer estimates that of the forty-one states that *officially* permit alternate certification, perhaps only nine are really active. This includes the main three—New Jersey, Texas, and California—plus some activity in Kentucky, North Carolina, Maryland, Georgia, Florida, and Pennsylvania.

Intimidated by the Establishment, most states refuse to really push alternate certification as an intrusion that could eventually destroy the teaching monopoly of education schools, most of which are run by the states themselves. Some states try to co-opt the system by *pretending* to be interested while giving outsiders short shrift. One of the most successful in this ploy is Connecticut, which trains only 125 noneducation graduates for teacher slots each summer at Wesleyan University—an insignificant number compared with the some 3,000 teachers it hires annually.

Each state that participates has slightly different motives. In some the impetus for alternate certification is that they desperately *need* teachers, especially for schools with large minority enrollments.

"Because of our new policy of smaller class sizes of twenty for grades K–3, we need a large number of teachers," explained a spokesman for the California alternate teacher program. "This year, of some 30,000 new teachers, about 5,800 came in through the alternate route. In about ten years we expect that number to grow to 10,000, about one-third of all teachers."

He stressed that although they have to meet the same standards as the others, the alternate-route teachers are somewhat different, and in some ways superior.

"They have a better one-year retention rate—87 percent versus 67 percent for traditional-route teachers," the California spokesman explained. "Forty-five percent are from ethnic or racial minorities, versus only 20 percent among traditional teachers. They are more mature—average of thirty-five years of age versus twenty-five. And while only 10 percent of elementary school teachers are men, 30 percent of alternate-route teachers are male. In terms of quality, we find that they more speedily assume leadership positions than other teachers. This might be due to the fact that they are older."

Judging from that litany of praise, one wonders why we put trainees through education schools at all. But the California spokesman, a staunch supporter of the regular system, thinks both are necessary. "We don't believe in trashing the traditional way of training teachers. They can exist side by side."

In Texas, the third state with a strong program, one senses that they view alternate certification in two ways—as a way of filling their teacher shortage and as a goad to regular teachers.

"We find that those who apply for alternate certification have more background in content even though they have no training in education," said a spokesman for the Education Agency of Texas. "They generally have higher grade point averages and SAT scores. Those who intend to teach math, for instance, have a stronger background in the subject than math majors in education programs. To teach math in Texas, you need 24 credits, but to get a B.S. in mathematics you need 35 credits. So alternate-certification applicants, who are all college graduates, are better prepared in that way."

Texas has already had what it believes is a small revolution in teacher training. As a result of an earlier protest, they have tried to de-emphasize education courses while building up content instruction.

The legislature has put in a cap of 18 education credits, and trainees can take no more. No longer does the state grant an undergraduate degree in education; candidates must major in something else. But much of this is window dressing. They still have vast numbers of undergraduate education students, no matter what they call them. And as the spokesman pointed out, they are less well trained in content than those who come in from the outside.

Once college graduates apply for alternate certification in Texas, they are put through a rigorous five-month training, part of it in classrooms. It runs from spring until they begin to teach in September. The greatest drawback of the program is that, sur-prisingly, *they are not paid at all for that period.* In fact, the train-ing actually costs them money, anywhere from $2,000 to $7,000.

If anyone was paranoid, they might think the Texas Establish-ment was putting obstacles in the way of outlanders threatening to overrun its territory.

Texas has a number of mavericks in education, who have been sniping at the Establishment for years. Many of these advo-cates for reform are convinced not only that those outside the Establishment are superior, but that regular training of teachers is an unnecessary waste of time, produces too little talent, and is detrimental to the education of our children.

They see the alternate route as the future, attracting more mature, more academically advanced, more steadfast teachers.

"The tradition route to teacher training is not working," says Delia Stafford, president of the Haberman Education Founda-tion and former chief of alternate certification in Houston, Texas. "What we're doing now is turning out twenty-two-year-old teach-ers who are not mature enough and who are still searching for a way of life. About 40 percent of the graduates never teach, and of the remainder, many quit in the first three years."

Stating that the present traditional system of selecting and training teachers is "broken," Ms. Stafford goes on to show, as do others, that the alternate-route teachers are more mature and reliable. "They average thirty-eight years of age," she reports, "have had other careers, are serious about wanting to teach, and stay on the job. Many of our alternate-route people come from a minority background, which is important. Right now, the children who need it the most are getting the worst teachers."

The fight between regular teachers trained by the Establishment and alternate teachers from the outside is just warming up. The strongest example of a current battle is Teach for America, a program for bright young people who, unlike other alternate-certified candidates, are mainly right out of college.

The program is not large—it puts only 500 new teachers into our urban and rural schools each year—but it has the optimism and crusading manner of a domestic peace corps. In fact, the major sponsor of the group is AmeriCorps, the federal volunteer group, which contributes about one-fifth of its annual $7 million budget.

The most extraordinary aspect of this alternate route is that it was dreamed up by a Princeton senior, Wendy Kopp, in 1989. She scrounged for seed money, including $500,000 donated by Ross Perot in 1990. The first class started teaching in September of that year, and the program has placed over 4,000 teachers in schools since then.

The young teachers are recruited from 200 campuses nationwide and are excellent students. They average 1,159 on their SATs (200 points more than education school aspirants) and come from such top schools as the University of Michigan, Georgetown, Berkeley, Stanford, Boston University, Cornell, Harvard, and Yale. They train for five weeks at a service center in Houston, Texas, then go into such needy communities as the South Bronx, Central Los Angeles, and the Mississippi Delta, where they fulfill a pledge to teach for two years.

How well do they do teaching in the classroom? A survey conducted by the research firm of Kane, Parsons showed they were stars in the eyes of their supervisors. In relation to other beginning teachers, principals graded them well above average—in intellect, 88 percent; in motivation, 88 percent; and even 70 percent in "managing a classroom environment conducive to student learning and growth."

What does the Establishment think of Teach for America?

Many hate the program, probably because these youngsters are smarter and teach better than their own progeny, according to their own principals. The Establishment claims that sending fresh graduates without education training into schools is dangerous, that five weeks of instruction is inadequate. Results show exactly the opposite, however, which is the mainspring behind Establishment anger.

The alternate route to teaching is still embryonic, but the argument is going to heat up as states like New Jersey, California, and Texas hire more and more from the outside. This movement will surely spread to other states, especially if public opinion forces state education commissioners and legislatures to support this educational reform.

In this battle of systems, the Establishment has the power, the ear of politicians, the votes of millions of teachers and support staff, and a public that knows little about the problem.

But on the other side, there is the simple fact that alternate-route teachers are more mature, have better academic credentials, stay on the job longer, and are less indoctrinated with "ed psych" and the often-nonsensical learning theories of the Establishment.

If we invited a literate visitor from Europe, perhaps a reincarnation of Alexis de Tocqueville, to examine American education, we can be assured that the alternate-certification method would win his approval.

"I am encouraged enough," says Dr. Emily Feistritzer, "to believe that the alternate route to teaching will be the key that will one day turn around the failing public education system."

10

MIDDLE SCHOOL AND HIGH SCHOOL

Legions of Abandoned Minds

"I travel around the country and visit many schools," a staff member of the National Assessment of Educational Progress (NAEP) told me. "I find that children in the 4th grade are eager and anxious to learn. By the time they are in the 8th grade, they can take it or leave it. And when they finally get to high school, you get the feeling that they'd rather be anyplace except there."

Though this is a harsh portrait, for many secondary students it's a true one. But their social life is often quite the opposite, one filled with friends, fads, and football, a kind of Disney World coming of age. They have companionship, the sharing of adolescent joys and fears, and sometimes sex.

As we've seen, a minority of high schoolers are stimulated enough by learning to take honors classes, or advanced placement college-level work, beginning the life of the mind. For most fifteen- to eighteen-year-olds, though, it is a period of scholarly torpor, even boredom. They tread academic waters until they can realize the exciting prospect of college—where they will be forced to become somewhat serious about learning.

In interviews with a teenage magazine, seniors in a suburban Chicago town put the American high school into their perspective—as a place to hang out, make friends, and grow up, with few comments about learning. As they wait for responses on college admission, their thoughts are on their social and personal lives, surprisingly much more so than those of college students, who have already gone through the most trying phases of adolescent adjustment.

"I wore this skirt the other day. It was so cool, people told me they liked it, and I said, 'I made it,'" one eighteen-year-old related, then went into a detailed description of her social life, complete with fantasies about what appeared to be the prime concern of the six graduating students—the upcoming prom.

That fantasy included playing video games at someone's house, going to a diner and dancing to the jukebox, then dancing at a pier where the theme song would be "I Will Remember You," then the school-sponsored prom, after which there would be a trip over the state line to Wisconsin for night swimming, bungee jumping, and "paint ball." During all this, the young woman would be wearing a dress similar to the one in *Titanic*, which she planned to make in clothing class.

Another eighteen-year-old, this time in Texas, assessed her time in high school, summing up what she had learned in those four vital years: "Academics isn't what it's about. It's about growing up, going places with your friends, learning about guys, learning about yourself, learning about how you react to situations, to heartbreaks. Anybody who doesn't go through all that is really missing out—which is why I never understood why people drop out."

The competition between "growing up" and learning is powerful, and in the present school environment, created by the Establishment, learning usually comes out second best—by a country mile.

"Large numbers of students in both urban and suburban schools drift through their high school careers largely apathetic to learning," writes Dan McGraw in *U.S. News & World Report*. "By one estimate, as many as two-thirds of the nation's public secondary school students are 'disengaged' from their schoolwork. Factors such as drugs, television and uninvolved parents are partly to blame. But in many instances, schools fail to give students good enough reasons to learn."

As graduation (virtually assured no matter how they perform) approaches, some high school students and parents wake up, if often too late. The scurrying competition for admission to college begins, as does the cramming for the SAT and ACT tests. Despite the general failure of high school as a training ground, college is no longer an option but a near necessity for the 2.5 million high school graduates each year, almost 70 percent of whom will go on to some form of higher education in the 1999–2000 academic year.

The attraction is heavily economic, as college—not high school—becomes the entry point for a career in the global economy. The spread between what high school and college graduates will earn continues to widen. A recent study conducted by the Census Bureau shows that the median income of men and women with a bachelor's degree is some 54 percent higher than that earned by those with only a high school diploma.

Parents are becoming aware of this, but they are ignorant of the failure of high schools to prepare their children for the increasingly powerful competition.

"Our secondary schools are a shambles," says Professor Richard Pipes, a history scholar at Harvard. "[High school] does not perform its proper function of preparing youth either for citizenship or for higher education. . . . In contacts with Harvard freshmen, presumably the cream of the country's high school graduates, I have been struck by their cultural rootlessness. Interviews with applicants for my freshman seminar reveal that they are almost totally unfamiliar with the world's great literature. . . . I find this very depressing."

In global terms, as measured by the poor performance of American high schoolers in international competition, this has grave significance for the future. Our younger students hardly excel, but most do perform at average or somewhat below average levels in these contests—until they get to high school. By then the absence of scholarship becomes discouragingly evident, as our seniors score near or at the bottom on tests of academic performance.

We make a semantic error in calling secondary education "high," which connotes elevated learning. That it is not. Before World War II, high school graduation was an achievement, producing relatively well-tutored youngsters. *The secret was that at the time, high school was separated from elementary school, much as college is today.* It attracted both faculty and students intent on learning. A high school diploma meant something, in some ways as much as a deflated college degree does today.

It was then usual for people to begin their lives as adults at the age of eighteen. In 1940, only 1 in 4 Americans held a high school diploma. The majority worked, then married within a few years. *Today that maturity is delayed, and the waiting room is high school.* It is as if the students are too old for the academically immature school environment.

In his book *Community of Scholars,* the late Paul Goodman spoke of the medieval period's tradition of young men of the mind living away from their parents as they absorbed the knowledge of the ages. That endeavor often began at the age of *thirteen* as an adolescent apprenticeship in scholarship. At great institutions such as the Sorbonne, young men just entering puberty became full-time scholars, paying to hear lectures by the brilliant minds of the time.

There was a biological reason for beginning university work at thirteen. At puberty, youngsters are perfectly primed for learning, as the early universities and later preparatory schools in England and America understood. It was generally too early for association with women, which helped to focus their minds. Educators knew that if students could be taught early in their hormonal awakening, scholarship could become an integral part of their makeup. They would be introduced to the life of the mind, which would stay with them forever.

Prior to puberty, children can absorb information. But the independent concept of *intellect*—intelligence stored up, then arranged in equational form—begins at puberty. From thirteen on, intently for perhaps five years more, the mind is extra active, more so than at any time before or after, developing methods of taking in, processing, and organizing information.

If we miss that early opportunity, and we generally do in public middle and high schools, we may never again be able to ignite the instinct of scholarship. By not acting on that glorious chance, we leave many students permanently marred by boredom and without the love of learning.

Every day, public school educators are carelessly abandoning these teenage minds, as early as the 6th grade in middle school up through the 12th grade, the very years when students are primed to absorb and integrate the most complex material. It is a betrayal of the highest order, one perpetrated by an unknowing, smug Establishment that fails regularly, then hails each consecutive failure as a victory.

How is the damage done?

Mainly by treating high schoolers like younger children, placing them under the control of education school graduates with an abysmal record of scholarship. High school teachers have studied more advanced subject matter than have elementary teachers, but the thrust of their work and their degrees reflects the same biases ingrained in teacher education. Many secondary school teachers even claim (or admit) that the basis of their professionalism is not math or history or science, but how to teach their limited knowledge of those subjects.

How limited is that knowledge? As we've seen, a high school math teacher needs less training in mathematics than a simple baccalaureate in the field. Under this ludicrous arrangement, math teachers seeking advancement and a pay raise don't usually take a master's degree in mathematics. Instead their graduate degree is typically in "math education," hardly a boon for students. In fact, most high school math teachers don't have enough math credits to be admitted to a regular master's program in mathematics. The same is generally true of public school science teachers.

The result? Government surveys show that only 18 percent of math teachers and 15 percent of science teachers have a graduate degree in their major field.

No matter how bright they may be, and results of the Graduate Record Exam show high school teachers to be brighter than those teaching elementary school, they are trapped within the ignorant limitations of the Establishment.

Being tied to the Establishment restricts high school teachers not only educationally but in pay as well. Most people don't realize it, but the Establishment insists on paying a physics teacher in high school the same salary as an instructor guiding finger painting in kindergarten—a reflection of the disdain for scholarship that permeates the American public school system.

In the world of modern education, teachers are all treated the same, with the same unfortunate results. How do schools expect to attract scientists or historians to teach in middle and high school if they pay them the same salary as a 1st grade teacher? That mystery has been solved: They cannot. Thus the shortage of well-trained teachers for the upper grades.

We even tolerate the common practice of secondary school students being taught by people with virtually no training in their fields. In science, as we've noted, a *majority* of teachers did not major in science, while in mathematics, only a bare majority (55 percent) did. These figures are somewhat better among high school teachers but are even lower in middle school, where teacher specialization begins.

So overall, almost half the math and science teachers are what are called "out-of-field" instructors, doing an uninformed, ad hoc job in one of the most vital of all educational tasks.

Today we are facing a dilemma in scholarly learning in high school. Fifty years ago, before the Establishment grabbed total control of secondary education, there was a scholarly tradition of sorts. High school *instructors* (a word no longer used) earned more money and gained more respect both in the community and the educational world. The work attracted some scholars and many near-scholars and was often compared with teaching college—professors *manqué*.

School administrators often had the freedom to hire bright high school teachers without credentials in education, as was routine practice in private schools. New York City's scholarship schools, for example, had an exemption from the education law, allowing principals to hire whomever they wanted.

That separation of high school from elementary school was a distinguishing characteristic and a vital contributor to quality of teaching, one that has now disappeared. Once the Establishment abolished the separation, high school became, as it is today, a mere continuation of elementary school. *It has denied teenagers the chance to come of age intellectually as well as biologically. Once that opportunity is lost, as it usually is today, it can seldom be recaptured in college, which then becomes a mere continuation of high school.*

What, really, is meant by *scholarship*? How does it differ from, say, a fourteen-year-old taking basic algebra and getting an A? Isn't that an example of a studious boy doing scholarly work? Not really. That, as educators say, is "age-appropriate" learning.

Perhaps I can explain it through my own experience at Stuyvesant High School, which then had an exemption from the certification law and hired only scholars for its staff. My history teacher was a Ph.D. in history (not education); my favorite math teacher, Dr. Baker, who was personally impossible, was a consultant for IBM on computers, then an infant field; my English teacher was a frequent book reviewer for the *New York Times* and WQXR radio.

They had no training in "how to teach." Their techniques were highly idiosyncratic, if they existed at all. They took the stance that they knew everything, and if you were smart, you'd want to imitate them and become equally smart. They were models, and their demands were often extreme. There was little quarter given to "emotions" or "socialization" or anything else.

All expressed their high standards in different ways. My English teacher played a trick on us that became my model for youthful scholarship and I believe changed my life. In the 10th grade, after graduating from junior high school, I entered Stuyvesant as a good student but with no understanding of true scholarship. I had merely done what my junior high teachers asked.

But at Stuyvesant, which required an exam for entrance, I learned the truth about learning at age thirteen. My English teacher asked us to write the traditional composition about what we had done over the summer vacation.

When the class next met, he called out in his sonorous voice, "Mr. Gross, you're the smallest guy here. Come up front and stand on this stool. Everyone hand him your papers."

At first we enjoyed this touch of madness. But that soon turned to dismay.

"All right, Mr. Gross. Tear up all the papers."

A low wail filled the room, only to be dismissed with a wave of the teacher's hand.

"You used to be boys, but now you're men," he began. "Forget those childish essays. I want you to go to the 42nd Street library and get copies of professional journals in any one of the sciences—biology, physics, astronomy, anything."

From the front of the room, I recall the quizzical expressions on the faces of my fellow students. What in the world was he up to?

"I want you to read as many copies of a journal, in one subject, as you can. Three weeks from now I want you to hand in a paper ready for publication in that journal, with bibliography and footnotes."

I distinctly remember thinking the man was crazed. No matter what he said, weren't we still children? But dutifully I went to the library and spent Saturdays and some late afternoons going through journals in physics, which then interested me. One subject stood out in the pre–atomic bomb era: early discussions of nuclear theory. Hahn and Strassman had described nuclear fission, and the pages were full of speculation. The subject was of common interest among physicists but a revelation for a curious thirteen-year-old boy. I wrote my paper, "The Future of Atomic Energy," and grew up in three weeks. To this day I offer my gratitude to that "madman," who had never been to a school of education, where they teach age-appropriate learning.

It is now obvious that to make high school the scholarly environment it should be, grades 9–12 must be clearly separated from elementary school. High school needs to abandon the public school model and adopt that of the university and better private schools.

A proper high school system requires a faculty untrained (or barely trained) in education and with scholarly standards similar to those of college. Each school district needs its own *superintendent of secondary education,* with a Ph.D. in a true discipline, whether medieval history or organic chemistry, much like headmasters of good prep schools or even university presidents. His jurisdiction would cover both middle and high school.

We need to rewrite the education law in all states so that public high school principals can hire any scholar they want, regardless of a background in education. To fill this new high school system with faculty, we need to look outside the present pool of education school applicants. There are several fruitful areas, including those with master's degrees and Ph.D.s who teach in community and four-year colleges but who are only employed part time without tenure. And we need to seek out other scholars who have wandered into private industry after doing graduate work.

David Miller of Fremont, California, a former university teacher, wrote to the *New York Times* about this dilemma. "One reason for the dearth of academically gifted recruits to the elementary and high school teaching profession is a public school culture that is antagonistic to prospective teachers with college teaching experience," he stated, adding that they form an ideal pool of talent.

Naturally the Establishment ignores this advice, knowing it couldn't meet the competition from true scholars. It has carefully excluded them as not knowing "how to teach" high school seniors, even though these same people have successfully taught college freshman—many of whom were sent to the university poorly schooled in high school and, in many cases, needing remedial work.

Middle School and High School

If politicians could learn what is needed in the schools and had the courage to buck the Establishment lobby, which now frightens most of them, secondary school in America under my system could truly claim to be "high" learning.

To make this changeover to scholarship would require upgrading the curriculum, beginning in middle school. The federal government has developed a curriculum for a mythical James Madison High School, which calls for three years of math, science, and social science, four years of English, two years of a foreign language, and a half-year of computer science.

This ideal is considerably better than most current curriculums, but it is still too limited if scholarship is the goal. *Since students are in high school for four years, we should require four years of English, math, science, and history (not social studies), three years of foreign language, a year or two of geography, and a full year of computer science. And there should be three additional required subjects that are now seldom taught: economics, physics, and trigonometry.*

The actual curriculum in high schools is much weaker than the government's James Madison recommendation, let alone my suggestion. A study published by the National Center for Education Statistics, covering the period 1993–94, lists the high school graduation requirements of twenty-six states. Only three states were up to the Madison High level.

The other twenty-three were satisfied to go their own merry antieducational way, with only two years of math and science. Among the states not reporting, many required only a year of each. Some high schools go beyond the state requirements, but by and large, most are happy just to comply with the minimum.

Since then, there has been a change for the better in some states, one of the few promising signs in American education. According to a 1998 study of all fifty states by the Council of Chief State School Officers, some seventeen states now have standards equal to that of James Madison High School. But thirty-three states still lag far behind.

(Only one state—surprisingly, Alabama—now meets my requirement for four years of both math and science.)

Another failing in the high school curriculum is the excess of fun-filled nirvana, the happy student electives. Because high school students often prefer "snap" courses, most electives reduce any emphasis on scholarship that exists.

"Students generally spend less time on core courses than is commonly assumed, and avoid the rigorous courses necessary for advanced work," states a U.S. Department of Education report. In over a dozen states where students can call many of the academic shots, almost half of all high school credits are in these electives. Critics have labeled this "cafeteria-style" learning, geared to such "junk food" courses as cooking, driver ed, even "bachelor living." When added to makeup and remedial courses, they comprise one-fourth of all high school credits.

Another block to good scholarship is lack of homework, a widespread national failing. The Establishment refuses to admit its error, even though research shows that learning is closely tied to the amount of homework given to students.

Youngsters listening to a classroom lecture can choose not to take notes, or take poor notes, or be diverted by an attractive member of the opposite sex. Or be seduced by balmy weather, or be engaged in heavy daydreaming. But homework is the ground zero of study. In the privacy of the home, the textbook or assignment *has* to be focused on and mastered. It is the core discipline of scholarship, the lonely pursuit of knowledge.

How much homework do Americans students do?

Too little.

The most conclusive studies have been made by the NAEP evaluators, who questioned students taking their nationwide tests. Judging from these studies, which were done in both 1984 and 1996, homework is in a sorry state and shows no sign of improving. Among nine-year-olds, little homework is assigned or done. Twenty-six percent did none. Four percent did not do the homework assigned by teachers. Fifty-three percent did less than an hour a day. In rounded averages, the typical 4th grade student appears to have perhaps thirty minutes of homework a night.

That amount increases as the child ages, but not considerably. In the thirteen-year-old group, most of whom are in the 8th grade in middle school, 22 percent were assigned no homework, which is rather shocking. Thirty-seven percent had less than an hour; while 35 percent were given an hour or more. It appears that these typical middle school students were given an average of only 45 minutes a night of study at home.

The figures are similar for seventeen-year-olds. The most disturbing aspect of the survey is that 23 percent of high school seniors had no homework at all, while another 13 percent of fun-loving students didn't do what was assigned. That makes 36 percent of students who are totally out of the homework-studying loop. *Another 28 percent, or a total of almost two-out-of-three seniors, had less than an hour's homework. If one suspected that America's secondary schools are hopelessly lax, this is final proof.*

Is it important? Apparently it is vital.

Across the board, the more homework given and completed, the higher the NAEP test scores, which proves the strong correlation between homework and performance. Among high school seniors, the average NAEP reading score for those who did no homework was 273. For those who did less than an hour, it was 288, some 15 points higher. And for those who did one to two hours of homework, the average score rose to 295. The score escalated even higher, to 307, for students who did more than two hours of homework a night. A nose in the textbook—at home—is obviously the route to school success.

What are students doing instead of homework?

Exactly what parents know and everyone else can guess. *They are watching television, a total of twenty-one hours a week, some four times the amount given over to homework.*

While parents vocally claim to be interested in their children's school performance, they are obviously unwilling to do anything about it. The typical American parent permits excessive television watching instead of insisting that children do their assigned homework and pressing lax school officials to assign still more. Since homework and test results are so closely related, one would think that status-striving American parents would at least put a partial lock box on the family—or the student's own—television set.

Reading assignments in high school are just as lax as homework. One study reported that seniors are asked to read only ten pages of text each evening, for all their classes *combined.* The NAEP study showed that outside reading is also a prime casualty of lax schools and compulsive television watching, taking up much less than two hours *a week,* a reflection of the visual, not literary, era in which children live.

Teachers have to take the blame for inadequate homework assignments—a symbol of their laxity.

But why do they assign so little? One reason is the general ethos of American middle and high schools, where rigor is considered to be unwarranted, outmoded, authoritarian, even perhaps injurious to the supposedly fragile student psyche. Another reason is that some teachers feel it is too much trouble to read and grade the papers.

Still other teachers are afraid to assign too much homework lest they stand out from the more permissive faculty and make students dislike them. Perhaps the greatest deterrent to homework is that many teachers were poor or mediocre students as youngsters and found homework an onerous task. Why inflict it on their students, they now ask?

Middle School and High School

The lax homework policy may also result from the Establishment's educational philosophy that "enough is enough." A Texas professor of education, writing in the *High School Journal*, admits that homework can improve a youngster's grades and knowledge. But, he warns, it will cut into the student's "leisure time and the autonomous pursuit of individual interests." As if there's not already enough of that around to satisfy a generation, or two.

Like homework, another important failure of scholarship in our public schools is the inattention to gifted children, a situation that is worsening each year. They fall victim to many of the ills of the Establishment, especially weak curriculum and poorly trained teachers.

For perhaps a hundred years, the teaching profession has placed students of higher ability together in one classroom in order to accelerate and deepen their learning. That was the next best thing to superior specialized schools such as New York City's eight institutions, from Stuyvesant to Townsend Harris. This is called "tracking," and it has shaped a raging argument, mainly between parents of bright students and a reluctant Establishment.

In high school, tracking is not traditional. Instead, honors classes and advanced placement courses take its place. This generally involves one in five students, those most interested in learning.

The argument especially involves middle school, where tracking was traditional but is now being attacked as *elitist*.

"Don't use the word *tracking*," says a spokesperson for one Connecticut school district. "Educators don't like it."

That's quite true. Tracking, or grouping students by ability, triggers Establishment psychobabble about "educational egalitarianism," and "democratic schooling," all part of teachers' tendency to identify with students of lower ability or performance.

Tracking reminds many educators about their own schooling, when many waxed envious as smarter students were placed on a fast track, leaving them behind.

The argument rages most fiercely in middle school, where the curriculum is often weak, and tracking—thus far—seems to be the only answer to a better education for bright young adolescents just coming of intellectual age.

Beginning in the 6th grade, middle school youngsters set off on the great adventure of moving about the school, leaving their home room to study math in one setting and history in another. Supposedly these specialized teachers are well equipped, but as we have seen, from the "out-of-service" statistics, at least half the children are being taught by nonspecialized instructors who are merely winging it academically.

Middle school itself is a relatively new phenomenon. Traditionally, the thirteen-year public school cycle (K–12) was divided into three parts: elementary school, grades K–6; junior high school, grades 7, 8, and 9; and senior high school, grades 10, 11, and 12.

Those who went to school up through the 1960s mainly attended junior high. In 1970, when the middle school expansion began, covering grades 5 or 6 through 8, there were 7,750 junior highs. But their numbers have decreased rapidly over the past three decades, to only 3,700.

Meanwhile, the middle school has had a reverse record. While there were only 2,080 in 1970, there are now 10,499. More come onstream regularly as junior highs are converted to middle schools, making the senior high a four-year experience.

The middle school is a puzzling dilemma for the Establishment. Since teachers and administrators are psychologically oriented, they find the age level of these young adolescents (ten through fifteen), and thus the teaching, confusing. High school students (ages fifteen through eighteen) are obviously full-blown adolescents, who have been psychologically picked over by the Establishment. Although assessments show the students failing academically, educators are convinced they *understand* their high school charges and thus are helping them.

Middle school educators, on the other hand, seem to have difficulty figuring out their students. In a report entitled "This We Believe," the National Middle School Association tries to define these youths.

"Young people undergo more rapid and profound personal changes during the years 10–15 than at any other period of their lives," they state. "These developmental processes, while natural and necessary, often constitute challenges for youngsters as well as for their teachers, parents and others entrusted with responsibility for their healthy development and education. . . . With young adolescents, the achievement of academic success, for example, is highly dependent upon their other development needs being met."

This view of middle school as a development clinic is an obvious attempt to explain away teacher failure in the classroom. A more candid evaluation comes from the Carnegie Corporation, which focuses more on the academic disaster.

"That half our nation's youth is at serious or moderate risk is cause enough for alarm," it states in *Turning Points*. "But even among those at little or no risk of damaging behaviors, *the pervasiveness of intellectual underdevelopment* [italics mine] strikes at the heart of our nation's future prosperity. American 13-year-olds, for example, are now on average far behind their counterparts in other industrialized nations in mathematics and science achievement."

The report goes on to point out that "the critical reasoning skills of many American adolescents are extremely deficient." In NAEP tests requiring analytic or persuasive writing, fewer than one in five 8th graders wrote "adequate or better essays." The

Carnegie group takes a needed swipe at middle schools as possible centers of edugenic damage. "Yet all too often," it states, "these schools exacerbate the problems of young adolescents."

Tracking for brighter students in 6th, 7th, and 8th grades is probably the only escape from the mundane intellectual environment. By separating out what are often called TAG (talented and gifted) children, schools can develop a superior curriculum. By placing the best and the brightest together in one class, most middle schools can muster a handful of superior teachers to instruct them. Ideally this should be done for all children, but that would require an internal revolution within the school system.

In affluent Greenwich, Connecticut, tracking begins in the 3rd grade, where children are observed and tested for a week, using the Stanford Achievement Test and the School College Ability Test. "What we're looking for," the program chief explains, "are the traits of creativity, persistence, and curiosity." A committee chooses the younger TAG children, who are periodically pulled out of their regular classes for enrichment courses.

In middle school, tracking is more complex. By 6th grade, students are evaluated in three areas—math, science, and language arts. They go to a special TAG room five hours a week to study an enriched curriculum in each of the subjects for which they have qualified. Only 10 percent of the youngsters achieve TAG status in all three areas, which would grant them fifteen hours a week of enhanced education.

One key to this tracking system is that students are taught by TAG teachers who have been specially chosen for their academic backgrounds. "For example," says the spokesperson, "the language arts TAG teacher has a master's degree in literature from Harvard, after which she took a master's in education."

The head of the program states that the TAG teachers she has personally hired generally *do not have an undergraduate degree in education*, which is the typical, inferior route of American educators. She adds that though the TAG program is very demanding, not enough is asked of other students in the school, a classic Establishment case of low expectations.

Part of the Greenwich TAG program involves accelerated learning, making the curriculum of gifted American students closer to that of the average student in Europe. For example, algebra is taught in the 7th grade in the TAG program (instead of the 8th or 9th as in most schools) and geometry in the 8th grade.

Tracking should need no defense, but the program angers much of the Establishment by showing up the stark difference in accomplishment between TAG students and other students mired down in school inefficiency and low expectations.

One argument advanced by opponents of tracking is that since mobility between tracks is not common, those in low tracks may never advance beyond them. The result is a push toward "detracking," a movement strangely under way throughout the nation.

That detracking campaign seems to be working. In one study, more than half the schools reported that they were cutting back on tracking, and only 15 percent reported regular grouping of students by ability. On the other hand, a study conducted by the Educational Testing Service and the National Urban League reported that even schools that claim they do not track, do separate math students by ability.

What is the Establishment's answer to tracking?

It has developed a theory called "cooperative learning." In this latest of failed Establishment concepts (read fads), children are not separated by ability. Instead they are placed in small heterogeneous groups, which might include the brightest student, some average children, and some slow youngsters. The theory is that they will work collaboratively on classroom projects and "share responsibility" for the success or failure of the group.

In this plan, teachers are no longer "dispensers of knowledge," as one proponent of the scheme says, but "guides and senior partners." The theme is student "interaction" in which the smartest students are supposed to learn as they teach.

"Cooperative learning" has all the resonance of other Establishment theories, which are brilliantly worded exercises in anti-intellect that often convince the uninitiated. Rather than bringing the typical youngster up to the level of the smartest student, more than likely it will decrease the amount of knowledge gained by all. As critics writing in *Gifted Child Quarterly* say, poor lessons taught cooperatively are no better than poor lessons taught using more traditional methods.

The ethos of middle school includes the early awareness that by the 10th grade, the ground zero of testing will arrive—the PSATs, or preliminary SAT tests, the opening salvo in the war for superior college admission. In the 11th grade, the actual SATs are taken and the scores sent off to several schools by the prospective enrollee.

Reams have been written about the SATs, but no one should underestimate its power among the 3,000 cooperating colleges and universities. (Only about 300 colleges refuse to use it.) Admissions people like to play down the importance of the scores, but most are lying. Some 1.7 million seventeen-year-olds take it each year, and without at least a 1,150–1,200 score, one can seldom get into a relatively good state university. Demands in the Ivy League are much higher, ranging from 1,300 to 1,400. The SATs may not be life or death, but it often seems that way to ambitious parents and teenagers.

The normative, or mean, score on the SAT is 1,016 for verbal and math sections combined, out of a total of 1,600. The 1,600 *perfect* score is really 1,200, since testees are given 200 points on each test just for signing their names. So of the 1,200 *actual* score, the norm of 1,016 is actually 616, or about 52 percent of the possible points.

Middle School and High School

At one time, a *perfect score* meant just that. In 1990, only one student in the entire nation achieved the magic 1,600. And today? Yielding to the powerful pressures of educational laxity, the standards of the SAT have been lowered significantly. In 1998, 673 students were magically elevated to a scholarly nirvana with a "perfect" 1,600 score—even though they made several errors on the test. This naturally enhances their self-esteem, but it also falsely presents these youngsters to the world as geniuses.

In business since 1926, the test is designed and executed by the Educational Testing Service of Princeton, New Jersey, for the College Board in New York. For years, the norm decreased, eventually running closer to a mere 900. To fight the trend, ETS merely "recentered" the test in 1994, which added approximately 100 points to the typical score.

The SATs are de rigueur for students in the East and in California, while the competitor, the ACT (American College Testing) assessment, published in Iowa City, is more popular in the South and the Midwest, covering an area of twenty-six states. It too tests some 1.7 million students a year, with about a 15 percent overlap of students who take both exams. The ACT comes in four parts—English, Math, Reading, and Science. Each test is scored from 1 to 36, then the four scores are averaged, resulting in a composite score, also from 1 to 36.

"The mean score is 21," states a spokesman for ACT. "The typical state college wants to see a 21–22 score, and the University of Iowa generally wants a 23–24 score. The prestige Ivy League schools like their students to score 27 or better."

(One interesting aspect of the ACT is that like the SATs, those students who intend to become teachers score *below* the mean, at about 20.3. This contrasts with seniors who hope to study in the field of "letters" with a 24.7; engineers, at 22.8; and mathematicians, at 24.4. Even the "undecideds"—at 20.8—do better than would-be teachers.)

The Conspiracy of Ignorance

Since the SAT and ACT tests are so important to students and their prospective colleges, a great deal of time is spent preparing for them. The SAT gives sample tests to high schools, many of which help students study them in class. Some schools even offer free after-school review sessions. But the paid business of coaching students for the SAT and ACT goes far beyond that, creating an estimated $100 million-plus industry. Two major players are the Kaplan Education Centers, with branches throughout the nation, and the Princeton Review, which is mainly in the East.

Individual tutors, like Aran Alagappan, a Princeton-trained scholar and graduate of Harvard Law School, charge up to $415 for just one session, while the less expensive Kaplan Education Centers and Princeton Review charge some $800 for a group course of study that takes up to eight weeks. The claims in the field are high: from a 100-point increase on the SAT by most, to over 200 points by Alagappan. His company, Advantage Testing, has tutors nationwide whose fees can run into the many thousands for individualized help.

What tutors do, in addition to helping students practice for the test, is to give them a series of tips—ranging from darkening the multiple choice ovals from the middle outward, to using their calculators (yes, it's allowed) to convert fractions into decimals for easier comparison before answering.

The actual content of the tutoring involves making up for what the high schools have failed to accomplish. For instance, a key part of the verbal test is vocabulary, in which most high schoolers are notoriously poor. Tutors require students to memorize hundreds—in some cases thousands—of words so that they can deal with them on the SAT. (This, of course, is "rote memorization," the bête noire of the Establishment.)

The coaching also forces students to do *critical thinking*, a skill educators talk about but seldom teach. At the last moment, about to face their scholastic Maker, many students accomplish in coaching class what they never learned to do in high school. In fact, as a general rule, the tutors are making up for the deficiencies of the high school curriculum and its failure of rigor.

There are coaches for the SAT I, which has math and verbal, usually referred to as English, sections. Then, for students who hope to compete for the top universities, there are tutors for the SAT II achievement tests, which are increasingly valuable in the tough admissions game.

One mother of two college-age girls in affluent Westchester County recalls that she sent them both to tutors for the SAT I and II. "The tutor for the SAT II English, who lives in the next town and costs about $75 an hour, stressed grammar and writing," she says. "One of my daughters took that test several times after the tutoring and ended up with a very high 600s score, out of 800, which made it possible for her to get into a really good university in the Midwest. One of my girls increased her math score over 100 points through tutoring, which made all the difference."

This alert mother says the local school districts suggest to anxious parents that they hire a tutor for the crucial SATs. "In my area, it's almost mandatory—if one wants to compete—for parents to hire tutors for their kids for the tests. One neighbor even had the Alagappan organization send a tutor to her house from New York City."

One can imagine the bill, since Alagappan's group charges some $300-plus an hour for its tutors, plus travel time from New York to Westchester.

The SAT people refute the coaching industry's claims of success, offering their own study, which indicates that coaching provides students with only a meager rise in scores. A study done by two SAT researchers, Donald E. Powers and Donald A. Rock, for the College Board states that the average gain on the verbal section is only 6 to 12 points, and 13 to 26 points on the math. Even if students use two major coaching services, they say, they can raise their scores an average maximum of 19 points on the verbal and 38 points on the math. They also believe that much of this gain can be achieved just by taking the test twice—without coaching. In fact, they claim that over one-third of SAT verbal scores do not change, or actually fall, after coaching.

Who is correct? It's hard to know, except that the financial health of the coaching industry indicates that the SAT people are being defensive. The best coaching for the crucial test, the College Board says, is "rigorous academic preparation over time, including the completion of challenging academic high school courses and extensive outside reading."

That makes infinite sense. Unfortunately, they must be talking about high schools in other nations, which of course is why the coaching industry is so profitable.

No one really knows if the SAT is an intelligence test, an aptitude test, or even an achievement test. Whatever it is, it has become a roadblock to success for those who don't master it, either on their own or with help. Many educators pooh-pooh the SAT, saying it measures nothing. But since it obviously measures something of academic importance, and can change lives, for better or worse, it is essential for young Americans to master it, on their own or with help, from school or outside coaches.

The basic problem is that most American high schools are not preparing students for either the academic level of SATs or for college itself. Creating a superior high school and middle school to do that job is not easy, but here are some avenues we need to explore immediately.

- Every school district should definitely separate high school from elementary school, then hire a scholarly superintendent of secondary education who is not trained in education but has a Ph.D. in a content subject. Nor should he or she hold the typical, and inferior, Ed.D., Doctor of Education, degree, as we shall see.

- No high school teacher should be hired who has an undergraduate degree in education. The degree should be in the teacher's area—math, history, science, etc. Ideally, the teacher would have a master's degree in that subject as well, something quite rare in today's high schools.

- Tracking should be instituted throughout the middle school population, then in the high school, without having to rely on honors or advanced placement classes. *However,* there should be an easy opportunity for students to switch from a lower to a higher track when they show progress and determination.

- Middle school and high school teachers should *never* be out-of-field people pressed into service in subjects they know little or nothing about.

- The weak high school curriculum must be upgraded to a required four years of math, English, science, and history, eliminating the catch-all social studies.

- The required curriculum in high school should also include at least a year each of geography, economics, trigonometry, and physics.

- The middle school curriculum should be accelerated in most subjects in an attempt to compete with European students, who tend to be a year or two ahead.

- High school electives in nonacademic subjects should be cut back and academic elective choices increased.

- Perhaps most important, middle school teachers should receive higher pay than elementary teachers, and high school instructors even more.

Once we have done all that, students will not have to rely on Kaplan to make them eligible for admission to one of our better colleges. And our seventeen-year-olds will no longer have to suffer embarrassment in international intellectual battles.

Are there any good signs on the horizon? Yes, one is the annoyance of a handful of educators like New York State Education Commissioner Richard P. Mills, who is threatening to withhold high school diplomas from underperforming youngsters, who are often the victims of underperforming teachers and schools. Previously, New York set up an official policy of laxity, which permitted students to decide whether they would get a meaningful Regent's diploma or a typical one, which in the common parlance, some of them "couldn't even read."

Now Mills has decided that *all* New York State students will have to take a three-day, six-hour Regent's exam in English before they can graduate from high school. The program is supposed to go into effect in the year 2000, and if prior tests are any guide, 27 percent of high school seniors in the state will not get their diplomas, a figure that will rise to 37 percent in New York City.

Furthermore, if his plans are permitted to go forward (and that's a mighty *if*) by 2003, seniors will have to pass exams in five subjects to graduate.

The program, which has yet to pass the test of public acceptance, makes a great deal of sense and should be one of the reforms duplicated everywhere despite student and teacher fear of not passing.

Failure or success in middle and high school is crucial to the nation's future. If a culture is to prosper, its adolescents must receive a more than satisfactory secondary education, one that prepares them *well* for college and life.

That is not happening in America, as all segments of the society are failing our children—parents, the states, and especially the Education Establishment. If middle and high school are to become the training grounds for successful citizens, those schools need to be radically reformed—a hard challenge the community and its politicians must face up to immediately.

11

THE TEACHERS' UNIONS

Using Schools as a Political Tool

"The fact is, in city after city across the country, public school systems are grossly mismanaged and are abjectly failing in their education mission. The fact is that teacher unions, by and large, have not done enough to protest these failures. We do a great job of protecting our members from these dysfunctional school systems. But we can and must do more to protect children who are the real victims of these systems."

This statement was not made by an outraged critic of public education, but by Bob Chase, the head of the National Education Association (NEA), the major teachers' union. As if he were a visiting schoolteacher from Mars, Chase seems to remove himself and the union from most of the guilt, when of course his teacher-members are a major cause of the debacle.

As he himself states, his union does an amazing job of advancing the needs of teachers, but very little for the victims of the system they have fashioned, in both the vast suburbia and in the failing schools of the urban areas.

This has been the course of the NEA for the last thirty years—pretending that its interests are the same as those of parents and students when, in reality, the NEA and to a lesser extent its competitor, the American Federation of Teachers, has been a highly efficient group advancing its own interests while ignoring the decline in educational quality.

The teachers' unions have fought, and are still fighting, every attempt to raise standards in their profession. They have countenanced the haphazard selection and training of teachers in inferior curriculums in inferior colleges. They have fought every attempt to tighten licensing criteria and weed out the army of incompetent teachers, who after they graduate from education colleges, enter the classroom and become members of the unions. They have done little or nothing to raise the level of curriculum and testing.

The intellectual inadequacy of teacher trainees is a dirty secret within the unions. Even the late head of the AFT, Albert Shanker, expressed his disdain. "By and large we are getting people who wouldn't be admitted to college in other countries," he confessed.

But the unions have achieved their power by effectively moving mountains to ensure the pay, retirement, tenure, and benefits of teachers.

The problem begins with the name, the National Education Association. Though it makes the group sound similar to such professional groups as the American Bar Association, it is a misnomer. The NEA is not an association but a *trade union*, a fact that has hindered professionalism. Despite its rhetoric, it is little different from the Teamsters or the United Auto Workers. But unlike those organizations, which are frank about their vested worker interests, the teachers' unions have masqueraded for years as professional groups intent on raising the quality of education.

In reality, they are following the model of industrial unions, which have little or nothing to do with the quality of the product—in this case, the education of 88 percent of American schoolchildren.

This charade has finally reached the consciousness of some leaders, Bob Chase among them. In that same speech he asks for a "new unionism," conceding that "there has been fierce resistance within the NEA" to change. This might be an understatement. Four Wisconsin NEA affiliates signed a letter to Chase comparing his new unionism to the policy of appeasement of the Nazis in the 1930s. To people like them, the enemy is school management, which translates into school boards, which of course are the elected representatives of the people. In all this, the children become secondary.

Chase tells the story of an NEA affiliate in Florida, which held a meeting to discuss union priorities. One member rose to challenge the supposed new policy. "Your job isn't to look out for the children," she said angrily. "Your job is to look out for me."

This new unionism, says Chase—who should be given *some* credit for attempting even a halfhearted reform of the NEA—is an effort to change that. Considering its past, skeptics—including this writer—see that effort as rather hopeless. The union, Chase says, must be bold in initiating reform, such as a program of "counseling" teachers who are "just not cutting it in the classroom." Perhaps, he posits, in extremis, even asking for their dismissal. Pilot programs of this "peer review" concept are being tested in Columbus, Ohio, and Seattle, Washington.

It is as if the removal of a handful of teachers can excuse the union's longtime lack of concern for quality education. All these years, the NEA has given its imprimatur to massive numbers of academic incompetents, placing its dedication to its members—as Chase himself says—at the expense of our children's minds.

The worst victims are perhaps those he singles out, the students in inner-city schools who are not reading or learning. He concludes that "to this end, we must insist on schools that give every child the enabling civil right of a quality public education."

The theme is correct and the rhetoric grand, but the message is thirty years late, with little hope that the present union membership has a true desire to correct their ways. *When the community—as we have seen in Massachusetts and North Carolina—finally decides that teachers must possess a minimum academic competence, the NEA is there, fiercely fighting against the reform, even to the extreme, in North Carolina, of taking the state to court.*

Before simple tests of literacy for teachers became the rule, the NEA even opposed them. When California administered 65,000 such easy tests in 1995, 20 percent of the teacher candidates flunked. For years the union fought the use of screening tests for teacher certification, and many states, including Massachusetts—which is now on the warpath—had none. Students just took specified courses in education college and became teachers, even if they were barely literate. Finally the NEA, kicking and screaming, has accepted the typical if highly inadequate screen of teacher competence.

The NEA is now aware that its hard-nosed tactics have gotten it in trouble with the public. Realizing that there was increased dissatisfaction with its ways, the union commissioned a survey to evaluate its standing, known as the Kamber Report. The results have not been released because of its negative conclusions, but some of the report has leaked out. Reportedly it states that many view the NEA as a "heavy-handed, selfish Washington special-interest group that is the primary obstacle to needed education reform." Another comment in the study says that Americans view the union as "the number one obstacle to better public schools."

How has the union achieved its power and its accompanying bad reputation with the public?

One reason is their politicization of the nation's teachers. As individuals, teachers may be Republicans, Democrats, or Independents. But as the result of potent union lobbying in state legislatures, their union dues can be used to advance the cause of one party. When I called the NEA for information during one presidential election, the receptionist's opening response shocked me: "ELECT CLINTON-GORE," she began.

In thirty-four states, the unions have the monopoly power to represent *all* teachers. Whether they like it or not, teachers are required—by law in those states—to recognize a union as their representative in collective bargaining. In addition, the school district is required to collect the dues for the union, at no cost to the union, through direct deductions from teacher paychecks. These dues, which run to over $1 *billion* a year, go for union activities, including politics with which the teachers may not agree.

This forced arrangement is being contested in federal courts. The Supreme Court, in landmark decisions in three different cases (*Abood, Hudson,* and *Lehnert*), established employees' rights to refrain from union membership and political activity. The Supreme Court ruled for teachers who refused to join the union, but insisted that whether they were members or not, they had to pay the union an "agency fee" as compensation for bargaining for them.

(Extracting a fee from union nonmembers seems blatantly unconstitutional, but that hasn't stopped the Supreme Court over the years from making this and other capricious decisions.)

"Many teachers don't know that they can refuse to become union members, so they just join up," says a spokesman for the

National Right to Work Legal Defense Foundation, which is handling some seventy-five teacher court cases. "The school boards are involved because many of their contracts with the union contain a clause that everyone in the unit must be a member of the union in good standing."

The "agency fee" is usually some 80 to 90 percent of the full dues, and many teachers are suing to get some money back. Class-action suits in California and Washington have awarded the teachers reimbursement for union money spent on politics and other items. Many cases are still in litigation, concerning both agency fees and forced membership in the union, according to the foundation.

Surveys indicate that only 40 percent of teachers consider themselves Democrats (the rest are evenly split between Republicans and Independents), but according to the Federal Election Commission, 98 percent of the money dispensed by the teachers' unions' political action groups—NEA-PAC and AFTCOP—goes to Democrats. Because a handful of dollars goes to Republicans, the unions pretend to be bipartisan. (This jibes with my own phone call introduction to NEA partisan politics.)

In the 1996 congressional elections, says the Federal Election Commission, the NEA gave $2.3 million to 382 Democratic candidates and only $11,850 to 13 Republican candidates. The AFT followed suit, with $1.59 million to 305 Democrats and only $19,750 to 4 Republicans. Most of the NEA money was spread around among many Democrats, but in one case it zeroed in to fight a Republican politician it didn't like, spending $151,000 in an "independent" campaign against Congressman Frank Cremeans of Ohio and helping to defeat him. Little wonder public officials are afraid of its clout.

The 1998 races were similar. The two teachers' unions spent a total of $3.14 million helping friendly congressional representatives, 96 percent of the funds going to Democrats. This politicization of the teachers' unions is confirmed by the fact that their members made up 11 percent of the delegates to the Democratic National Convention, a group larger than that from the state of California.

Since states pass the ultimate legislation affecting education, unions put money behind their lobbying muscle there as well, which pays off in pro-union legislation. In most states, teachers' unions are the largest contributors to political campaigns. In addition, the NEA spends $39 million a year on field organizers to help lobby legislators and school boards.

Are the unions bashful about their outright political activity?

Quite the opposite. In its house organ, the NEA boasts that "contributions to NEA-PAC, NEA's political arm, fund TV and radio ads designed to expose the records of anti–public education members of Congress. In the 1996 elections, NEA-PAC ads appeared in four Congressional races—and helped defeat incumbents in three of them."

Neither is the NEA beneath playing unabashed hardball to get its way. In one bizarre case, NEA delegates to its annual convention voted to boycott Florida orange juice unless that state's department of citrus stopped sponsoring the radio show of conservative commentator Rush Limbaugh. Florida knuckled under to NEA pressure and withdrew its sponsorship. One can easily assume that the NEA union is more political than educational in its outlook.

The NEA's political views are seldom challenged by member teachers, who are pleased with its collective bargaining clout. For instance, though one might assume that teachers would be even more opposed to illegal immigration than the average citizen—since it makes teaching more difficult—the NEA was one of the main backers of the fight against California's Proposition 187, aimed at curtailing education and welfare spending on illegal immigrants.

The citizens of California voted overwhelmingly for Proposition 187, and presumably so did teachers in the privacy of the voting booth. But the union was unrepentant.

Ezola Foster, a prominent African-American teacher in Los Angeles, was quoted in *Forbes* magazine about teacher attitudes toward Proposition 187: "There's a lot of low morale in my school because of the union position. . . . They know that members are hurting because of overcrowding and bilingual education. They never do anything to help."

The NEA and the AFT together have 2.4 million teacher-members, some 85 percent of all teachers in the nation. Despite teachers' educational failures, it should be clear that they do need to organize. In prior days their salary levels were so low that in some states they didn't even receive a living wage. Today the situation is much better, and the unions deserve credit for what they have accomplished—if only for teachers.

That said, the NEA has failed our students in many ways. Bob Chase of the NEA and Sandra Feldman, president of the AFT, both public-spirited citizens who say they want better education, especially for minorities, make great public pronouncements, backed by radio, television, and magazine ads about the need for reform.

Chase has even outlined a four-point "quality" program. While it is welcome, it is not backed with any strong action by the NEA:

1. Create a "new deal" for first-year teachers in which they get "high-quality mentoring" and "professional development."

(A simpler way to improve quality is to use the Massachusetts state licensing test to eliminate large numbers of academic incompetents before they ever get to the classroom. Naturally, the NEA has been fighting this effective exam.)

2. Help 100,000 NEA members achieve national board certification.

(This is like saying that only 1 in 27 doctors should be board-certified and that we should tolerate the incompetence of the other 26. At present, only 2,000 teachers out of 2.7 million—1 in 1,350 in the entire nation—are board-certified.

3. Champion universal literacy by the end of the 3rd grade.

(The reading disaster in urban schools, *created by poor teaching,* has crippled learning in all subjects. Only a few anti-Establishment educators like Irwin Kurz in Brooklyn's P.S. 161 have a sterling record of bringing minority students' reading scores up to respectable levels. As the former education commissioner of New Jersey, Leo Klagholz, says, "If we had to teach children to speak in school, a lot of them wouldn't speak.")

4. Rescue low-performing schools.

(If we had to leave this to the union, the schools would never perform well. That requires a total reform of the craft, something the NEA, despite its "new unionism," has no intention of doing.)

Criticism is slowly, if too slowly, forcing the teachers' unions into the twenty-first century. One critic of blind unionism was Albert Shanker, the late president of NEA's competitor, the AFT. Shanker, who wrote a weekly syndicated column, "Where We Stand," was a firm union advocate, but he was also an early advocate of national standards, which have created such advances as the NAEP testing, the first opportunity to learn how badly our students are doing. However, many of Shanker's reforms were voted down by his own executive council.

The NEA, like the old American Medical Association, however, has always been the last to know what to do to serve the general community. At first the union bitterly opposed national education standards, fearful—correctly—that teachers would be blamed for poor performance. (Who else should be? The children?) Then, dragging their feet, they finally supported that reform.

The Conspiracy of Ignorance

One of the major drawbacks to quality education is union support of strong tenure laws, which protect the enormous number of inadequate young teachers being produced each year by schools of education. Of the 150,000 new teachers each year, it is no exaggeration to estimate that at least 50,000, and probably more, are academically inadequate. They should never have been enrolled in those schools in the first place, or graduated, and surely not placed in a classroom as teachers. Once they've been in the classroom for two years, tenure protects almost all of them—irrationally, but quite legally.

With their enormous political power, the unions have lobbied to pass laws that force school districts to retain teachers who have proven inadequate. If a superintendent wants to fire a teacher for incompetence, it typically takes up to three years and can cost hundreds of thousands of dollars in legal fees and other costs, including paying the teacher while the proceedings go on.

In a document titled "A Blueprint for the Professionalization of Teaching," the New York School Boards Association showed that under that state's tenure system, it takes an average of fifteen months and $177,000 to fire a teacher. Worse yet, if the firing is appealed, the cost shoots up to $317,000.

(On the other hand, private school teachers, unprotected by the state, generally sign short-term contracts, and their performance is evaluated before the contracts are renewed.)

Public school teachers insist on full protection against the loss of their jobs, which is a hindrance to good education. "The system is deeply flawed because it provides dollars no matter what happens in schools," says Joe Nathan at the University of Minnesota's Hubert H. Humphrey Institute. "Unions have certainly contributed to that."

In a school district in California, one teacher, whose assignments apparently made no sense, whose speech was unintelligible, and who refused to answer student questions, was dismissed but fought her termination. After years of hearings and court proceedings, her teaching license was suspended for only one year. The cost to the district in legal fees was $300,000.

If one doubts the power of tenure, one has only to look at a ludicrous case in New York City. A special education teacher was sent to jail for selling cocaine to an undercover policeman. He collected his salary in jail for several years while school officials failed to get him fired.

The unions claim that they only want their teachers to get a fair hearing, but contracts are usually so loaded down with protection clauses that dismissal of incompetent teachers is almost impossible. A California school board lawyer says it's so difficult that many superintendents don't even bother. Instead they make deals with the unions to give doubtful teachers a good rating in exchange for allowing them to be transferred elsewhere. The technique is colorfully known as the "dance of the lemons."

University professors, both liberals and conservatives, need tenure to protect them against being fired for their pronouncements in class, or their writings, especially when academic fashion is against them. Public school teachers, especially in high school, should have the same right, but only in relation to what they say in class, or write. The tenure law should not protect incompetent teachers.

Today tenure is usually granted after only two years on the job, although reform-minded Pennsylvania has extended that to three years. In New York State, Assemblyman Craig Doran sponsored a bill to replace lifetime teacher tenure with five-year contracts that can be renewed based on performance. But the bill has made no progress.

"The union pressure has a great deal to do with keeping this bill buried," Doran has said, adding that the legislators need the political and financial backing of the teacher unions. "There is a lot of money out there, and it's going to everyone." Even Doran got $150.

What tenure protection should teachers have?

Teachers should be required to serve five years on the job before receiving tenure, and that right should remain only as long as they pass recertification (including written exams) and a performance review every seven years.

One of the gravest problems is that the union considers a teacher a teacher—that they are all interchangeable. As we have seen, a teacher of science in high school gets the same salary as a kindergarten teacher, hardly an incentive for talented people to become teachers and a sharp reversal of the policy half a century ago, when secondary school teachers were better paid. Neither is merit pay permitted in most union contracts.

Seniority also rules the day, an archaic system that broke the power of most industrial unions. The more years teachers have in the system, the more money they make. When people have to be let go, it is "last hired, first fired," regardless of talent. This happened to a history teacher with a Ph.D. who was named Minnesota's Teacher of the Year. But she was the least senior of five social studies teachers. When the district wanted to lay someone off, she was, by union contract, the victim. Finally she quit teaching.

Unions have a long record of opposing many reforms, including the new charter schools. Charter schools are designed to be sponsored by various groups and individuals in the hope that the stifling bureaucracies can be eliminated and the necessity to hire poorly trained state-certified teachers can be avoided. When the movement began, the NEA came out squarely against them. Since then it has relented, but only on its own narrow terms.

Bob Chase now points proudly to the NEA's sponsorship of six charter schools but manages to omit the union's insistence that only state-certified teachers can teach. This is a denial of the philosophy of charter schools as independent entities with much of the power of private schools, which can hire whomever they want, one of the secrets of their success.

In a symposium, Chase talks about his "vigorous support" of the charter school movement. But, he adds, "in a number of states, charter school laws have been misused as a vehicle to attack teachers' collective bargaining rights."

To add even more clout to the teachers' unions, the two major ones—the NEA and the AFT—started talking about a merger. The matter was brought by Chase before the NEA's 1998 annual convention, where it was voted down 58 to 42 percent, much to his chagrin. However, in retrospect, it was probably good for parents and students because it would have swallowed the AFT, which has been more progressive and more interested in change than the academically reactionary NEA. More than likely, a united NEA would be an even greater danger to good schools than it is today.

For instance, in response to a *New York Times* editorial criticizing teachers' unions, the AFT's Sandra Feldman, who has taken Shanker's place as president of the AFT, in a letter to the editor reminded people that her own organization has not impeded progress and reform.

Says Feldman: "We opposed lowering the passing grade in Massachusetts when so many prospective teachers failed the test. We've supported alternative credentials for highly qualified candidates, like those in the Teach for America program." The inference was clear: The AFT has not been a roadblock to reform as has the reactionary NEA. Perhaps it is an exaggeration, but there is some merit to Ms. Feldman's argument.

Lest anyone think the NEA is really entering the twenty-first century, we are reminded that it is merely an *industrial trade union* and not a professional organization. Its latest move is to increase its membership of nonteachers, the "support personnel" in school districts throughout America, a typical strategy of industrial unions.

In its magazine, *NEA Today,* the union recently boasted that it took in 500 new members in Puerto Rico, from secretaries to school guards. In New Mexico, the NEA and the AFT teamed up to win an election for 88 custodial workers and are working on bringing in 600 Las Cruces food service workers and educational assistants.

Nonteachers should be unionized if they want to be, but not in the NEA or the AFT. Though teaching is not a true profession, taking in nonteachers destroys any professional emphasis they might attempt and is akin to the American Medical Association enrolling those who help out in hospitals. Both the NEA and the AFT have to decide if they are simply trade unions or even quasi-professional organizations. They cannot be both, as they are now, unless learning is to suffer—as it is.

The worst aspect of union power is the excess of benefits it forces school districts, and thus taxpayers, to support. One of these is accumulated sick leave. Teachers should have the use of sick leave, *if they get sick.* But in many school districts, teachers are paid accumulated unused sick leave when they retire. This can reach as high as $50,000, which is ridiculous.

Teachers receive liability insurance from the union, low-interest credit cards, and long paid vacations that average eleven weeks. In all, teachers work some 180 days a year, while most people work 234 days, or 30 percent longer. Teachers have holidays off—often including both Christian and Jewish holidays—plus a week or ten days between sessions. The retirement plan is rich, with the average school board adding to the teacher's own contribution.

Another benefit, this a hidden one, is that taxpayers, through their school districts, subsidize virtually all union activities. They give teachers time off to do union business, time to bargain for their contracts, and even time off to place their grievances.

The NEA, like the AMA twenty years ago, is waking up to the fact that the American people do not like the hypocrisy of special interest groups that disguise their real intentions under the false umbrella of civic goodness.

The teachers' unions have always placed our public school children *last* on their agenda, which is why the organization is universally disliked, even hated. Bob Chase, in his attempt—or pretended attempt—to reform the group, has laid it out plainly:

"Too often our association became focused on the welfare of our members to the exclusion of that of our students. In the face of troubled schools, we simply threw up our hands. We refuse to do this any longer. As teachers, we know all too well the lessons of history. We do not want to share the fate of steel workers and other unions who felt that quality was not their responsibility."

A nice mea culpa. But thus far the rhetoric is high-flown and the work toward quality education and better, smarter teachers is virtually nil.

The teachers' unions, and those they represent, and the Establishment of which they are a part, are the perpetrators, not the rescuers, of the failed American public education system.

12

THE ESTABLISHMENT
AND THE COMMUNITY

Unscholarly Administrators,
Weak School Boards,
and Pliant PTAs

n every community in America there is one individual whose head is always a touch higher than those of the citizens and the politicians. It is not the mayor of the town or the county executive. Instead it is the superintendent of schools, the person responsible for educating the children of the community, from kindergarten to the completion of high school.

If we want a cutaway look at the school system, we can do no better than examine a profile of the individual who is responsible for the hiring and firing of teachers and support personnel and who—unless the school board intervenes—has control of the curriculum and the day-to-day running of the district's schools, along with setting the academic standards of the system.

Firstly, are superintendents paid enough to attract superior people, who will then translate their will throughout the classrooms? Absolutely. According to figures supplied by the American Association of School Administrators, their pay is top-drawer, perhaps even excessive. In districts of 25,000 or more students, the mean salary for superintendents is $133,702. In large cities it approaches a mean of $175,000, typically a higher salary than the governor of the state. In New York City, as we have seen, the chancellor (superintendent) earns $235,000, more than the president of the United States.

According to industry studies, the education chiefs are typically males, about fifty years old, who generally come from small town or rural backgrounds and from poorly educated blue-collar families. They are representatives of Main Street, and generally unconnected to the true academic world. They are, as the report of their association states, "typical" Americans.

Though the industry is mainly composed of women, they are poorly represented in the ranks of superintendents. Only 6 percent of superintendents are women, and 4 percent are members of minorities.

Part of the mystique of the superintendents is their exalted title of Doctor, which is *always* used in introducing or identifying them. When one thinks of doctors, it is generally in terms of medical doctors, or perhaps professors with Ph.D.'s, especially in the sciences.

However, in the world of education the title is much less exalted. It generally doesn't mean a Ph.D. at all, but rather an Ed.D., a doctor of education. Superintendents are most often possessors of that inferior sheepskin. Initially developed for working school administrators, it is now the *basic doctorate* in the field. As one spokesman for a graduate school of education explained, the Ed.D. degree now outnumbers the more difficult Ph.D. by some five to one.

That Ed.D. degree has lower academic requirements than the Ph.D. in virtually every respect. The thesis of an Ed.D. tends to be a "practical" dissertation on some school specific situation rather than a universal academic concept. Perhaps as important, certain Ph.D. requirements, such as mastery of a foreign language, are usually waived as being "unnecessary" for Ed.D. candidates.

More accurately, the language requirement is often too difficult for education administrators, who are seldom scholarly individuals, either in personality, background, or training. Yet mastering a foreign language has long been a tried-and-true requirement for the Ph.D.

One suspects that the Ed.D. degree began to be awarded for two reasons: (1) it was a shorthand reward for people already working full time in the field, (2) worse yet, it was created because many administrator doctoral candidates were not intellectually capable of earning a Ph.D.

Altogether, 42 percent of superintendents are "doctors," a figure that rises close to 100 percent in large metropolitan and suburban areas. The typical citizen or parent views that individual—with his enormous power in the school system—as a learned person, one who can be trusted to ensure that their children will become as learned.

The public is naive. If they are in awe of the school superintendent, it is because they assume—falsely—that he ranks high in intelligence and education, far above the other members of the teaching cadre. It is also assumed that he has been promoted for his superior intelligence and skills in the classroom. That is one of the great fallacies of modern education. In fact, most superintendents are not learned people at all, having come up through the administrative, rather than by the academic or even teaching route. They generally have a less cultured background than the typical college-educated parent.

As we have already seen, schoolteachers and would-be teachers score at the bottom on the Graduate Record Exam, the screening device for entry into a master's program. Perhaps the most revealing aspect of the GRE score is that those who intend to take a master's degree in school administration—the pool from which principals and superintendents are eventually drawn—score near the nadir. *Not only do they score much lower than high school teachers, but even lower than elementary classroom teachers, by over 50 points.* Hardly the profile of scholars.

The desire to become a doctor of education is strong because of the opportunity it brings for advancement and increased salary. Teachers with doctorates earn pay raises, and the degree greases the route to principalships, then superintendencies. So strong is the desire for doctorates that we have developed a virtual assembly line for doctoral degrees in our graduate schools of education.

In the most recent recorded year, according to the U.S. Department of Education, we produced 6,676 doctorates in the field of education, the overwhelming majority of which were the inferior Ed.D. degree. Of the 1,200 schools of education, 300 are certified by the states to offer doctoral programs in educational administration.

How does this doctoral production compare with other fields? Unfortunately, it overwhelms them. *There are more doctorates in education than in any other discipline, beating out chemistry, engineering, mathematics, physical sciences, and social sciences.* In fact, more doctors of education graduate each year than doctors of business, English, math, philosophy, and religion combined.

How does one become a superintendent, with all the accompanying money, power, and pay? First, one must be certified as a teacher and, in most states, teach school for three to five years. Then it requires a master's degree in administration, the prerequisite in most states, usually followed by the doctoral training program.

Our fantasy of a doctor of education in the form of a principal or superintendent of schools is that of an academically versatile person rich in general knowledge and able to direct a diverse group of specialists in all fields. The reality is quite the opposite. Perhaps no group of people in the Establishment are as academically weak, a fact that eventually dilutes the entire school environment and keeps it from rising to the Goals 2000 level so enthusiastically trumpeted by Washington.

To substantiate this, we have only to look at their graduate school curriculum. Administrators generally come from undergraduate schools of education, where they studied barely more arts and sciences than a graduate of a two-year community college. Then they go on to take a master's and a doctorate in educational administration.

What do these programs look like in content? Are they well balanced between administration and the liberal arts?

Hardly. They are narrow courses devoid of noneducational learning. Here are some of the courses required for the Master of Arts in Educational Administration at New York University, which requires 42 credits:

- Organizational Theory I
- Introduction to Management and Information Science
- Foundations of Education
- Economic and Legal Dimensions of Schooling
- The Principalship
- Educational Policy

It appears that there is not a single required course in conventional knowledge, whether literature, or science, or math, or history, or philosophy.

In the typical administrative doctoral program, the Ph.D. is designed for those who intend to pursue careers in research and academe. The Ed.D. is for those working in the field—administrators of various ranks, from assistant principals to superintendents.

What does the Ed.D. doctoral program look like? More of the

same. Like the master's in educational administration, it is one of Establishment nuts and bolts. Here are some of the courses involved:

- Organizational Theory II
- Professional Administration
- Politics of Education
- Research in Educational Administration
- Electives in educational communications, counseling, and technology

Lest one conclude that NYU is an exception, here are excerpts from the curriculum of the University of Connecticut's graduate school of education for those seeking the state's Intermediate Administrator Certificate. The courses follow the same narrow route:

- Budgeting and Resource Management
- Business Administration of Educational Organizations
- Personnel Evaluation
- Seminar: Time Management and Personal Organization
- Seminar: The Leadership Role of the Teacher Union
- Administration in Multicultural Settings
- Legal Aspects of Education

To be kind, there is one course, "Program Evaluation for School Improvement," which, though vague, might touch on classroom content.

What kind of academic training is that? What about excellence in general knowledge? What do they know about literature and philosophy, let alone math and science? If they know little or nothing about history, how can they design, or even approve, a course of study in American history? If they have never taken physics or chemistry, how can they design or approve a rigorous curriculum in science? Of course they cannot, nor can most principals with similar administrative backgrounds.

They become the leaders of the school community, but if they are not sufficiently educated, or cultured, how can we expect our children to excel? More than likely, educators tend to replicate themselves. Apparently that has happened, resulting in often disastrous student performance in the classroom.

The course of study of administrators is not unlike that taken by management people studying to be business executives, only in this case it is directed to public schools. In fact, studying the curriculums in school administration, one would be tempted to change the title of the superintendent of schools to that of business manager, or school manager, since the course of study hardly deserves a doctorate. The title of Doctor seems primarily designed to impress impressionable parents.

Considering the grave liabilities of superintendents, what can the average community do to make up for them? I offer two suggestions for our school districts nationwide, recommendations designed to buttress the academic default created by Ed.D. training:

1. Hire a school manager, who has completed the prosaic courses in educational administration to run the practical day-to-day activities of the district. This person would not have earned a doctorate and would not be addressed as "Doctor," with the title's false impression of scholarship.

In fact, the Ed.D. degree should be eliminated by state legislation as being academically insufficient. The only doctoral level degree awarded in education should be the Ph.D., which includes mastery of a foreign language plus strong scholarly content outside the field of education. This would dictate a largely different universe from which to draw and train principals and superintendents.

2. Hire a true scholar as superintendent of schools. *Such a person should be a Ph.D. in any subject except education,* much

the same qualifications as for headmasters of prep schools and university presidents. The job of superintendent would be to improve the curriculum, the testing, and the quality of teaching and to set new, much higher standards for teachers and students. Only he, or she, should be addressed as "Doctor."

The bias against excellence in learning that permeates the training of administrators was openly demonstrated by a prominent official at a large Texas university that runs a doctoral program for would-be principals and superintendents, most of whom will receive the inferior Ed.D. degree.

The education professor in Connecticut whom I had interviewed denigrated facts—or knowledge—as "trivia," claiming that the main goal of teaching was to direct children in "learning to learn," whatever that means. Similarly, I had a lengthy discussion with the doctoral professor in Texas, who offered equally peculiar, but quite Establishment-like, opinions about education. These were directed at the selection and scholarship of school administrators.

When I asked whether the Ed.D.'s, with their lower GRE scores and limited scholarly training, were the right candidates for principalships and superintendencies, he fumed. Shouldn't they be trained in and tested on general academic knowledge before they are given an education doctorate, I asked?

This annoyed him beyond his tolerance. He insisted that using standardized tests to evaluate individuals for competence and ability, whether the SAT, GRE, or any other instrument, was outmoded.

"Don't you understand that we educators no longer consider testing important in the selection of candidates?" he asked, adding that testing was a passé idea in educational circles. Not only that, but he strongly believed that the evaluation of candidates for entrance to or graduation from doctoral programs by means of exams of general knowledge was an "elitist" concept. It was, he claimed, a case of "snobbery."

If we don't test people to gauge their ability or knowledge, what criteria should we use? I asked.

"Portfolios," he quickly responded, referring to the stage-managed file of "work" that he was sure was more accurate than testing in determining academic talent. We should, he insisted, purge any tendency toward the old "elitist" concepts and make sure only that would-be doctors had both the "opportunity" and the "determination" to succeed.

Once more, I was witnessing intellect, intelligence, and knowledge—other than narrow training for a trade or craft—denigrated as antidemocratic criteria, while excellence was labeled as snobbery. This bias has found its way into the school through many avenues, including the office of the superintendent of schools, who, it seems, need not be smart, only determined.

So lax is their procedure for choosing and training Ed.D.'s that our vision of a student typically spending years in the ivory tower is also apparently wrong. It seems that at this Texas university, perhaps the largest producer of teachers and superintendents in that state, many people study for their Ed.D. degree while working full time. Most come to the school only on weekends, at night, and during vacations, with occasional paid time off from their school districts, to pursue their doctoral training. But part-time study is hardly an environment in which to stimulate a love of contemplation and scholarship.

Knowledge and aptitude for learning aside, this is not to say that superintendents of schools do not do a good job in the administration of our school districts. Their work is quite challenging, sometimes excessively so. They have to deal with teachers, the unions, the community, custodians, contractors, budgets, politicians, and an ever-increasing number of lawsuits from special interest groups. It is a most demanding position, and we should be thankful for their energies and administrative skills. Someone, after all, has to do this often onerous job.

But in the most vital area—that of creating a studious environment with a broad curriculum—they are failing miserably. It is a job for which they are not trained, and for which they seem to have little background, understanding, or disposition. *As with so much in the Establishment, superintendents of schools are the wrong people, at the wrong place, with the wrong training if we hope to achieve a quality education for our children.*

And school principals, who are supposed to implement superior learning, have much the same narrow administration background.

One area where administrators have done a reasonable job is in dealing with the school boards of the nation. (Politics, not learning, seems to be their bailiwick.) America has a highly localized, unique, and semiautonomous system of education, one that we rightly prize. Constitutionally, education is a function left to the states, not to the federal government. The states then delegate that authority—most of the time—to local communities, which then elect school boards of citizens to run the system.

These boards are the ones that name the superintendents and have the overall responsibility for the success, or failure, of education in their communities. All complications in the schooling of our youngsters eventually devolve onto them, for the members to remedy or ignore.

The idea of democratically elected school boards is a good one. However, like district superintendents, school boards are also failing the students. Though their authority is near-total, surpassed only by the state itself, they have not provided a quality education in most communities.

The reasons are many, including the fact that the boards usually represent only a small segment of the population and are often childishly naive in their trust of the hired help. Though *theoretically* the board members set educational policy, in reality they usually abdicate that responsibility. Unfortunately, the Establishment often runs them instead of vice versa.

There are 14,800 school boards, each of which controls a system averaging 3,000 students and 300 teachers and support personnel. Some are smaller, and others, like New York City, are mammoth operations whose attempts to have community school boards take over much of the authority have failed. In one state, Hawaii, all education is centralized and local school boards have been eliminated. Cities throughout the nation often have central school authorities, much removed from the citizenry.

However, small towns and suburbs pride themselves on local control, which enables individual parents and groups to maintain communication with, and pressure on, the school boards, which are the final arbiters of curriculum and standards. Above them, of course, are the state authorities, which dictate goals and do statewide testing, most of it at a minimum level.

Who are the school board members?

They are, we might say, the lowest—or highest—rung of politicians. Nothing, including apple pie and the World Series, is as archetypically American as our democratically elected school boards. Some 94 percent of the 97,000 school board members in the nation are elected by the people.

Though it epitomizes local control, that democratic process is often lame, even crippled, by the lack of voter participation in school board elections. Only some 50 percent of citizens on average vote for the president of the United States, 40 percent for Congress, 20 percent in state primary elections, and a meager 12 percent in school board elections—which should be the most vibrant aspect of our democracy.

The number of people running for that office is declining as well. Board members receive no pay, and although the job is supposedly part time, increasingly it consumes a great deal of time and energy. Perhaps most important in these educationally contentious times, members are usually elected by only a small, if vocal, minority of the people. Since the turnouts are low, school board members generally represent a mere handful of people.

In many towns, school board elections hang on the vote of an active, committed minority, whether from the left or the right, from the NEA cohorts to the Christian Coalition. Most elections are nonpartisan, but in some areas the Democrats and Republicans intrude. Such party participation in something that should be none of their business tends only to increase the ideological wars, which are severe enough.

In one community, Greenwich, Connecticut, the two parties have joined in an agreement, permitted by state law, to manipulate the school board elections. In fact, that election is rigged by the political parties working as an antidemocratic cabal. For example, when the Democrats—who represent only 20 percent of town voters—put up their school board candidate, he is automatically elected even if he receives only one vote!

The most disturbing aspect of school board elections is that the teachers' unions are committed to influencing who is named to those offices. It is an attempt, often successful, to control management as well as labor, which should be illegal. The reason for this excess union influence is that both teachers and administrators consider themselves members of the same Education Establishment and too often view parents and citizens as outsiders.

The unions are not bashful about their attempt to control school management through board elections. By influencing the vote, they can not only campaign for higher salaries and benefits, but can exercise their wrath on their enemies, especially superintendents. In its house organ, *NEA Today*, the giant teacher union is frank about its infiltration of management. "ELECT FRIENDS OF EDUCATION TO THE SCHOOL BOARD," it shouts, trying to set up the false equation that a friend of education is a friend of the union.

As an example, the NEA offers a case history from Colorado, where the union worked to get rid of a disliked superintendent by electing friendly school board members. They said the official was "domineering," "supported budget cuts," and had fired a media technician.

The support personnel had formed a union, the Classified Employees Association. But the school board wouldn't recognize it. Members of the CEA backed two pro-union candidates with a vigorous election campaign. They made phone and house calls and dropped 10,000 leaflets in homes in one day. They held coffee klatches and placed nine-foot-long campaign signs in strategic locations, including one directly across from the district's administration building. They won, and the superintendent left.

In such contests, unions can throw in large numbers of activists to defeat school board candidates they do not like. Usually this is not necessary, because the unions typically have the support of the local Parent-Teachers Association (PTA), which helps them maintain a "friendly"—meaning pro-union and pro-Establishment—school board by getting out the vote.

Founded in 1897 as the National Congress of Mothers, the organization later became the PTA when teachers were allowed to join, which in hindsight was an error. By 1927 they had only a million members, but that rose after the depression and nearly doubled by the end of World War II. Membership peaked at 12 million in 1966 and then headed downward. Today the membership is only 6.5 million despite the rise in student enrollment.

Why?

The PTA claims it is because most mothers are working, which is partially true. But perhaps the major reason for the PTA's decline is that its reputation is changing, much for the worse. For decades—until perhaps 1970—the PTA was seen by parents and voters as an impartial organization devoted to better education. But as time went on, it became obvious that the national PTA as well as most local units had become politicized. They aligned themselves with the teachers' unions and the educational status quo, more interested in supporting collective bargaining than in reforming the system.

Whatever the NEA proposes—such as their opposition to vouchers for the poor—the PTA seems to endorse. This is true even though most parents polled in minority communities are in favor of vouchers as the only hope for a quality education in the inner cities. When Governor Christine Todd Whitman of New Jersey introduced a very limited charter school and voucher program for two grades in Jersey City, mainly minority schools, the New Jersey PTA delegates saw this as a "frightening" threat to public education—even though parents in the area favored Governor Whitman's move.

Today the PTA is correctly seen as a loyal adjunct of the teachers' unions, while still waving false credentials as a parents' group. The teacher half of the organization most often has the upper hand, yet parents are not usually aware that many PTA activists are classroom teachers with union affiliations.

Still, the connection between the PTA and the teachers' unions is becoming obvious. As a result, a revolt is beginning by some parents seeking to form alternative PTAs. In Loudon County, Virginia, John Taylor, then president of the PTA at a local middle school, attended his first state convention and was shocked at the open politicization shown by PTA officials.

Expecting a discussion on how to improve schools, he says, he mainly heard attacks on then-governor George Allen's educational reform programs. "I don't mind people being political at all," Taylor said at the time, "but I do mind if they don't allow others to express dissimilar views or if they only tell one side. They were anti-Republican."

(The dispute seems reminiscent of the educational politics in California, where a simple matter of the best reading system became the center of a politicized conservative-liberal fracas.)

Most parents at the Seneca Ridge Middle School agreed with Taylor and voted to abolish their PTA unit and form a replacement, a Parent-Teacher Organization (PTO), an independent group that, unlike the PTA, did not send members' dues to any state or national organization.

Other PTA units in the area have also voted to leave their national organization and become independent local PTOs. In Loudon County, almost half of the forty-two local schools now have PTOs instead of PTAs. In Prince William County, also in Virginia, at last count, twenty-one schools had PTAs, but thirty-five had PTOs. The rebellion is moving forward, but the national PTA and its locals are still quite strong, and still a supine adjunct of the unions and the Establishment.

School communities throughout the nation are beginning to face still another challenge to superior education, a teacher shortage. Created by the baby boomlet—the children born to baby boomer parents—it is rapidly becoming a reality. In addition, there has been a wave of immigration in the 1990s, and high school dropout rates are being reduced. The result is that the graph of student enrollment looks much like that of a volatile Internet stock.

Enrollment rose steadily after World War II, through 1970, when it reached a peak of some 47 million public schoolers. It leveled off as the boomers grew up, then started to drop, almost precipitously. Beginning in the middle 1980s, it started to rise again. Today it is back to its old high of 47 million, and still rising.

The Census Bureau estimated a 15 percent growth in student enrollment between 1990 and 2005, but we seem to be exceeding that. The present increase is running at almost 2 percent per year. That will give us a public school student population of 50 million by 2003, and 55 million by 2008. The rise is everywhere, but greatest in high-immigration cities such as Los Angeles, Chicago, and New York, plus such states as Florida and Texas. The student increase is in all grades, but heaviest in senior high schools as the boomlet children age. The increase in senior highs is estimated at 28 percent in those same fifteen years.

"This is not a blip," says Education Secretary Richard Riley about the rise in student enrollment. "It's a constant trend, and we're going to have to deal with it."

The crush of students requires new buildings. In one recent year, 512 new schools were built; 667 newly constructed schools, including replacement buildings, were opened; and 2,225 schools, mainly in burgeoning California and Texas, were operating on a year-round schedule, a threefold increase since 1990.

In Broward County, Florida, one of the fastest-growing areas in America, eighty-seven new schools were built in a recent seven-year period, but it was still not enough, and students had to study in trailers, called "portable classrooms."

As the boomlet children fill our schools, the roster of teacher retirees has simultaneously started to rise with the "graying" of the teaching force, adding to the future teacher shortage. Estimates are that we will need an additional 2 million new teachers in the next decade, a 21 percent growth in demand. The U.S. Department of Education believes that school districts will have to hire 220,000 teachers each year for a decade as against the usual 150,000. This problem becomes more acute when we realize that of the students receiving teaching credentials each year, some one-third do not go into teaching but take jobs elsewhere.

The largest shortfall will be in the ranks of special ed teachers to handle the programs fueled by federal IDEA (Individuals with Disabilities Education Act) legislation, which allows more and more students, most of them slow learners, to be defined as "at risk" and eligible for local, state, and federal benefits. Added to this is the push for smaller class size, an expensive, yet unproven goal of the Establishment. Naturally, the smaller the classes, the more teachers are needed.

The coming shortage, which has already hit some states, especially California and Texas, has had one salutary effect. Alternative certification programs are becoming important as more states promote the concept, Pennsylvania being the most recent. The alternative program has many benefits for communities: As we've seen, the alternate teachers tend to be smarter, more mature, and more apt to stay in the job. The growth in their numbers also tends to weaken the ineffective training monopoly of the Establishment.

The shortage seems to have put the tyro teacher in the driver's seat, at least until the boomlet babies graduate from high school. In Prince George's County, Maryland, a Washington suburb, new teachers are offered a free month's rent and low-interest loans. In nearby Howard and Frederick Counties, the districts are luring teachers by offering to pay their tuition for graduate work.

In Baltimore, new teachers are given reduced-rate mortgages. In New York City, the school board had to go to Austria to find competent math and science teachers. In El Paso, the city offered a $2,000 cash bonus for math instructors. Massachusetts has raised the ante considerably. Governor Argeo Paul Celluci granted a $20,000 cash bonus to the 200 most promising teachers who agreed to come to his state.

All this takes money. The public understands the possible need, but it is torn when it comes to higher school taxes, reluctant to spend new money on top of present levies. School taxes have become the fastest-rising component of the entire tax structure, sometimes going up 6 percent per year.

Covering the cost of schooling is a tripartite operation—the state, the local district, and the federal government. Washington contributes the smallest amount, some 7 percent. The remainder is evenly divided between the state and the local district, paying some 47 percent each, with the state portion rising slowly each year. In all, local communities must raise about $160 billion in school taxes each year, which can be a crushing burden on homeowners, whose property taxes pay the way.

As a general rule, three-fourths of all local taxes, which support 66,000 local governments, come from property taxes, the bread and butter of communities. Of that bundle of money, some 45 percent goes to pay for schools.

Citizens are particularly aggravated by school taxes because their basis is not equitable. Based on the assessed value of homes, the tax varies enormously even within a single town. Several factors, from local politics to favoritism to inaccurate assessments, play a part, as do appeals by homeowners who believe, often correctly, that they have been overcharged.

The present system, says the Tax Foundation, a nonprofit Washington think tank, has led to "unhappy taxpayers, who may see their assessment jump suddenly upon revaluation, or may see similar property owners pay substantially less tax." (In one year in my hometown, a reassessment of home values raised the average property tax by 27 percent!)

School taxes especially aggravate senior citizens, whose homes have zoomed in value along with their assessments due to real estate inflation. Meanwhile their incomes have gone in the opposite direction as they age. In many instances, high property taxes driven by the school levy have forced seniors to sell the family home. Young couples with children are more willing to pay school taxes, even if they sometimes become almost prohibitive. But for most citizens, the taxes have shaped a backlash, resulting in a large number of school bond issues being defeated at the polls.

Property and school taxes actually went down in the decade

of the 1970s because of an antitax rebellion led by Proposition 13 in California. But in the 1980s, they started upward again and have since been on a steeply rising graph. From 1980 to 1991, for instance, they rose 122 percent, almost double the increase in inflation. Since then, it has been much the same, with no relief in sight.

The argument over school taxes in many communities and states focuses on two points: their high cost and the equity of property taxes as the source of cash to support education. In Michigan, the governor and the legislature—on a bipartisan basis—decided that property taxes were not the best way to finance schools. Instead they have set a new precedent by eliminating property taxes as a source and substituting total state financing of education.

As a general rule, rich districts spend more per pupil, and poorer districts spend less—except for federal money, which mainly goes into poverty areas. The courts are starting to deal with this problem, often deciding that the states must resolve the disequilibrium and guarantee more equality of financing for all students. In several cases, the state supreme courts in New Jersey, Ohio, and Arizona have ruled that the disparity among districts in spending per pupil is not constitutional and has to be changed.

Thus far, some school districts are balking at change because people are willing to spend the exorbitant prices for houses in some upscale suburbs, and then pay equally exorbitant school taxes. To deprive them of this extra privilege—and burden—frightens them.

The public education crisis continues to compound each day, placing enormous pressures on communities, their school boards, and the state legislatures. In addition to the crisis of inferior teachers and schooling, we also have the problems of inadequate administrators, biased PTAs, overactive unions, a teacher shortage, rising school taxes, ineffectual school boards, and indifferent voters.

The chaos in education, which comes together most strikingly in the community, paradoxically has a silver lining. It presents an excellent opportunity for citizens to finally shake the complacency of the Establishment by developing a plan of action that will gain the attention of parents, the public, and perhaps even a few enlightened educators.

CONCLUSION

How to Reform, Rebuild, and Regain Our Public Schools

American public education occupies a peculiar position in American life. While all other professions and vocations have advanced in skill and substance over the last half century, teaching and learning in grades K–12 have actually regressed. That is, our children are less well educated today than at any time in history. The situation is particularly unusual because at no time has there been more to learn.

Medicine, science, and technology have moved ahead exponentially, while education has not only lagged, but is stubbornly less and less enlightened, substituting faddish theory for proven, time-tested fundamentals. Basic skills once taken for granted, such as reading, are no longer easily obtained. Although a certain level of information has always been considered essential for graduation from high school, that level no longer exists. Students now too often enter the adult world without the knowledge of an educated person.

Meanwhile, attempts to truly change the system for the better are blocked at every turn by the Establishment. Recently I spoke at length with Dr. Leo Klagholz, who was commissioner of education of New Jersey until 1999, when he resigned the post to become Distinguished Professor of Educational Policy Studies at a local university. Dr. Klagholz has been a major force for good as the father of alternate certification. In addition, he has been a skeptical thorn in the side of the Establishment.

"Were you forced out?" I candidly asked Dr. Klagholz.

"No, I had the confidence of Governor Whitman and could have stayed on if I wanted to."

"Then why leave such a prestigious and important post?"

"I had spent twenty years promoting educational change from within the system, often successfully but always against strong resistance from various segments of the Establishment," he responded. "I was approaching the end of my legal term as Commissioner anyway, and I felt the time had finally come to promote reform from the outside."

His views about the current Establishment are largely negative. He sees the public education system as "increasingly rigid and lacking a sense of urgency about the need to improve students' academic performance."

In Massachusetts, another leader of reform, Dr. John Silber, is the main target of the reactionary Establishment because of his tightening of the teacher certification exam, which is eliminating massive numbers of unqualified candidates. (He too, has recently resigned.)

Still another state where reformers are in conflict with the Establishment is Pennsylvania, where Secretary of Education Eugene Hickok is trying to crack down on poor teacher selection and training. He also has gained the enmity of the Establishment and the union, whose concern for students is superseded by their concern for teachers and administrators, a concept that flies in the face of quality education.

Hickok's latest move is a new set of standards that raises the entrance requirement for teacher trainees from a C+ average in high school to a B (3.0). This simple reform, which seems obvious, could eliminate the lower third of education students.

For years, the Establishment has stonewalled its critics. At first it used every public relations tactic to convince parents and citizens that change wasn't necessary. When finally the most stubborn of the status quo defenders admitted that reform was needed, the Establishment raced in front, saying, "Don't worry, we'll do it ourselves."

That false assurance no longer works. A program of *total* reform pressed from the outside is necessary. The entire structure of K–12 teaching in America, from teachers on up, is faulty, as is its performance.

In the opening chapter, I laid out an indictment of the Establishment with a promise to provide constructive changes. I have done that throughout this book, but it is now my intent to summarize the reforms needed to make American public education suitable for the twenty-first century.

Here then are the solutions to the Bill of Indictment (though not necessarily in the same order) against those who have robbed us of the precious heritage of public education.

1. RAISE LICENSING EXAM STANDARDS FOR NEW TEACHERS FAR BEYOND THE PRESENT 9TH OR 10TH GRADE LEVEL. Teacher certification tests should be made more rigorous, even more than the new Massachusetts screen. Licensing exams should be at least at the level of third-year college students, with emphasis on general knowledge, not educational theory.

Conclusion

2. STRENGTHEN THE WEAK K–12 CURRICULUM. Replace "whole language" with phonics education and the sounding out of words in reading. Drop social studies and teach history and geography separately and earlier. Four years of English, history, science, and mathematics should be required for graduation from high school, along with exams in all major subjects, as now contemplated by the New York State Board of Regents.

   Physics, trigonometry, and intermediate algebra should also be required in all secondary schools, along with philosophy and economics. Courses in the classics should be reintroduced, as many Protestant-based private schools are now doing.

3. MODIFY TENURE LAWS FOR TEACHERS. We should retain tenure for all teachers to protect their independence of expression, the same right granted to college teachers. However, tenure should be eliminated for incompetence. That should be judged by school boards, principals, and superintendents, perhaps even by teaching peers. We need to amend state laws accordingly.

4. CLOSE ALL UNDERGRADUATE SCHOOLS OF EDUCATION. This is a prime reform. By totally eliminating high school graduates from teacher training, we automatically raise the level of the education student. Teacher training should be *solely* a one-year postgraduate course in teaching methods and student teaching for college graduates with no prior education courses. Only those with good college grades, at least a 3.0 grade point average, should be admitted to training, yielding a smarter, more mature brand of teacher. The same reform in 1910 changed the face of medicine for the better.

5. REEVALUATE ALL TEACHERS AFTER FIVE YEARS ON THE JOB. At that time, they should be recertified and receive tenure

or be asked to leave the "profession" (a term that would then be more appropriate than it is today).

6. ELIMINATE THE INFERIOR DOCTOR OF EDUCATION DEGREE. Most principals and superintendents now possess the Ed.D. degree, which requires almost no study of the liberal arts and sciences. A Ph.D., with full foreign language and broad knowledge requirements, should be necessary for a teacher to advance to an administrative post. The Ed.D., a false doctorate, should be eliminated by law in all states.

7. REGULATE TEACHERS' UNIONS. The NEA and AFT claim to be both professional organizations and teachers' unions at the same time. State legislation is needed to separate the functions and create two separate groups. The unions now legally engage in political activity, which should not be permitted to a professional organization. Simultaneously, school districts should not act as collectors of union dues, nor should teachers be forced to use unions as their bargaining agent, as is now the case in most states.

8. DISBAND THE NATIONAL, STATE, AND LOCAL PTAS. They should be replaced by independent PTOs, which will act on behalf of parents and students. In the future, teachers should not be allowed to join such groups, which should have only parents as members. That would change the ineffective PTAs into pressure groups for better education instead of their present role as adjuncts of the Establishment and the unions.

9. AWARD VOUCHERS STATEWIDE FOR ALL CHILDREN IN FAILING SCHOOLS. Florida is leading this movement by permitting students, mainly minorities, to attend private schools with $4,000 yearly vouchers when the public schools fail to educate them, as is usually the case.

Conclusion

10. INCREASE THE NUMBER OF ALTERNATE-CERTIFICATION TEACH-
ERS. Since these teachers all hold a college degree in a
subject other than education, they are—almost by definition—better prepared and more mature teachers for our
children. Until undergraduate schools of education are
closed, alternate-certification teachers should gradually
take over the instruction of public school students.

Equally important: Permit principals and superintendents to hire brilliant college graduates to teach their
specialty in high school—*immediately*—without any education training at all, just as private schools now do.

11. ELIMINATE TOP-HEAVY SCHOOL BUREAUCRACIES AND EXCESS
SUPPORT PERSONNEL. Bureaucrats, who have more than
doubled in number from 98,000 to 217,000 in a generation, make up a powerful, expensive, top-heavy group in
the Establishment. Similarly, we have over 2 million non-
teacher support personnel, a phenomenon that does not
exist in other nations. The two groups should be cut back
by at least one-third and the money used to raise the salaries of teachers.

12. SEPARATE TRAINING AND SALARIES FOR HIGH SCHOOL TEACHERS.
Secondary school teachers should have much the same
training and status as college professors. At present they
take fewer courses in their specialties than do ordinary
college majors in the same subjects. Less than 1 in 5 high
school teachers of science and math have noneducation
master's degrees in their specialties. Properly educated
high school teachers deserve higher salaries than elementary grade teachers, and we owe it to parents to separate
secondary schools, with their own noneducation-trained
superintendent of schools, from the lower grades.

13. CUT BACK ON PSYCHOLOGY IN THE SCHOOL SYSTEM. There has
been a broad expansion of psychological services in pub-

lic schools, with 125,000 counselors and school psychologists now in the system. There is no evidence that it has helped students or parents, nor has it predicted or prevented violence. It violates privacy, divides students and parents, and is generally administered by undertrained personnel with excessive faith in personality and psychological tests, up to and including the Rorschach ink blots. I recommend a reduction in psychological personnel and new requirements: If they are not licensed to practice on the general public, they cannot be hired by the school system. We also need strict rules that information be shared with parents and that schools receive parental permission before delivering any psychological services to children.

14. REGAIN CONTROL OF SCHOOL BOARDS FROM EDUCATORS. At present most of the 97,000 elected school board members are controlled by the Establishment rather than vice versa. They are awed by educators' jargon and weak degrees and generally unaware of what is required for a solid curriculum and administrative competence. One reason is citizen passivity. Parents and others need to vote in school board elections and choose members sophisticated enough to know what is needed to improve the schools. Political parties should keep their noses out of our education system.

15. REJECT NEW, UNPROVEN EDUCATION THEORIES. Public school education wasn't broken in the 1930s, '40s, and '50s, yet contemporary teachers and education professors have since tried to change and fix it with faddish new theories, all of which appear to be false. They include new, then whole math, whole science, whole language, and the general thesis that innovation can substitute for time-tested ideas. The goal in public education should be to *return*

to tradition and superior curriculums that worked quite well.

16. STOP GRADE INFLATION. One reason parents have not revolted against the Establishment is that schools cleverly give false, inflated grades to students, which pleases proud parents. Grades are now generally one full level above what is normal, and exaggerated Honor Rolls proliferate. Inflation is so extensive among the Establishment that education students who were C+ students in high school, which is near the bottom, suddenly become A− students in college. Parents should trust standardized tests, whether the SAT or ACT, and especially exams administered statewide, and take teacher evaluations with a grain of parental salt.

17. DISCONTINUE "ED PSYCH" COURSES FOR TEACHER TRAINING. False science can lead the unsophisticated astray. Impressionable college sophomores and juniors studying to become teachers are overinfluenced by "human development" courses, which are generally inaccurate. Most important, as a result of this training, teachers adopt the social work/psychology model and de-emphasize their true role as instructors of the young.

18. STATE LEGISLATORS NEED TO SUPPORT THE PUBLIC, NOT THE EDUCATIONAL ESTABLISHMENT. Mainly ignorant of educational problems and in happy receipt of political contributions from the education lobby, state legislators—who have the final say in the public education of our children—tend to follow the lead of the Establishment, not citizens, parents, or reformers. Instead, they need to understand what leaders like Dr. Silber have done in Massachusetts and act accordingly in defending the rights of parents and students, not educators.

19. NAME A DIFFERENT TYPE OF EDUCATOR TO THE JOB OF SUPERIN-

TENDENT OF SCHOOLS. The school superintendent is just as important to the future of learning as the school boards. At present, most superintendents have extremely poor academic credentials and are trained almost exclusively in administration. If true reform is to take place at the local level, we need superintendents who—like prep school headmasters and college presidents—are trained in scholarship, not in education. This type of person would expand the horizons of public schools so that they rival private schools, most of which see the Establishment as a roadblock, not a facilitator, of good education.

The public needs to break out of its lethargy and its unjustified trust in the Establishment and become knowledgeable about schooling, much as they are about business or home buying.

The public must be in a position to challenge the system and warn the Establishment that if radical changes are not made, and rapidly, public education may be entering its last days as the bulwark of democracy that Alexis de Tocqueville envisioned— only to be replaced by a new, more responsive system.

A TEST OF STUDENT ACHIEVEMENT
A Student Inventory of Basic Knowledge

F ind out what your child really knows and doesn't know. What has he or she actually learned at school?

The truth is often quite different from what teachers tell parents. The reality can be at great variance from the A's and B's given by the school on over-generous report cards—all part of the "grade inflation" and "self-esteem" concepts now rampant in public education.

The following quizzes, which include one for the 4th grade, another for the 8th grade, and still another for high school seniors, will give you a truer insight into your child's academic performance and level of general knowledge. (The tests can also be used for the 3rd, 5th, 7th, 9th, and 11th grades, as mentioned.)

The questions are basic and representative of what a child should know at the appropriate age. Because the questions are not multiple choice queries, the tests can be given to children by their parents either orally or in writing.

If carefully used (not allowing students to see the printed answers), these quizzes can help you understand if your child is being properly tutored in school and if the grade level curriculum is sufficiently demanding.

Each of the tests contains sixty questions of general knowledge, covering history, geography, math, and science. A good student should answer at least fifty-two of the sixty questions correctly, with a score of 87 percent. A score below that indicates that the school is not doing its job in educating your child. (To learn even more about your child's grasp of general knowledge, you might quiz him or her on the test above and below the student's own grade level.)

Let's begin with a quiz designed for the 4th grade, which can also serve for third and fifth grade students.

1. Which ocean washes up on the East Coast of the United States?
2. Which ocean washes up on the West Coast of the United States?
3. What country is directly north of the United States?
4. What country lies directly to the south of the United States?
5. In what year did Columbus discover the New World?
6. How many states are there in the United States?
7. Why did the Pilgrims come to America?
8. From what country did they come?
9. In what area—now a state—did they settle?
10. In what direction does the sun rise?
11. In what direction does it set?
12. Who wrote the Declaration of Independence?
13. On what day in what year?

14. What gas in the air keeps us alive?
15. In what country is Paris?
16. In what country is London?
17. In what country is Rome?
18. How many colonies joined to form the United States?
19. Name six of them.
20. Without using pencil and paper or a calculator—what is 9 times 9?
21. What is 6 × 9?
22. What is 7 × 8?
23. Who was the first president of the United States?
24. Who is the president now?
25. How many quarts are in a gallon?
26. What is the capital of the United States?
27. What is the capital of your state?
28. Can you name fifteen of the fifty states?
29. Who is the vice president of the United States?
30. Name one state that borders on your state.
31. Without pencil and paper, add 12 and 13.
32. Divide 24 by 3 in your head.
33. Add 7 and 26 without writing it down.
34. In reading, what is the sound of the letters "t-i-o-n" when they come at the end of a word?
35. How many inches in a foot?
36. How many ounces in a pound?
37. How many feet in a yard?
38. About how many inches in a meter?
39. How do we see the force called "gravity" at work?
40. What material does a magnet attract?
41. When organic matter burns completely, what element is mainly left?
42. What is photosynthesis?
43. Name one city in Canada.

44. At what temperature Fahrenheit does water freeze?
45. At what temperature Fahrenheit does water boil?
46. What is the Emancipation Proclamation?
47. Who wrote it?
48. What is the largest city in the United States?
49. Can you name either the second or third largest cities?
50. Around what body in space does the Earth revolve?
51. How long does it take for one complete revolution?
52. Name three planets in addition to the Earth.
53. What are the first three notes of the musical scale?
54. What word is the opposite of "neat"?
55. What word has the same meaning as "error"?
56. What is the name of the Queen of England?
57. What is H_2O?
58. What two elements make up this compound?
59. In your head divide 300 by 15.
60. Who invented the airplane?

This is the quiz for 8th graders, which may also be taken by students in 7th and 9th grades.

1. Divide 64 by 8 in your head.
2. On what continent is Israel?
3. On what continent is Formosa?
4. On what continent is Turkey?
5. If X is 9 and Y is 4, what is X minus Y plus seven divided by three? (You can use pencil and paper but not a calculator.)
6. In what country is Newfoundland?
7. Who first flew solo across the Atlantic Ocean, in 1927?
8. What is the brightest "star" in the evening sky?
9. Who was the president of the United States before the present one?
10. Who was his vice president?

11. On what continent is Brazil?
12. On what day and in what year was Pearl Harbor bombed to begin America's entry in World War II?
13. Name four countries in the Far East.
14. Who was president of the United States during World War II?
15. Name one play written by William Shakespeare.
16. How much is 4 squared?
17. What is the highest mountain in the world?
18. Who was Patrick Henry and for what was he famous?
19. Name the first five presidents of the United States.
20. What city did the Puritans found when they came to America?
21. Where did they come from?
22. What is sodium chloride?
23. What two countries fought in the War of 1812?
24. About how many days are there between each full moon?
25. If five children are the following ages: 5, 7, 8, 9, and 11, what is their average age? (You can use paper and pencil but not a calculator.)
26. What body of water keeps England from being very cold?
27. Without using paper and pencil, how much is 11 × 12?
28. Who invented the telegraph?
29. Who invented the telephone?
30. How many letters in the alphabet?
31. In the progression 2, 5, 8, 11, what is the next number?
32. In the progression 6, 10, 7, 11, 8, 12, 9, what is the next number?
33. How many senators are there in the U.S. Senate?
34. What were the last two states to be admitted into the Union?
35. What American author wrote *Tom Sawyer* and *Huckleberry Finn?*

36. What type of engine runs most automobiles?
37. What type of engine runs most large airplanes?
38. How many feet in a mile?
39. Name two cities in Russia.
40. Name two cities in Great Britain.
41. What is the capital of Ireland?
42. Name two cities in France.
43. What is the longest river in the United States?
44. What is the longest river in South America?
45. On what continent is India?
46. What explorer sought the Fountain of Youth and discovered Florida?
47. What was *Sputnik?*
48. What is the longest river in China?
49. What American general led the Allied invasion of Europe in World War II?
50. Who became president when Franklin D. Roosevelt died?
51. When was the Civil War fought?
52. Who was Thomas Paine?
53. From what country did we get many of our western states?
54. In what country is Prague?
55. On what continent is the Cape of Good Hope?
56. What was the Louisiana Purchase?
57. What American president bought the Louisiana Purchase from France?
58. Who was Benedict Arnold?
59. Who was Alexander Hamilton?
60. Who was John Quincy Adams?

This quiz is designed for high school seniors, most of whom will go on to college. The test is equally valuable for 11th graders.

A Test of Student Achievement

1. Name eight of the presidents who served before Abraham Lincoln.
2. Name the most recent eight presidents beginning with the present one and going backward.
3. Name four of the states taken from Mexico in the Mexican War.
4. When was it fought?
5. Who was the president at the time?
6. In a right triangle whose base is five and perpendicular leg is also five, what is the length of the hypotenuse to the nearest whole number? (You can use pencil and paper but not a calculator.)
7. Who was the president of the Confederate States?
8. Who was the victorious Union general?
9. When Lincoln was assassinated, which vice president became president?
10. Name three plays written by William Shakespeare.
11. What was the name of his theatre?
12. Mention two of the levels of air surrounding the earth.
13. If X is 3 and Y is 2, how much is X^2 plus Y^3? (You can use pencil and paper but not a calculator.)
14. Who was president of the United States during World War I?
15. What was the Marshall Plan?
16. Who was the vice president who became president after the assassination of President Kennedy?
17. Who was the hero of the Battle of New Orleans who later became an American president?
18. What was the Great Society?
19. What is meant by Greenwich Mean Time?
20. About how large is the earth around the equator?
21. Who was the dictator of the Soviet Union during World War II?

22. Who was the dictator who won the Spanish Civil War in the 1930s?
23. There are twenty countries in NATO, the North Atlantic Treaty Alliance. Name ten of them.
24. Who wrote the novel *Ulysses?*
25. Name two books by Ernest Hemingway.
26. What was the picture writing of ancient Egypt called?
27. In grammar, name four prepositions.
28. Who wrote *Pride and Prejudice?*
29. What is CO^2?
30. What is CO?
31. What element is the basis of atomic energy?
32. Which isotope of that element provides the energy?
33. Name five countries that border on the Mediterranean Sea.
34. What is the capital of Hungary?
35. What is the capital of the Czech Republic?
36. What is the capital of Denmark?
37. What is the capital of Sweden?
38. What is the capital of Norway?
39. Name three U.S. states that border on the Gulf of Mexico.
40. Name two Greek writers or philosophers.
41. What lighter-than-air gas is used in blimps?
42. Who was the prime minister of Great Britain during most of World War II?
43. Who was the King of England during World War II?
44. Who is considered the Father of the American Constitution?
45. Where are the Dardanelles?
46. How many members are there in the House of Representatives?
47. Madame Curie discovered what element?

48. What fundamental law of science was discovered by Sir Isaac Newton?
49. In what country was the Magna Carta signed?
50. Who was the artist who sculpted the statue *David* in Florence, Italy?
51. What is the Sistine Chapel? Where is it?
52. If the length of the radius of a circle is 3, what is the circle's circumference, to the nearest whole number?
53. Who discovered the fact that the sun is at the center of our planetary system?
54. What four areas make up the United Kingdom of Great Britain?
55. From which country did the United States buy Alaska? About when?
56. Who assassinated Abraham Lincoln?
57. Who painted *The Last Supper*?
58. What were the Articles of Confederation?
59. In what city was George Washington inaugurated as our first president?
60. Who was Aaron Burr?

The answers appear on separate pages at the end of these quizzes. Do not let your child see them. Either cover them up or tear out the pages before giving the test to a student.

A Test of Student Achievement

The following are the answers to the three quizzes.

Quiz for 4th graders (as well as 3rd and 5th graders)
1. Atlantic Ocean
2. Pacific Ocean
3. Canada
4. Mexico
5. 1492
6. Fifty
7. Religious freedom
8. England
9. Massachusetts
10. East
11. West
12. Thomas Jefferson
13. July 4, 1776
14. Oxygen
15. France
16. England
17. Italy
18. Thirteen
19. New Hampshire, Massachusetts, Rhode Island, Connecticut, New York, New Jersey, Delaware, Pennsylvania, Maryland, Virginia, North Carolina, South Carolina, Georgia
20. 81
21. 54
22. 56
23. George Washington
25. Bill Clinton
26. 4
27. Washington, D.C.
28. Capital of your state

29. Al Gore
30. States around your state
31. 25
32. 8
33. 33
34. "shun"
35. 12
36. 16
37. 3
38. 39
39. Things are pulled down toward earth.
40. Iron
41. Carbon
42. Method by which plants create their food
43. Toronto, Montreal, Ottawa, Vancouver, Quebec, Winnipeg, etc.
44. 32 degrees
45. 212 degrees
46. Document that freed the slaves
47. Abraham Lincoln
48. New York City
49. Los Angeles and Chicago
50. The sun
51. One year
52. Mercury, Venus, Mars, Jupiter, Saturn, Uranus, Neptune, Pluto
53. Do, re, mi
54. Sloppy
55. Mistake
56. Elizabeth
57. Water
58. Hydrogen and Oxygen

59. 20
60. Wright Brothers

Answers to Quiz for 8th Graders (As well as 7th and 9th graders)

1. 8
2. Asia
3. Asia
4. Europe and Asia
5. 4
6. Canada
7. Charles Lindbergh
8. Venus
9. George Bush
10. Dan Quayle
11. South America
12. December 7, 1941
13. Japan, China, Taiwan, South Korea, North Korea, Indonesia, Malaysia, Singapore, Thailand, Vietnam
14. Franklin Delano Roosevelt
15. *Romeo and Juliet, Macbeth, Hamlet, Taming of the Shrew, Midsummer's Night Dream, The Tempest, All's Well That Ends Well, Othello*, etc.
16. 16
17. Mt. Everest
18. Patriot who said "Give me liberty or give me death."
19. George Washington, John Adams, Thomas Jefferson, James Madison, James Monroe
20. Boston
21. England
22. Salt
23. The United States and Great Britain
24. 27 days
25. 8

26. Gulf Stream
27. 132
28. Samuel Morse
29. Alexander Graham Bell
30. 26
31. 14
32. 13
33. 100
34. Hawaii and Alaska
35. Mark Twain
36. Internal combustion
37. Jet
38. 5,280
39. Moscow, Saint Petersburg, etc.
40. London, Manchester, Edinburgh, Glasgow, etc.
41. Dublin
42. Paris, Marseilles, Nice, Toulon, etc.
43. Mississippi
44. Amazon
45. Asia
46. Ponce de León
47. First space satellite, built by Russia
48. Yangtze
49. Dwight Eisenhower
50. Harry Truman
51. 1861–1865
52. Revolutionary War writer, author of *Common Sense*
53. Mexico
54. Czech Republic
55. Africa
56. Land between the Mississippi and the West
57. Thomas Jefferson
58. Revolutionary War general who defected to Britain

59. Early patriot who was a Federalist
60. Sixth president and son of John Adams

Answers to the Quiz for 12th Graders (As Well as 11th Graders)

1. Washington, Adams, Jefferson, Madison, Monroe, John Quincy Adams, Jackson, Van Buren, Harrison, Tyler, Polk, Taylor, Fillmore, Pierce, Buchanan
2. Clinton, Bush, Reagan, Carter, Ford, Nixon, Johnson, Kennedy
3. Arizona, New Mexico, Nevada, Colorado, Utah
4. 1846–1848
5. James K. Polk
6. 7
7. Jefferson Davis
8. General Grant
9. Andrew Johnson
10. *Romeo and Juliet, Macbeth, Hamlet, Taming of the Shrew, The Tempest, All's Well That Ends Well, Midsummer's Night Dream, Othello,* etc.
11. Globe
12. Atmosphere, stratosphere, ionosphere, exosphere
13. 17
14. Woodrow Wilson
15. Aid to Europe after World War II, named after the Secretary of State
16. Lyndon Johnson
17. Andrew Jackson
18. Name of Lyndon Johnson's social program
19. Global time beginning in Greenwich, England
20. 25,000 miles
21. Josef Stalin
22. Francisco Franco
23. United States, Great Britain, Germany, Canada, France,

Italy, Denmark, Norway, Iceland, Luxembourg, Belgium, Netherlands, Norway, Portugal, Greece, Turkey, Spain, Hungary, Czech Republic, Poland

24. James Joyce
25. *Farewell to Arms, For Whom the Bell Tolls, The Snows of Kilimanjaro, The Old Man and the Sea*
26. Hieroglyphics
27. of, from, to, by, in, since, etc.
28. Jane Austen
29. Carbon dioxide
30. Carbon monoxide
31. Uranium
32. U-235
33. Spain, France, Italy, Greece, Turkey, Syria, Lebanon, Israel, Egypt, Libya, Tunisia, Algeria, Morocco
34. Budapest
35. Prague
36. Copenhagen
37. Stockholm
38. Oslo
39. Texas, Louisiana, Alabama, Florida
40. Aristotle, Plato, Socrates
41. Helium
42. Winston Churchill
43. George VI
44. James Madison
45. In Turkey, straits separating the Mediterranean Sea and the Black Sea
46. 435
47. Radium
48. Gravity
49. England
50. Michelangelo

51. Chapel at the Vatican in Rome painted by Michelangelo
52. 19
53. Copernicus, a Polish scientist
54. England, Scotland, Wales, and Northern Ireland
55. Russia, 1867
56. John Wilkes Booth
57. Leonardo da Vinci
58. The compact that bound the states prior to the Constitution
59. New York City
60. Vice President under Thomas Jefferson

ENDNOTES AND BIBLIOGRAPHY

CHAPTER ONE

Details of international competition, including South Korea and the United States, from "International Assessment of Educational Progress," *A World of Differences: An International Assessment of Mathematics and Science,* 1989.

"The Geography Learning of High School Seniors," National Assessment of Educational Progress (NAEP), 1990, U.S. Department of Education.

"The U.S. History Report Card," National Assessment of Educational Progress (NAEP), 1990, U.S. Department of Education.

"Results of October Test for Prospective Educators Released" (press release), November 9, 1998, Massachusetts Department of Education.

"January Educator Candidates Tests Results by Higher Education Institution Are Released," (press release), February 17, 1999, Massachusetts Department of Education.

Education as the nation's prime priority from surveys done in 1997, 1998, and 1999 by the Pew Research Center for the People and the Press, Washington, D.C.

Haberman, Clyde, "Vital Lessons for Students Is Workaday: Many Graduates Lack the Skills to Win Over a Potential Employer," *New York Times,* September 25, 1998.

Figures on the economic value of education, "Usual Weekly Earnings of Employed Full-time Wage and Salary Workers by Educational Attainment, Age, Sex, Race and Hispanic Origin, 1997 Annual Averages," Current Population Survey, U.S. Bureau of Labor Statistics, New York City, N.Y.

"Science and Engineering Doctorate Awards: 1996," Division of Science Resources Study, National Science Foundation, Arlington, Virginia.

"Statistical Profiles of Foreign Doctoral Recipients in Science and Engineering," November 1990, National Science Foundation, Arlington, Virginia.

Various statistics on public education from the National Library of Education, Office of Educational Research and Improvement, U.S. Department of Education.

"Black-White Test Score Gap, Long Term Trends, 1973–1996," National Assessment of Educational Progress, U.S. Department of Education.

Comments on poor student performance and socio-economics, Fuller, Bruce, "Debate Over Testing Doesn't Add Up," *Knight Ridder/Tribune News Service*, July 27, 1998.

Pay scale of teachers from the National Education Association, Washington, D.C., and departments of education in Connecticut, New York, and New Jersey.

Comparative figures on teacher earnings by state from "Estimated Average Annual Salary of Teachers in Public Elementary and Secondary Schools, By State, 1969–70 to 1997–98," U.S. Department of Education.

"Getting By: What American Teenagers Really Think About Their Schools," A Report from Public Agenda, 1997, New York City, N.Y.

De Tocqueville, Alexis, *Democracy in America* (two volumes), 1966, A.A. Knopf, New York.

Conant, James, *The Education of American Teachers*, McGraw-Hill, 1963, New York.

CHAPTER TWO

Honor Roll statistics from the Greenwich Schools, Greenwich, Connecticut.

Advanced placement figures from the College Board, New York City.

Endnotes and Bibliography

Lerner, Barbara, "America's Schools: Still Failing After All These Years," *National Review*, September 15, 1997.

NAEP and other student performance results, Finn, Chester E., Jr., "Can the Schools Be Saved?" *Commentary*, September 1996.

Details on poor student performance, Finn, Chester E., Jr., and Ravitch, Diane, "Is Educational Reform a Failure?" *USA Today Magazine*, November 1996.

Finn, Chester E., Jr., "Will They Ever Learn" (decline in student performance), *National Review*, May 29, 1995.

Material on remedial college classes, Ravitch, Diane, "Do It Right The First Time," *Forbes*, February 10, 1997.

Performance of American students in international competition, Lewis, Anne C., *Phi Delta Kappan*, December 1996.

Performance of American students in science in international competition, Wheeler, Gerald, *Science*, March 13, 1998.

Poetter, Thomas E., "International Assessment of Student Achievement," *The Clearing House*, March–April 1998.

Material on decrease in math performance in international competition with age, Lewis, Anne C., "Math and Science," *The Education Digest*, September 1997.

Comment on American performance on TIMSS international tests, Elmore, Richard F., "The Politics of Education Reform," *Issues in Science and Technology*.

"Pursuing Excellence: Eighth Grade Findings from the Third International Math and Science Study," (Video presentation), National Center for Education Statistics, U.S. Department of Education.

"Pursuing Excellence: A Study of U.S. Fourth-Grade Mathematics and Science Achievement in International Context," National Center for Education Statistics, U.S. Department of Education.

"School Spirit," (U.S. low test scores versus our robust economy), *The New Republic*, March 23, 1998.

"Trends in Average Scale Scores for the Nation" (in science, math, reading and writing), Report in Brief, NAEP 1996 Trends in Academic Progress, National Assessment of Educational Progress, National Center for Education Statistics, U.S. Department of Education.

"Percentage of Students at or above the Reading Achievement Levels for the Nation, 1992, 1994, and 1998," NAEP, U.S. Department of Education.

"Report Card for the Nation and the States: NAEP 1996 Science," National Center for Education Statistics, U.S. Department of Education.

"Report Card for the Nation and the States, NAEP 1996 Mathematics," National Center for Education Statistics, U.S. Department of Education.

"SAT Table 1: Average SAT Scores of Entering College Classes, 1967–1998," Educational Testing Service, Princeton, New Jersey, 1998.

Change in SAT Scores from "SAT Table 1: Average SAT Scores of Entering College Classes, 1967–1998," College Board, New York City, N.Y.

SAT statistics on grade inflation, "Rising Grades and Falling Test Scores May Indicate Grade Inflation: 1988, annually through 1998," Educational Testing Service, Princeton, New Jersey.

Material on National Education Goals Panel, Schrof, Joannie M., "What Kids Will Have to Know: See If You're Good Enough to Compete with Students at a World-Class Level," *U.S. News & World Report*, April 1, 1996.

Relative costs of education in various nations, from the Organization for Economic Cooperation and Development (OECD), which includes 39 nations, headquartered in Washington, D.C.

"Public Expenditure on Education as a Percentage of Total Public Expenditure by Level of Education (1995)," OECD Washington Center, Washington, D.C.

Klebnikow, Paul, "What Are Condoms Made Of?" (French schools have higher performance at lower cost than U.S.), *Forbes*, September 11, 1995.

Endnotes and Bibliography

Peltzman, Sam, "What's Behind the Decline of Public Schools," *USA Today Magazine*, March 1994.

"Current Expenditures per Pupil in Average Daily Attendance in Public Elementary and Secondary Schools, by State, 1959–60 to 1995–96," National Center for Education Statistics, U.S. Department of Education.

Cost of public education, from "Summary of Expenditures for Public Elementary and Secondary Education, by Purpose, 1919–20 to 1995–96," *Statistics of State School Systems*, National Center for Education Statistics, U.S. Department of Education.

Class size in various private schools from "Average Class Size for Teachers in Departments and Self-Contained Classrooms, by Selected School Characteristics, 1993–1994," *Schools and Staffing Survey*, National Center for Education Statistics, U.S. Department of Education.

Class size in public schools, "Average Class Size for Teachers in Self-Contained Classrooms and Departments, by State: 1993–1994," *Schools and Staffing Survey*, National Center for Education Statistics, U.S. Department of Education, Washington, D.C.

Pupil-teacher ratios from "Public and Private Elementary and Secondary Teachers and Pupil-Teacher Ratios, by Level: Fall 1955 to Fall 1998, *Statistics of Public Elementary and Secondary Day Schools*, National Center for Education Statistics, U.S. Department of Education.

Figures on class sizes internationally from "Average Class Size at Grade Level to Which Most 13-year-old Students Are Assigned, According to School Administrators, by Country: 1991," *Education in States and Nations, 1991*, U.S. Department of Education.

Feldman, Sandra, president of the American Federation of Teachers, "Think Small" (class size), *The New Republic*, March 23, 1998.

"Sizing Up Class Size," Editorial, *Wall Street Journal*, September 30, 1998.

Parkinson, Northcote C., *Parkinson's Law and Other Studies in Administration*, 1957, Houghton Mifflin, Boston.

Endnotes and Bibliography

Statistics on expenditure per pupil in New York State from the Department of Education, Albany, New York.

Hartocollis, Anemona, "Most 4th Graders Fail Albany's New English Test," *New York Times*, May 26, 1999.

Details on reading success of minority students at P.S. 161, Brooklyn from interview with its principal, Irwin Kurz.

More on same from Ravitch, Diane, "Success in Brooklyn, But not in D.C.," *Forbes*, June 2, 1997.

Same from Siegel, Jessica, "The Jewel in the Crown." *Teacher*, October 1997.

CHAPTER THREE

Hickok, Eugene, Secretary of Education, Pennsylvania, "Higher Standards for Teacher Training," *Policy Review*, September–October 1998.

Personal interview with Dr. Leo Klagholz, then Commissioner of Education, New Jersey.

"1998 Profile of College-Bound Seniors College Plans" (22 vocations correlated against SAT scores), Educational Testing Service, Princeton, New Jersey.

"General Test Percentage Distribution of Scores Within Intended Broad Graduate Major Field," Graduate Record Exam (GRE), Educational Testing Service, Princeton, New Jersey.

Scores on GRE from "Graduate Record Examination 1997–1998 Guide to the Use of Scores," Educational Testing Service, Princeton, New Jersey.

Further statistics on SAT and GRE exams of education students from Educational Testing Service (ETS), Princeton, New Jersey.

America's Teachers: Profile of a Profession: 1993–4, National Center for Education Statistics, U.S. Department of Education.

"Teacher Education and Qualifications," *Schools and Staffing Survey: 1993–4*, Chapter 3, National Center for Education Statistics, U.S. Department of Education.

Endnotes and Bibliography

"Years of school completed by persons aged 25 and over and 25–29, by race/ethnicity and sex: 1910 to 1997," U.S. Department of Education.

Koerner, James, *The Miseducation of American Teachers*, 1963, Houghton Mifflin, Boston.

Schwartz, Sheila, "Teaching's Unlettered Future" (poor quality of education students), *New York Times*, August 6, 1998.

Relation of student performance and teacher training, "State Indicators of Science and Math Education, 1997," Council of Chief State School Officers, State Education Assessment Center, Washington, D.C.

Sowell, Thomas, *Education: Assumption Versus History*, 1986, Hoover Institution Press, Stanford University.

Sowell, Thomas, *Knowledge and Decisions*, 1996, Basic Books, New York.

Comments on teacher accreditation by NCATE, Dyrli, Odvard Egil, "More Teacher Training Urged," *Technology and Learning*, January 1998.

Interview with Assistant Headmaster (formerly Vice Principal) at Choate.

Interview with chairman of the education department at a Connecticut state university.

J. Sykes, Charles J., *Dumbing Down Our Kids*, 1995, St. Martin's, New York.

Hirsch, E.D., Jr., *The Schools We Need & Why We Don't Have Them*, 1996, Doubleday, New York.

Regnier, Paul, "The Illusion of Technique and the Intellectual Life of Schools," *Phi Delta Kappan*, September 1994.

Kramer, Rita, *Ed School Follies*, Free Press, 1991.

Basinger, Julianne, "Federal Report Urges Better Teacher Training," *The Chronicle of Higher Education*, September 25, 1998.

Grenier, Richard, "U.S. Teachers Lead Race Toward Education's Nadir," *Insight on the News*, March 30, 1998.

Schmidt, Peter, "State and Federal Officials Push for Improvements in Teacher Education," *The Chronicle of Higher Education,* February 28, 1997.

Ishler, Richard E. "The Future of Schools of Education: Is There One?" *National Forum,* Fall 1996.

Furnham, Adrian, "The Power of Negative Thinking" (teacher's low expectations for students), *Across the Board,* November–December 1995.

Material on higher degrees for teachers and how it affects students, Goldhaber, Dan D., and Brewer, Dominic J., "When Should We Reward Degrees for Teachers?" *Phi Delta Kappan,* October 1998.

CHAPTER FOUR

Interview with Marion Josephs.

Comment on rote learning from Barlow, Dudley, "The Teacher's Lounge," *Education Digest,* March 1997.

"The Reading Excellence Act," *Right to Read Report,* December 1998, National Right to Read Newsletter.

Duff, Christina, "How Whole Language Became a Hot Potato in and out of Academia" (Whole Language versus Phonics), *Wall Street Journal,* October 30, 1996.

Steinberg, Jacques, "Teaching Children to Read: Politics Colors Debate over Methods," *New York Times,* May 11, 1997.

Interview with William Honig, former state superintendent of education, California.

Anderson, Duncan, and Warshaw, Michael, "How 'Hooked on Phonics' Got Whacked by the Blob," *Success,* April 1996.

Sweet, Robert W., Jr., "Don't Read, Don't Tell: Clinton's Phony War on Illiteracy," *Policy Review,* May/June 1997.

"Is Whole Language Dead?" *Investor's Business Daily,* September 28, 1995.

Endnotes and Bibliography

"Report Card for the Nation and the States—NAEP 1992 Reading," National Center for Education Statistics, Department of Education.

"Report Card for the Nation and the States—NAEP 1994 Reading," National Center for Education Statistics, Department of Education.

Bronner, Ethan, "Turnaround in Texas Schools Looks Good for Bush in 2000," *New York Times*, May 28, 1999.

"Report Card for the Nation and the States—NAEP 1998 Reading," National Center for Education Statistics, Department of Education.

"Grade 4 Reading Achievement Levels, NAEP Trial State Assessment in Reading, Public Schools Only," 1993–1994, National Center for Education Statistics, U.S. Department of Education.

"Percentage of Students at or Above the Reading Achievement Levels for the Nation, 1992, 1994, and 1998" (and other measures of reading), National Assessment of Educational Progress (NAEP), U.S. Department of Education.

Goodman, Ken, *The Whole Language Catalog*, 1991, American School Publishers.

McGuiness, Diane, *Why Our Children Can't Read and What We Can Do About It*, 1997, Free Press, New York.

Hancock, LynNell, and Wingert, Pat, "If You Can Read This. . . . You've Learned Phonics. Or So Its Supporters Say," *Newsweek*, May 13, 1996.

Mendel, Ed, "Read Their Lips: Phonics Is Back," *The San Diego Union-Tribune*, October 12, 1995.

Levine, Art, "The Great Debate Revisited," (phonics and whole language methods of reading), *Atlantic Monthly*, December 1994.

Thomas, Cal, "The Phonics Revolution Keeps Growing," *Human Events*, June 21, 1996.

Archibold, Randal C., "Reading Scores Are Steady; A Few States Gain," *New York Times*, March 5, 1999.

"Grade 4 Reading Achievement Levels, NAEP Trial State Assessment in Reading, Public Schools Only," National Assessment of Educational Progress, U.S. Department of Education.

"1994 Average Grade 4 Reading Proficiency by Race/Ethnicity, Public Schools Only," National Assessment of Educational Progress, U.S. Department of Education.

"Report Card for the Nation and the States: NAEP 1998 Reading," National Center for Education Statistics, U.S. Department of Education.

CHAPTER FIVE

Archibold, Randal C., "How Schools Measure the Talent to Teach," (teacher certification tests), *New York Times*, September 13, 1998.

Interview with a spokesperson of the Massachusetts Teachers Association.

North Carolina NEA attack on new licensing standards. "Testiness in the Tarheel State," *NEA Today*, September 1998.

"Massachusetts Teacher Tests: Communication and Literacy Skills Test, Sample Test Items and Responses," 1998. Massachusetts Department of Education.

Toch, Thomas, "Some 'Horibal' Test Results," *U.S. News & World Report*, July 13, 1998.

"January Educator Candidate Test Results by Higher Education Institution Are Released" (Press Release), February 17, 1999, Massachusetts Department of Education.

"Results of October Test for Prospective Educators Released" (Press Release), November 9, 1998, Massachusetts Department of Education.

"Massachusetts Teachers Fail First Independent Review; State Urged to Suspend Administration and Audit Exam," Ad Hoc Committee to Test The Teacher Test, Boston College, Chestnut Hill, Mass.

Sample questions on Praxis I from Educational Testing Service (ETS), Princeton, New Jersey.

Argument within the NCATE. Sutton, James H., "Reaching for Understanding—Response to Jonathan K. Parker," *Phi Delta Kappan*, May 1994.

Endnotes and Bibliography

Response to James H. Sutton on teacher accreditation, Parker, Jonathan K., "NCATE, PC and the LCME," *Phi Delta Kappan*, May 1994.

Material on NBPTS from that organization and from interview with spokesperson.

Comment by Senator Jeff Bingaman from Selingto, Jeffrey, "Colleges Oppose Senator's Plan to Improve Quality of Teacher Training," *The Chronicle of Higher Education*, May 15, 1998.

Forte, Lorraine, "Teachers Make a Class Act Using a Teaching Standard Program," *Education Digest*, December 1994.

Needham, Nancy R., "One Giant Step for Teaching," (National Board certification), *NEA Today*, December 1994.

Ballou, Dale, and Podgursky, Michael, "The Case Against Teacher Certification," *The Public Interest*, Summer 1998.

Reising, Bob, "National Certification for Teachers—What's New In . . . ," *The Clearing House*, July–August 1995.

CHAPTER SIX

"Report to the Nation and the States, NAEP 1966 Mathematics," National Center for Education Statistics, U.S. Department of Education.

"The 1994 High School Transcript Study Tabulations," September 1998, National Center for Education Statistics, U.S. Department of Education.

Academic assignment versus training from *America's Teachers: Profile of a Profession, 1993–94*, National Center for Education Statistics, U.S. Department of Education.

Joftus, Scott, and Berman, Ilene, "Great Expectations?—Defining and Assessing Rigor in State Standards for Mathematics and English Language Arts," Council for Basic Education, January 1998.

"More Difficult Courses Pay Off," Society for the Advancement of Education, *USA Today Magazine*, April 1996.

Endnotes and Bibliography

"Professional Standards for Teaching Mathematics," National Council of Teachers of Mathematics, Reston, Virginia.

Romberg, Thomas, "Creative Math or Just Fuzzy Math?" Op-Ed piece, *New York Times*, August 11, 1997.

Jennings, Marianne, "Why Our Kids Can't Do Math," *Readers Digest*, November 1997, Reprinted from the *Wall Street Journal*, December 17, 1996.

Interview with Marianne Jennings of Mathematically Correct.

Interview with Dr. Richard Askey, professor of mathematics at University of Wisconsin.

Comment about order of science teaching, quoting Leon Lederman, from Mervis, Jeffrey, "U.S. Tries Variations on High School Curriculum," *Science*, July 10, 1998.

Comments by Nobel Prize scientists on school curriculum, Coombs, Marian Kester. "More Rigor, Less Wonder," *Insight on the News*, July 27, 1998.

Material on teaching physics first, from Lederman, Leon M., "Getting High School Science in Order," *Technology Review*, April 1996.

Collins, Rhoda Power, "Middle School Science," *The Clearing House*, September–October 1994.

Holloway, Lynette, "Report Says Schools Lack Math and Science Needs," *New York Times*, March 2, 1999.

"Report to the Nation and the States: 1995 NAEP Science," National Center for Education Statistics, U.S. Department of Education.

"NAEP 1994 Geography: A First Look; Findings from the National Assessment of Educational Progress," National Center for Education Statistics, U.S. Department of Education.

Interview with Dr. Osa Brand, president of the Association of American Geographers, Washington, D.C.

"Red, White—and Blue—Conflict over a New History Curriculum," *Newsweek*, November 7, 1994.

Endnotes and Bibliography

Cross, Christopher T., and Lieberman, Myron, "Do Public Schools Need State-Mandated Educational Standards?" *Insight on the News*, February 17, 1997.

Hirsch, E. D., Jr., *Cultural Literacy: What Every American Needs to Know*, 1987, Houghton Mifflin, Boston.

Material on school curriculum from Core Knowledge Foundation, Charlottesville, Virginia, 22902.

"National Evaluation of Core Knowledge Sequence Implementation," Center for Organization of Schools, Johns Hopkins University, January 1999.

"K–5 Curriculum Guide for Parents," Greenwich Public Schools, Greenwich, Connecticut.

"Greenwich High School, Course of Study Guide 1999–2000," Greenwich Public Schools, Greenwich, Connecticut.

Results of national history tests, "NAEP 1994 U.S. History: A First Look," National Center for Education Statistics, U.S. Department of Education.

"History in the Making: An Independent Review of the Voluntary National History Standards," Special Report, January 1996, Council for Basic Education, Washington, D.C.

"1993 National Study of Postsecondary Faculty," October 1997, National Center for Education Statistics, U.S. Department of Education.

"National Standards for United States History: Grades 5–12 Expanded Edition," National Center for History in the Schools, University of California, Los Angeles.

"Baccalaureate and Beyond, Longitudinal Study: Second Follow up Field Test Report, 1996," May 1997, National Center for Education Statistics, U.S. Department of Education.

Weisberg, Jacob, "Old Ball and Cheney," (Lynn Cheney criticizes proposed National history standards), *New York*, May 27, 1996.

"Performance Standards: English Language Arts, Mathematics, Science, Applied Learning," National Center on Education and the Economy, Rochester, New York.

CHAPTER SEVEN

Numerous personality tests used in the school systems of Pennsylvania, supplied to this author by Representative Sam Rohrer of the state legislature.

Interview with Mr. Rohrer.

Figures on number of school guidance counselors from the National Library of Education, Department of Education, and the American School Counselors Association.

Figures on the number of school psychologists from the National Library of Education, U.S. Department of Education, and the National Association of School Psychologists.

Leo, John, "Don't Listen to Miranda," *U.S. News & World Report,* June 16, 1997.

Interview with an official of the American School Counselors Association.

Statistics on IDEA program from the National Library of Education, U.S. Department of Education.

Information on and interview about the Special Ed program in Greenwich, Connecticut, from the Greenwich Schools.

Statistics on school psychologists who have Ph.D.'s in psychology from the National Association of School Psychologists.

Interviews with school counselors and school psychologists in Westchester County, New York, and Fairfield County, Connecticut.

Gross, Martin L., *The Brain Watchers,* 1963, Random House, New York.

CHAPTER EIGHT

Information from Sidwell Friends School in Washington, D.C.

SAT scores of public and private school students from the ETS, Princeton, New Jersey.

Endnotes and Bibliography

"Report to the Nation and the States, NAEP 1996 Science," National Center for Education Statistics, U.S. Department of Education.

Information on tuition from private schools involved.

Information on independent secular private schools from the National Association of Independent Schools (NAIS), Washington, D.C.

Information on Catholic schools from the National Catholic Education Association, Washington, D.C.

Derek, Neal, "Measuring Catholic School Performance," *The Public Interest*, Spring 1997.

Quote regarding Catholic schools from *New York Observer*, Buckley, Gail Lumet, *America*, April 19, 1997.

Golway, Terry, "Nowadays the Products of Parish Schools Hold Their Heads High," *America*, September 16, 1995.

Donohue, John W., "See the Catholic School Walk a Fiscal Tightrope," *America*, March 11, 1995.

Hales Franciscan school in Chicago, "Answered Prayer: Education," *The Economist*, April 5, 1997.

Lieberman, Myron, "Catholic Teacher Unions: A Non-Catholic Perspective," *America*, February 28, 1998.

Interview with Tom Scott, spokesperson for the Association of Christian Schools International (ACSI), Colorado Springs, Colorado.

"Scores on Protestant school achievement," Association of Christian Schools International, Stanford Achievement Test, Spring 1997.

"Students Score Above the National Average at Every Grade," *Stanford 9*, Christian School Edition, Spring 1998.

Comments on Jewish private school education, Shapiro, Svi, "A Parent's Dilemma: Public vs. Jewish Education," *Tikkun*, November–December 1996.

Material on Milwaukee voucher program from various interviews with individuals named in the book, plus information from the Milwaukee

Endnotes and Bibliography

Public Schools, Office of Governmental Relations, Milwaukee, Wisconsin.

Public school teachers in Milwaukee enrolling their children in private schools, McGroarty, Daniel, "Teachers Know Best," *National Review*, September 25, 1995.

Interview with Terry Craney, who heads the Wisconsin Education Association Council, the state teachers' union.

Statistics and comment on Cleveland vouchers from interview with Bert Holt, director of the Cleveland Scholarship and Tutoring Program, Ohio Department of Education.

Crew-Giuliana dispute, Barry, Dan, "Crew Threatening to Resign His Post as Schools Chief," *New York Times*, March 4, 1999.

Herszenhorn, David, "Crew Softens Threat to Quit over Vouchers," *New York Times*, March 7, 1999.

Hartocollis, Anemona, "Crew Puts Off Threat to Resign as Clash Over Vouchers Eases," *New York Times*, March 3, 1999.

Janofsky, Michael, "Ohio Justices Strike Down Voucher Plan in Cleveland," *New York Times*, May 28, 1999.

Bragg, Rick, "Florida Will Award Vouchers for Pupils Whose Schools Fail," *New York Times*, April 28, 1999.

Comment on vouchers, Levine, Arthur, President of Columbia Teachers College, "Why I am Reluctantly Backing Vouchers," Op-Ed, *Wall Street Journal*, June 15, 1998.

"A National Study of Charter Schools: Second Year Report," Office of Educational Research and Improvement, 1998, U.S. Department of Education.

Finn, Chester E., Jr., and Manno, Bruno V. et al., "Charter Schools in Action: Final Report," Hudson Institute, July 1997.

Manno, Bruno V., and Finn, Chester E., Jr., et al., "How Charter Schools Are Different: Lessons and Implications from a National Study," *Phi Delta Kappan*, March 1998.

Endnotes and Bibliography

Ravitch, Diane, "Education with Accountability," (charter schools), *Forbes*, March 10, 1997.

Edison Project, privatization, "Can the Public Schools Be Saved," *The Economist*, June 4, 1994.

Privatization of public schools, Toch, Thomas, "Selling the Schools," *U.S. News & World Report*, May 2, 1994.

Doyle, Denis P. "The Role of Private Sector Management in Public Education," *Phi Delta Kappan*, October 1994.

Zuckerman, Mortimer B., "Schools Our Kids Deserve" (Editorial on the advantages of charter schools), *U.S. News & World Report*, September 23, 1996.

Forstmann, Ted, "School Choice, by Popular Demand," Op-Ed piece, *Wall Street Journal*, April 21, 1999.

Kattelus, Susan C., and Goenner, James N., "Accounting for Charter Schools," *Michigan CPA*, Fall 1997.

"Free At Last: Charter Schools," *The Economist*, July 2, 1994.

Nathan, Joe, "Heat and Light in the Charter School Movement," *Phi Delta Kappan*, March 1998.

Additional material on charter schools, Wells, Claudia, "A Class of Their Own," *Time*, October 31, 1994.

Geiger, Philip E., "The Charter School Choice," *American School and University*, May 1998.

Glassman, James K., "Class Act: How Charter Schools Are Revamping Public Education in Arizona—and Beyond," *Reason*, April 1998.

Glazer, Nathan, "Homegrown," (on value of charter schools), *The New Republic*, May 12, 1997.

"The School Choice Juggernaut," *The Weekly Standard*, April 26, 1999.

CHAPTER NINE

Anecdote about President George Bush from Delia Stafford, former head of alternate certification in Houston, Texas.

Endnotes and Bibliography

Interview with Dr. Leo Klagholz, then Commissioner of Education, State of New Jersey.

Interview with Dr. Emile Feistritzer, president of the National Center for Education Information, Washington, D.C.

Interview with spokesperson for alternate certification program of California.

Interview with spokesperson for alternate certification program of Texas.

Interview with Delia Stafford, now president of the Haberman Education Foundation, Houston, Texas.

Dill, Vicky, and Stafford, Delia, "School Based Teacher Education, *Phi Delta Kappan*, April 1994.

"Who Should Teach?" I & II, editorials on teacher alternate certification, *Wall Street Journal*, July 15, 1998 and July 17, 1998.

Facts from Teach for America, 20 Exchange Place, NYC, 10005.

Feistritzer, C. Emily, and Chester, David C., "Alternate Teacher Certification: A State-by-State Analysis, 1998–99," National Center for Education Information, Washington, D.C.

CHAPTER TEN

Comments on high school by teenagers. Littman, Margaret, "Senior Class," *Teen Magazine*, March 1999.

Quote on high school apathy, McGraw, Dan, "Inspired Students," *U.S. News & World Report*, January 18, 1999.

Goodman, Paul, *Community of Scholars*, Random House, 1962.

"Teacher Education and Qualifications," *Schools and Staffing Survey: 1993–94*, National Center for Education Statistics, U.S. Department of Education.

State course credit requirements for high school graduation from "State Education Policies," Council of Chief State School Officers, 1998, Washington, D.C.

Endnotes and Bibliography

Figures on homework from "NAEP 1996 Trends in Academic Progress," U.S. Department of Education.

Figures on outside reading, homework, and television, "A Profile of the American Eighth Grader," National Center for Education Statistics, U.S. Department of Education.

Hinchley, Pat, "Why Kids Say They Don't Do Homework," *The Clearing House*, March–April 1996.

Statistics on the number of junior high and middle schools from the National Library of Education, U.S. Department of Education.

Figures on television viewing from "A Profile of the American High School Sophomore in 1990," U.S. Department of Education.

This We Believe: Developmentally Responsive Middle Level Schools, National Middle School Association, Columbus, Ohio.

Turning Points: Preparing American Youth for the 21st Century, (abridged version), Carnegie Council on Adolescent Development, Carnegie Corporation of New York.

Burnett, Gary, "Alternatives to Ability Grouping: Still Unanswered Questions" (discussion of tracking), *ERIC/CUE Digest*, Number 111, Clearinghouse on Urban Education, New York, N.Y.

Information on TAG program for gifted students from that department at the Greenwich, Connecticut, schools.

Statistics on SAT tests from the Educational Testing Service, Princeton, New Jersey.

Statistics on the ACT test from American College Testing, Iowa City, Iowa.

"Taking the SAT I: Reasoning Test: SAT Program; Free Sample Test and Tips," The College Board, 1998–99, New York, N.Y.

Schwartz, Tony, "The Test Under Stress," examination of the SAT and coaching, *New York Times Magazine*, January 10, 1999.

Powers, Donald E., and Rock, Donald A., "Effects of Coaching on SAT I: Reasoning Scores," College Board, New York, 1998.

Endnotes and Bibliography

"New Studies Document Limited Value of Coaching on SAT Scores," College Board On Line, College Board, New York, N.Y.

"Dispute Over SAT Coaching Courses Resurfaces; Stewart (Donald Stewart, president of the College Board) Responds," College Board On Line.

Gilstrap, Robert L. "New Developments in Preparing Teachers for the Middle Grades," *Childhood Education,* Spring 1994.

CHAPTER ELEVEN

Chase, Bob, "Restoring the Impulse to Dream" (Speech by president of the NEA), *Vital Speeches,* October 15, 1997.

Chase, Bob, "Paradigm Lost," (reported shift in union emphasis), *NEA Today,* March 1997.

Shanker, Albert, "Quality Assurance: What Must Be Done to Strengthen the Teaching Profession," *Phi Delta Kappan,* November 1996.

Shanker, Albert, "Where We Stand—What Standards?" advertisement column in *New York Times,* April 7, 1996.

Material on legal aspects of teacher union membership from the National Right to Work Legal Defense Foundation, Washington, D.C.

Feldman, Sandra, "The Challenges and Opportunities: Education Reform is Working," (Speech by president of the American Federation of Teachers), *Vital Speeches,* August 15, 1998.

Details of political contributions from the NEA and AFT from the Federal Election Commission, "Candidate Supported/Opposed" list.

Material on state legislatures and teacher tenure, Chinni, Dante, "Teacher's Pets," *Washington Monthly,* January–February 1997.

Lieberman, Myron, "What to Do About Teacher Unions: Children, Teachers, PTA and Politics," *Vital Speeches,* August 15, 1998.

Brimelow, Peter, and Spencer, Leslie, "Commupance" (critique of NEA), *Forbes* February 13, 1995.

Endnotes and Bibliography

Worth, Robert, "Reforming the Teacher's Unions," *Washington Monthly*, May 1998.

Larson, Reed, "More Teachers Challenging NEA's Clout," *Insight on the News*, July 7, 1997.

Hitt, Greg, "Proposed Merger of Teachers Unions Is Rejected in Vote," *Wall Street Journal*, July 6, 1998.

Toch, Thomas, "Why Teachers Don't Teach," (effect on teachers' unions on education), *U.S. News & World Report*, February 26, 1996.

Toch, Thomas, and Garrett, Major, "Will Teachers Save Public Schools," *U.S. News & World Report*, July 20, 1998.

CHAPTER TWELVE

Statistics on superintendents from Glass, Thomas E., "The 1992 Study of the American School Superintendency," American Association of School Administrators, Arlington, Va.

Statistics on number of education degrees awarded, "Earned Degrees in Education Conferred by Institutions of Higher Education, by Level of Degree and Sex of Student: 1949–50 to 1995–96," Higher Education General Information Survey (HEGIS), National Center for Education Statistics, U.S. Department of Education.

Statistics on various doctoral degrees, "Doctor's Degrees Conferred by Institutions of Higher Education, by Discipline Division: 1970–1 to 1995–6," Higher Education General Information Survey (HEGIS), National Center for Education Statistics, U.S. Department of Education.

Salaries of school principals, "Principals Receive Small Salary Increase," February 26, 1999, news release from the National Association of Secondary School Principals.

Material on New York University graduate education curriculum from the *School of Education Bulletin, 1997–1999*, Department of Administration, Leadership and Technology, New York University, New York City.

Endnotes and Bibliography

Graduate education program, from Division of Educational Leadership, School of Education, University of Connecticut, Storrs, Ct.

Interview with head of graduate education training at a major Texas university.

Material on alternate Parent-Teacher groups, Nakamura, David, "PTA Alternative Embodies a Shift in School Activism," *Washington Post*, September 28, 1997.

Information on reform program in Pennsylvania from the Department of Education, State of Pennsylvania, Harrisburg, Pa.

Figures of growth of student enrollment from the U.S. Census Bureau, Department of Commerce, Washington, D.C.

Statistics on new schools from the National Library of Education, Department of Education.

Cost of education to communities, states, and the federal government from the National Library of Education, Department of Education.

CONCLUSION

Quote from Dr. Leo Klagholz on reasons for leaving the commissioner's post in New Jersey.

Information on reform movement in Pennsylvania from that state's department of education.

INDEX

Index

Index

Index

Doctor of education degree (Ed.D)
(cont.)
  Bill of Indictment on, 14
  candidates for, 44–46
  compared with other fields, 229
  curriculum of, 230–32
  evaluation of candidates for,
    233–34
  number of, 229
  proposed changes for, 232–33,
    250
Doran, Craig, 221–22
Douglass Elementary School,
    Houston, 81
Draw-A-Man Test, 142

Ed.D. *See* Doctor of education
    degree
Edgar, Jim, 169
Edison Project, 173
Educational psychology courses
  Bill of Indictment on, 14
  curriculum with, 52–53, 58–59
  proposed changes for eliminating,
    253
  teacher model influenced by,
    55–56
Educational Testing Service (ETS),
    26
  prospective teachers and, 43–44
  teacher exams and, 95
  tracking survey by, 203
Education departments. *See*
    Schools of education; State
    departments of education; U.S.
    Department of Education
Education Establishment
  as a closed circle, 10–11
  conspiracy of ignorance of, 11–12
  failure of reforms of, 9–10
  misconceptions about public
    school system student
    composition held by, 7–8
  power of, 11
  psychological testing and, 147–48
  teacher education and, 100–101
  theories of education held by, 8–9
  whole language instruction and,
    81–82

Education of teachers. *See* Teacher
    education
Education profession
  Bill of Indictment on, 14
  level of intellectual profession in,
    61–62
  resistance to change in, 86–87
Education Quality Assessment, 134
Eighth graders
  history curriculum and, 121–22,
    123
  proposed standards for, 29
  reading levels in, 73
Engineering, 7, 45
English
  high schoolers going on to higher
    education and preparation in,
    21
  home schoolers and performance
    in, 170
  college remedial courses in, 21
  spending per pupil in, 35
Establishment. *See* Education
    Establishment
ETS. *See* Educational Testing
    Service
Excel Academy, Michigan, 173
Expectations of teachers for
    students, 15, 51

Federal Election Commission, 216
Feistritzer, Emily, 179–80, 184
Feldman, Sandra, 218, 223
Ferguson, Ronald, 51
Financial support for education
  academic performance related to,
    29–35
  growth trends in, 30
Finn, Chester, Jr., 21, 22, 171
Fleming, Jeff, 159, 160, 161
Flexner, Abraham, 67
Florida, 94, 241, 250
Foorman, Barbara, 85
Foreign language teachers, training
    of, 46
Foreign students, 7. *See also*
    International competitions
    among students
Foster, Ezola, 218

Index

Index

High school students *(cont.)*
  history curriculum and, 121, 123–24
  homework for, 196, 198–99
  Honor Roll inflation and, 16–17, 27
  mathematics curriculum and, 106–7, 108
  percentage going on for higher education, 21
  proposed reforms in, 208–9
  science curriculum and, 115–16
  tracking in, 199–200
  undergraduate education programs and, 42–44
High school teachers, GRE scores of, 45–46
Hirsch, E. D., Jr., 61, 127, 173
Hispanic students. *See also* Minority students
  reading levels of, 82
History
  NAEP test on, 3–4, 22–23
  proposed standards for, 29
History curriculum, 72, 120–26
  Core Knowledge curriculum on, 127
  revisionist approach to, 124–26
  student performance in, 120–24
Holt, Bert, 163–64
Home schooling, 168–70
Home School Legal Defense Association (HSLDA), 168–69
Homework, 196, 198–99
Honig, William, 79, 86
Honor students, 16–17

Illiteracy
  in reading, 73, 74
  in science, 116–17
Illinois, 169
Individuals with Disabilities Education Act (IDEA), 138–40, 241
Intelligence tests, 142
Intel Science Talent Search, 18
International competitions among students, 1–2. *See also* Third

International Mathematics and Science Study (TIMSS)
  class size and performance on, 33
  increasing failure of U.S. students by age in, 19–20
  results of U.S. gifted students in, 18–19
International Reading Association, 87
Iowa, teacher education in, 100, 101

Japan, 19, 33
Jennings, Marianne, 113
Jewish schools, 157–58
Joseph, Marion, 83–84, 89
Journal of Human Resources, 51

Kamber Report, 214
Kane, Parsons, 183
Kaplan Education Centers, 206
Kearns, David, 6
Klagholz, Leo, 43, 177–79, 219, 247
Koerner, James M., 49
Kopp, Wendy, 183
Korean students. *See* South Korean students
Kramer, Rita, 67
Kurz, Irwin, 37–38, 164, 219

Labor Bureau, 6
Learning disabilities, 139–40
Learning theory, 56, 59–62
Lederman, Leon M., 115–16
Legislators. *See* State legislators
Leo, John, 135–36
Lerner, Barbara, 20
Levine, Arthur, 167
Liability insurance, 224
Liberals, 87–89, 113
Licensing and certification, 90–103.
  See also Alternate certification
  Bill of Indictment on, 13
  board certification and, 101–2, 218–19
  charter schools and, 172
  home schooling and, 169
  Massachusetts exams for, 4–5, 90–93, 97–98, 99, 103
  periodic reevaluation of, 249–50

Index

private schools and, 54–55, 151–52
proposed reforms in, 98–99, 101–3, 248
school psychologists and, 140–41
standards for certification tests in, 95–98, 103, 248
teacher education and, 53–54
teachers' reactions to, 93–94, 94–95
voucher programs and, 162
Limbaugh, Rush, 217
Literacy, 219
in reading, 73, 74
in science, 116–17
Los Angeles, charter schools in, 172
Louisiana, 80, 86, 117

McGraw, Dan, 187
McGraw Award, 172
McGuinness, Diane, 86
Magnet schools, 9
Maine, 117, 166
Maryland, 21, 242
Massachusetts
teacher certification exams in, 4–5, 90–93, 97–98, 99, 103, 151
home schoolers in, 170
Massachusetts Department of Education, 4, 90, 97, 99, 103
Massachusetts Teachers Association (MTA), 92, 99
Mathematically Correct, 113
Mathematics
college remedial courses in, 21
foreign students in higher education in, 7
high schoolers going on to higher education and preparation in, 21
NAEP test scores in, 3, 23–24, 47, 105–6
proposed standards for, 28
public awareness of problems in, 5
results of U.S. gifted students in, 18, 20
spending per pupil in, 35

TIMSS test scores in, 3, 104–5, 114
U.S. Department of Education on failure of teaching in, 19
Mathematics Association of America, 114
Mathematics curriculum, 72, 104–14, 156
calculator use and, 110–12
new math in, 108–12
student performance and, 104–8
teacher education and, 46, 108, 190–91
Math portfolio, 112–13
Mathland curriculum, 108, 113
Medical education, 66–67
Memorization
learning theory on, 59–62
spelling and, 78
Mental health team concept, 132–33
Mesa, Arizona, 173–74
Michigan, 169, 172, 173
Middle school, 20, 200–210
mathematics in, 105, 106, 108, 114
NAEP tests and, 201–2
proposed reforms in, 208–9
tracking in, 202–3
Miller, David, 194
Mills, Richard P., 210
Milwaukee Parental Choice Program, 159–63, 165–66
Minnesota, 166, 170
Minority students
Catholic school students and, 153–55
poverty and academic performance and, 35–37, 155
in the public school system, 7–8
reading curriculum and, 72, 82
voucher programs and, 163, 166
Mississippi, 80, 86
Montana, 117
Montessori method, 173
Montgomery County, Maryland, 21
My Beliefs—My Parents' Beliefs questionnaire, 135

NAEP. *See* National Assessment of Educational Progress

299

Index

Index

Powers, Donald E., 207
Praxis I and Praxis II, 95–96, 103
Primack, Robert, 50
Princeton Review, 206
Principals, 194
  administrative work of, 235
  Education Establishment as a
    closed circle and, 10
  education of, 229–30
  increase in number of, 31
Private schools
  academic performance and,
    150–51
  debate over vouchers for, 158–68
  dilemma about using, 149–50
  percentage of K–12 students
    enrolled in, 7
  pupil-teacher ratio in, 33
  teacher certification and, 54–55,
    151–52
Professionalization
  certification and, 53–54
  psychological testing and, 147–48
  teacher education and, 51, 52
Profession of education
  Bill of Indictment on, 14
  level of intellectual profession in,
    61–62
  resistance to change in, 86–87
Progressive theories of education, 5
Property taxes, 243–44
Proposition 13, 244
Proposition 187, 217–18
Protestant academies, 156–57
Psychology courses. 13
  curriculum with, 52–53, 58–59
  teacher model influenced by,
    55–56
Psychology testing, 129–48
  Bill of Indictment on, 14
  confidentiality and, 136–37, 144,
    145
  debate over use and misuse of,
    143–48
  intervention by guidance
    counselors after, 131–32
  learning disabilities and, 139–40
  longer-term intervention by
    school psychologist and,
    137–38

  mental health team concept and,
    132–33
  motives for, 134–35
  parents and, 135–37
  personality testing and, 129–30
  proposed changes for, 251–52
  special education students and,
    138–39
Psychotherapy, 137
Public Agenda for the Educational
  Excellence Partnerships, 10
Public opinion
  on NEA, 214–15
  problems in public education
    and, 5–6
  on superintendents, 228
  voucher programs and, 167
Public Opinion Quarterly (journal),
  24
Public school system. *See also* High
  schools
  annual costs of, 9
  building construction and, 241
  changes in direction and
    philosophy of, 12–13
  conspiracy of ignorance
    regarding, 11–12
  cost to business of problems in, 6
  failure of reforms in, 9–10
  funding of, 242–43
  growth of enrollment in, 240–41
  minority and white middle class
    students in, 7–8
  public awareness of problems in,
    5–6
  public confidence in, 24
  public relations in handling
    parents by, 24
  students' opinions of, 10
Pupil-teacher ratio
  academic performance related to,
    33
  financial support for increased
    number of teachers and, 30–33
  private schools and, 33

Race. *See* Minority students
Ravitch, Diane, 21
Reading Teacher (journal), 81–82

Index

Index

Index

Index

Index